Gone Feral

Unruly Women and the Undoing
of Normative Femininity

I0112413

Edited by Andrea O'Reilly and Casey O'Reilly-Conlin

DEMETER

Gone Feral: Unruly Women and the Undoing of Normative Femininity
Edited by Andrea O'Reilly and Casey O'Reilly-Conlin

Demeter Press
PO Box 197
Coe Hill, Ontario
Canada
K0L 1P0
Tel: 289-383-0134
Email: info@demeterpress.org
Website: www.demeterpress.org

Demeter Press logo based on the sculpture "Demeter" by Maria-Luise Bodirsky
www.keramik-atelier.bodirsky.de

Printed and Bound in Canada

Cover image: *Materna Sinistra* by Alexandra Carter, 2021
Cover design: Michelle Pirovich
Typesetting: Michelle Pirovich
Proof reading: Jena Woodhouse
Library and Archives Canada Cataloguing in Publication
Title: Gone feral: unruly women and the undoing of normative femininity /
edited by Andrea O'Reilly and Casey O'Reilly-Conlin.
Names: O'Reilly, Andrea, 1961- editor | O'Reilly-Conlin, Casey, editor.
Description: Includes bibliographical references.
Identifiers: Canadiana 20250111756 | ISBN 9781772585339 (softcover)
Subjects: LCSH: Femininity (Philosophy) | LCSH: Femininity. | LCSH:
Women–Identity.
Classification: LCC BD450.G66 2025 | DDC 128–dc23

Funded by the Government of Canada | Canadä | The publisher gratefully acknowledges the support of the Government of Canada

For feral women everywhere

Contents

Introduction

Andrea O'Reilly and Casey O'Reilly-Conlin

> If you have ever been captured, if you have ever endured hambre
> del alma, a starvation of the soul, if you have ever been trapped,
> and especially if you have a drive to create, it is likely that you have
> been or are a feral woman.
>
> —Clarissa Pinkola Estés, *Women Who Run with the Wolves*, 116

This collection probes the concept of ferality concerning traditional, patriarchal concepts of womanhood and femininity from multiple perspectives and diverse standpoints, with contributors from Australia, Canada, China, Ireland, Norway, Scotland, and the United States. More specifically, this collection explores how unruly women and their enactments of untamed or undomesticated femininity may be positioned and understood as resistances to patriarchal culture. The *Oxford Dictionary* defines "feral" as "being in a wild untamed state, especially existing in or returning to an untamed state from domestication; and of, or suggestive of, a wild animal; savage." A feral creature, in essence, was once wild and following a period of domestication has reverted to a wild or untamed state. However, because of the experience of domestication—which can strip wild creatures of their instincts—the loss of natural homelands, or the abandonment that often precedes their transformation into ferality, feral beings most often exist in a state of dereliction and flux.

The term "normative" is ascribed to social systems of proper conduct, which are naturalized and idealized. To exist outside or on the margins of the normative renders one suspicious, defective, or aberrant. Under patriarchy, the dictates of normative femininity are male defined and male controlled. As Toni Morrison notes, "Outlaw women are fascinating—not always for their behavior, but because historically women are seen as naturally disruptive and their status is an illegal one from birth if it is not under the rule of men" (qtd. in Gaitskill). Therefore, feminine displacement from patriarchal culture, predicated as it is on feminine submission and subjugation, whether by choice or force, can be viewed as a source of resistance or even empowerment.

Susan Fraiman argues that feminist thinkers and writers have, for decades, explored the notion that women and animals are linked together as avatars of nature:

> ... that they are similarly debased by their shared association with body over mind, feeling over reason, object rather than subject status; that men are rational subjects, who therefore naturally dominate women and animals alike; that masculinity is produced in contradistinction to the feminine, animal, bodily, emotional, and acted upon; that degree of manliness is correlated to a degree of distance from these and other related categories—physicality, literalness, sentimentality, vulnerability, domesticity, and so on. (99)

Kelly Struthers Montford and Chloë Taylor note that "One way in which women have been oppressed has been through their relegation to the domestic sphere and through the exploitation of their domestic labour" (6). To go feral, then, can be viewed as a liberation—a thrust towards freedom from a patriarchal culture that has long snared feminine potential, caged feminine spirits, and neutered feminine authenticity. Struthers Montford and Taylor elaborate:

> We are drawn to the liminal animals who are apart from the society in which they nonetheless live. Although being liminal in the case of nonhuman animals may often be less voluntary, the liminality of these animals has parallels to being feminists in a misogynist society.... Beyond this precarious sense of identification, we are drawn to the feral because at least some ferals

> represent the prospect of escape from a former relationship of domination and control. (6)

However, it is important in a discussion of ferality not to fall prey to the traps of romanticism. Once the feral has gnawed through the chains of captivity and bounded towards freedom, there is no longer a wilderness for them to return to, no safe haven of salvation that awaits them. As Struthers Montford and Taylor observe: "Just as there is no 'outside of power' for Foucault, there is arguably no longer any possibility of 'going wild'" (9). Therefore, as the authors continue: "On the one hand, we can celebrate the freedom of ferals from human [or male] domination and control, but on the other hand, we should recognize that ferals are often abandoned, desperate, and highly vulnerable... [and] suffer from the stigma of being seen by the dominant population as illegitimate, alien, contaminants, trespassers, or invaders" (5). To be feral, then, is to be acutely vulnerable and extraordinarily brave.

This collection uses the concept of ferality to explore how subjugated beings carve out, by choice or circumstance, spaces of survival and resistance under the continued dominion of the dominant culture. It questions how unruly women—whether they are deemed mad, eccentric, incorrigible, weird, deviant, dissident, aberrant, or heretical or labelled as witches, shrews, bitches, spinsters, sluts, crazy cat ladies, femme fatales, or bad mothers—navigate their lives on the margins of society proper. It further explores how such women, and other feral animals, resist normative social regulations and blur, or evade entirely, seemingly fixed definitions and categorizations and why this is met with such suspicion and hostility by the dominant culture.

The collection is organized into two sections. The first explores how unruly women undo normative femininity and how it is lived and enacted, and the second examines how these enactments and lived experiences are represented in art, media, poetry, and literature. Because the paths chosen by the feral are often nonconventional, nonlinear, and resistant to traditional categorizations and binary thinking, there is some overlap between these two sections.

Enactments

In the opening chapter to this collection, "Taken by Others: The Danger of Being Feral," Martina Cleary examines how the murder of Bridget Cleary, known as the last witch burning in Europe, was linked to collective and cultural fears of the feral. By feral, Cleary means a woman seen to have strayed beyond the domestic and transgressed the confines of what is permitted to her within the sociopolitical and symbolic order of her community or cultural context. To wander beyond this order and transgress an imaginal threshold was enough to ignite the flames. Cleary discusses this case within the socio-political and historical context of Bridget Cleary's time, but the author also relates it to more recent examples of how a fear of the feral continues to present dangers for women in contemporary Ireland.

The following chapter, "From Harlots to Irresponsible Economic Citizens: Shifting Discourses on Sole Mothers," by Emily Wolfinger explores historical and contemporary discourses on sole mothers across media, politics, and academia. It argues that in Australia (as in other Anglophone nations), sole mothers have been constructed as feral or bad mothers within three primary discourses over time: unmarried mothers, "kids having kids," and welfare mothers. Just as feral women exist on the figurative outskirts of society as regards normative femininity, feral mothers contravene normative prescriptions of motherhood and are thus positioned as bad mothers who require intervention and reform, if not control and punitive action. Although understandings of what constitutes feral or bad mothers are culturally and historically specific, they almost always include the figure of the sole or single mother.

Jessica Spring Weappa's chapter, "Gone Spielreinian: Maternal Ferality and the Suprahumanities," explores the overlooked contributions of Sabina Spielrein, a pivotal figure in twentieth-century psychoanalysis and developmental psychology, whose ideas were historically appropriated and misattributed to colleagues. Through a reflective scholarly narrative, the author examines Spielrein's biological, relational, and evolutionary theories, linking them to broader maternal themes often bypassed or excluded from the humanities and social sciences. Situating Spielrein's work in sexual difference studies, such as the symbolic order of the mother, the author suggests Spielrein's legacy could inform an emerging field known as the suprahumanities.

The creative prose piece "Three Little Witches" by Hillary Di Menna works with the idea of trinities. The fairytale looks at surviving abuse and breaking curses, as well as grief, girlhood, and growth. Di Menna wrote this piece while examining the deep maternal roots needed to nurture the dreams of future generations of wild kittens and witchlets.

What follows is a collection of poems by Joy Domingo. The speaker in these five poems is a survivor of father-daughter incest, marital rape, and postpartum depression. Informed by love, joy, and trauma, the poems are tragic and funny, heavy and lighthearted. They explore such themes as reclaiming agency over one's body and sexual experiences; postmenopausal sexual reawakening; and healing from sexual trauma.

The chapter "Feral Itch" by Caroline Carey explores a lifetime of trying to fit into an artificial world where you do not belong while still receiving gifts, messages, reassurances, and nudges from the primal, feral, and unreconstructed nature of womanhood. What does it take to break free and become the innate feral woman? What does it cost, and what do you gain?

"Mothers Born Feral: An Exploration of Birth Trauma" by Teela Tomassetti explores the taboo world of birth trauma and challenges the silence that exists for those mothers who do not begin their journey into parenthood beautifully domesticated. Tomassetti creates space to unpack an outcome that happens to many mothers yet leaves them feeling like an anomaly and identifies social media as a rebel community breaking free from the unrealistic expectations placed on those who give birth. By acknowledging the unkept and broken parts of birth society, we can understand how such systems are archaic and how to break them down to rebuild.

In the concluding chapter of this section, "The Mess House: Wildness in the Domestic Realm," Batya Weinbaum explores how being removed from the social roles of mother and daughter has freed her to be more expressive of herself in her own house. She discusses the ethos of Fuck Housework in early radical feminist culture, and how this led to a sense of the feral in private space. She draws an analogy between how we see our bodies and how we see our homes, comparing advocates of keeping a messy, expressive house to fat liberationists in terms of acceptance of the self over refined definitions of femininity. She draws upon the work of ecofeminist theorist Susan Griffin and early essays from the feminist movement, such as "The Politics of Housework." She includes documentary photographs of the wildness in her liberated abode.

Representations

This section opens with Alexandra Carter's artwork, "The Mother Shell," which explores the sensations of the female body through themes of fertility, maternity, and transformation, with a focus on the concept of the "monstrous feminine." Using acrylic inks on translucent drafting film (mylar), she creates fluid, figurative forms that highlight the resilience and power of the maternal body. Inspired by folklore, mythology, and her personal experiences of motherhood, Carter weaves imagery from her upbringing on a cranberry farm into her work, linking agricultural fertility to the physicality of the human body.

The following artwork by Catherine Moeller, "Strike a Pose," is based on ancient stories of women lifting their skirts and baring their vulvas before their husbands and soldiers to shame them. This wild skateboarding woman, displaying her defiance and power in a refusal of conventional morality, was an image created in self-love and personal support in response to an aggressive patriarchal male.

The following chapter "From Bold, Going Feral: Xiao Lu's Feminist Art and Ferality" by Li Yang explores the entwined themes of heterosexuality, motherhood, and nonconformist femininity as revealed by Xiao Lu's art practice over the past decades. Yang argues for the inherent vulnerability and blurred boundaries faced by women artists in embracing a feral stance. Specifically, Yang connects feral theory with the concept of feminist mothering, delving into how feminist untamed motherhood encompasses an in-between space where feral beings exist and move between set definitions of identity and seek interruption, redefinition, and empowerment.

The following poems by Victoria Smits respond to hegemonic roles placed on women, which are inextricably mixed within identity. The "Countess" series speaks to feminine desire and pleasure, a serving of self, extracted from expectations of the domestic. "Ode to the Mundane" and "Ode to Mahsa Amini" spirit the collective force and sacrifice women make while restrained within systems of oppression. As a whole, the poems claim an embodied empowerment, a repossession of what patriarchy has willfully taken.

In her chapter, "Unfaithful Domestics: Ferality and Domestic Disorder in John McPherson's *Strays*," Casey O'Reilly-Conlin uses the 1991 horror film *Strays* to probe the concept of ferality through its conjoined portrayal of women and cats and explores how this concept exposes man-made anxieties about the tenuousness of dichotomies, the porous boundaries between binaries, identities that exist in flux, and the beings/ beasts who defy and evade fixed definitions. Beginning with a brief overview of "naturecultures" (Haraway) as a concept through which human-feline cohistories and relationalities may be interrogated, O'Reilly- Conlin then focuses on two historical periods (the late Middle Ages/early modern period and the Victorian era) with particular significance to these relationalities, followed by a close analysis of McPherson's *Strays* and its portrayal of disobedient beings. The constant hostility towards and desire to punish such beings—those who dare stray from the rigid, predetermined pathways of society proper—affirms the continued threat that such beings pose to the illusion of impenetrable fortresses of fixed, binaristic categorization and highlights the latent societal fear that some beings can never be fully brought under control and are always at risk of straying.

In the following chapter, "Releasing the (M)other within: Jeanette Winterson's Feral Journey from *Oranges Are Not the Only Fruit* to *Why Be Happy When You Could Be Normal*," Else Werring explores the recurring mother-daughter motif in Jeanette Winterson's writing through a comparison between Winterson's debut novel *Oranges Are Not The Only Fruit* (1982) and her midlife memoir *Why Be Happy When You Could be Normal* (2011). Werring argues that Winterson's continued tarrying with her past and with motherhood links her work to the feminist philosophy of birth tradition. She reads the repetition-with-a-difference of the *Oranges* plot, performed by Winterson in her 2011 memoir, as a feral feminism linked to the Deleuzo-Guattarian concept of "becoming-animal" and to an Irigarayan subversion of matricidal culture."

Laura Bissell's chapter "From Pig to Dog: Becoming Woman/Becoming Mother" analyses novels written twenty-five years apart (Marie Darrieussecq's *Pig Tales* [1996] and Rachel Yoder's *Nightbitch* [2021]) to argue that species metamorphoses in the novels offer generative and creative becomings. Pigs and dogs are culturally conceived as animals that can be domesticated and feral and have also historically been associated with female bodies, which are frequently animalized for degrading or derogatory purposes. *Pig Tales* and *Nightbitch* celebrate these threshold creatures, animals that humans identify with or have relationships with but also can be repelled by or frightened of. Exploring ideas of the institution of motherhood, the conventions of womanhood, mothers, and others, and kinship with animals, this chapter argues that the social conventions governing womanhood and motherhood can be experienced as a form of captivity. The feral transformations within these novels provide an escape from gendered tropes and the opportunity for the creative potential of the protagonists to flourish.

In the section's concluding chapter, "Gone Feral: Deviant Mothers, Defective Mothering, and the Undoing of Normative Motherhood in Katixa Agirre's *Mothers Don't* and Yewande B. Omotoso's *An Unusual Grief*," Andrea O'Reilly explores how the two novels, in taking up two of the most tabooed maternal topics—infanticide and the suicide of a child—position mothers and their mothering as deviant and defective. More specifically, the chapter argues that the two novels, in their descriptions of maternal reluctance, ambivalence, discontent, and estrangement, and in positioning infanticide as understandable and a child's suicide as transformative, enact ferality to unsettle and undo normative motherhood.

Conclusion

Carl Jung once commented on the connection between women and cats. He said that cats resemble women "because cats are the least domesticated of the domesticated animals" (qtd. in Rogers 139). In theory and essence, all women possess the potential to go feral because the dictates, ideals, and confinements we are forced to live by and under are so rigid, contradictory, and unforgiving that it is impossible to abide by them without infraction. Such infractions—being loud rather than staying quiet, talking back instead of obeying, questioning in place of blind acceptance, choosing instead of complying, and acting rather than succumbing—are not without consequence. Feral beings are abandoned, neglected, outcasted, vilified, and killed. "Yet," as noted by Struthers Montford and Taylor, "these animals do not recognize themselves as killable, nor their peers as ungrievable. In fact, they show resilience, have complex methods of survival, and lead intricate social lives" (12). A call to the feral is a dare to embrace our authentic selves in the face of intense scrutiny and a recognition that if we were not such a threat, there would not be such a need to confine us.

Works Cited

Gaitskill, Mary. "Toni Morrison and What Our Mothers Couldn't Say." *The New Yorker,* 7 Aug. 2019, www.newyorker.com/books/page-turner/toni-morrison-and-what-our-mothers-couldnt-say. Accessed 16 Jan. 2025.

Fraiman, Susan. "Pussy Panic versus Liking Animals: Tracking Gender in Animal Studies." *Critical Inquiry,* vol. 39, no. 1, 2012, pp. 89–115.

Pinkola Estés, Clarissa. *Women Who Run with the Wolves: Myths and Stories of the Wild Woman Archetype.* Ballantine Books, 1992.

Rogers, Katherine M. *Cat.* Reaktion Books, 2006.

Struthers Montford, Kelly, and Chloë Taylor. "Feral Theory: Editors' Introduction." *Feral Feminisms: Feral Theory,* no. 6, 2016, https://feralfeminisms.com/wp-content/uploads/2017/04/ff_intro_issue6.pdf. Accessed 27 Jan. 2025.

I

Enactments

1

Taken by the Others:
The Danger of Being Feral

Martina Cleary

> There are witches in the hills calling my name
> Saying come join us sister, come kiss the flame
> Come dance in the moonbeams, ride the night wind
> Make love to the darkness and laugh at man's sins
> —Cowboy Junkies (1990)

In 1895, Bridget Cleary was burned to death over the hearth of her home in a rural part of County Tipperary, by a husband convinced she was a changeling, a creature more supernatural than human. This creature, he believed, had replaced his natural wife. He persuaded even her father to participate in a purging ritual that would lead to her being burned alive. Resonating with older Irish myths of the feral woman, a changeling creature who moved between worlds, the events of Bridget's life and death played out in a liminal zone—a place between the real and the imaginal, the contemporary and collective memory of older, never-quite-forgotten beliefs. Unconventional in her independence and childlessness, Bridget became a target and projection ground, a living embodiment of the wild, hybrid, and feral shapeshifter of myth. However, unlike this wild feral feminine archetype of bygone tales, Bridget the human woman was broken and subjected to public humiliation, torture and finally death. There was no transfiguration, no moment when she, as her husband maintained, would ride out restored from the fairy fort of Kylenagranagh. This chapter examines attitudes and beliefs about the feral as it relates to Irish folklore and myth and how this influenced the real-life fate of Bridget Cleary and continues to influence the treatment of certain women in present-day Ireland. Drawing parallels with contemporary cases, it explores how being considered feral poses real risks to women's lives—a problem that cannot be rectified until the underlying symbolic matrix of our postcolonial Irish culture, including its banishment of the feral feminine to a shadowy outcast othering, is made conscious, recognized, and acknowledged. The chapter introduces her story as it relates to the feral feminine including details of her fate. It then places events within the broader anthropological context of the role of myth and Indigenous beliefs surrounding ideas of the feral, often termed as "taken by the others," including how a "fear of the feral" was instrumental in her death. To conclude, I discuss echoes of her story in the contemporary cases of Imelda Riney, Emer O'Loughlin, and Sophie Toscan du Plantier.

The events of one small room in Ballyvadlea in County Tipperary on a dark March night in 1895 mark a threshold, a crossing over between worlds: the so-called primitive and the civilized, the ancient and the modern, the fantastical space of a mythopoetic worldview and one dictated by the norms of a rural conservative Irish Catholic society. Known as the last witch burning in Europe, the murder of Bridget Cleary over the open fire of her cottage by her husband and immediate in-laws is too uncomfortably close in both the time and accuracy of recorded court testimony to be dismissed as a relic of oral myth or the backwardness of another era. Her torture and death reveal the dangers for women perceived to be feral. By feral, I mean a woman seen to have strayed beyond the domestic and transgressed the confines of what is permitted to her within the sociopolitical and symbolic order of her immediate community or cultural context. To wander beyond, by transgressing a real, or in this case, an imaginal threshold, is enough to ignite the flames.

Pinkola Estes proposes that the feral woman is "one who was once in a natural psychic state that is, in her rightful wild mind—then later captured by whatever turn of events, thereby becoming overly domesticated and deadened in proper instincts" (213). To reclaim her authenticity, she advocates rediscovering this wild nature, conceived as an innately feminine closeness to the natural world: physically, psychically, or symbolically. This instinctual self, Estes suggests, knows how to escape the snares set to deaden, trap, or confine the soul, especially for those who are creative. The archetype of the Wild Woman as it survives in myths the world over, forms the basis of Pinkola Estes's psychological roadmap for women who need the space to wander freely—to rediscover, reconstitute and reclaim this aspect of their nature. It is however, important to consider how this archetypal psychology, drawn from the ancient wisdom of myth, may have consequences for real-life women. Myth is always of its own time; it emerges from a particular sociopolitical context and communal need to make sense of the unseen, the spiritual, and what defies easy rational human understanding. Where the feral may have once been a respected, even venerated aspect of divinity in its feminine form, for women living within societies and communities governed for millennia by a patriarchal symbolic order, its re-emergence can provoke raw fear and violence. In the absence, loss, or erasure of elevated symbolic forms and rituals through which to approach this aspect of the psyche, to be perceived as feral too often incurs the backlash of being othered to the point of dehumanization.

It's Not a Woman I'm Burning

Bridget Cleary was twenty-six years old when she was murdered. Court records describe her as a milliner by trade, living a simple domestic life in a labourer's cottage in a remote area of rural Tipperary. Married to Michael Cleary since the age of eighteen, he was seven years her senior. As Angela Bourke notes, Justice O'Brien described her as "a young woman in the opening of her life ... put to death". His words also reflect the strictly gendered social, even legal, expectations placed upon women of her time. He observed how Bridget had not transgressed; she was "guilty of no offence, virtuous and respectable in all her conduct and all her proceedings." Her husband was "bound to protect her," "having "sworn at the altar" to do so ("Reading a Woman's Death" 566).

Outwardly Bridget seemed the perfect wife, giving no cause to provoke the actions leading to her murder. So what possessed Michael Cleary to decide to burn his wife alive and for nine people from her family and local community to collude with him? The case was notorious, as it coincided with contemporary political debates on Home Rule in Ireland

and became a cause celebre for those supporting the continuation of British rule in Ireland. Bridget was murdered in 1895, a year when the political debate on Home Rule was particularly heated. As Euugenio Federico Biagini notes, from 1874 to 1914, the question of whether Ireland should be given a form of dominion status, allowing for a devolved parliament in Dublin, was high on the political agenda. Home Rule would have provided a form of independence and self-governance of domestic affairs in Ireland, ending centuries of direct rule by the British Empire. The debate was bitter and highly contentious, with strong opposition from the Unionists. Bridget Cleary's murder was used by certain factions as a case in point as to why the Irish were not fit to self-govern. The coverage in national and international papers at the time reflected this sociopolitical struggle; those in opposition to Home Rule took this outrage as an example of why such a backward and brutish race needed the civilizing hand of empire. The Irish, especially Irish womanhood, had to be protected from primitive customs and superstitions. The fact that Michael Cleary was not hanged, though sentenced to twenty years of penal servitude, and the leniency of the other sentences handed down reflected a certain kind of paternalistic pity for the tragically misguided actions of the primitive native mind, influenced by folk customs, pishogues and fairy lore. The women involved—her cousin Johanna Bourke, Johanna's daughter Katie, and Bridget's elderly mother, Mary Kennedy—were found guilty with the men but released. It seemed that those involved believed it was not a woman they were burning at all but a wild feral thing more animal than human. Bridget they believed, had been replaced by a changeling from the otherworld.

The belief in changelings is not unique to Ireland. This superstition existed in several European countries from the Middle Ages until the twentieth century. However, the fact that Bridget Cleary was an adult woman when this happened was unusual, as it was more often children who were believed at risk of this substitution. This may explain why Michael Cleary wavered between branding her a changeling or a witch. In the case of infants, superstitions warned of a "cuckoo child"—a nonhuman substitute resembling the original but who was instead a malevolent shapeshifter invading the home. This unnatural creature, withered and cantankerous, could bring disease upon the family and livestock. It could only be banished by fire, or burning the feet with hot shovels, a belief leading to inhumane even torturous treatment of children suffering from what today would be understood as physical or other disabilities. Contemporary researchers suggest that the changeling may have even been a means to explain autism presenting in children as they matured (Sexton and Fitzgerald). Contemporary understanding of neurodivergence and nonbinary gender identity suggests this may have been a way to other those who did not conform to traditional expectations. Bourke, who has written extensively on the case of Bridget Cleary, observes that fairy lore was a coded expression helping to explain disturbing and otherwise inexplicable events. It was a shared symbolic language to contain unease about difference. Kathleen Vejvoda also notes how "most folklore collections make clear ... fairies abduct only certain members of the community, usually those who are in a liminal state physically, or socially—for example, new-borns and nursing mothers" (45). The changeling substitution accounted for sudden changes in health, character, or temperament. To be "away with the fairies" could also be an allusion to altered psychological states, such as depression, postpartum depression, nervous breakdown, anxiety, and even anorexia. Those inflicted were described as suddenly changed, failing or wasting away, and completely altered in spirit though appearing to be themselves. Moreover, as Vejvoda comments, fairy lore "may have been a means to metaphorically allude to states of marginalisation, even alienation within a social context" (45). Childbirth was an especially dangerous time, and many stories tell of women being carried through the air by the Sídhe, expressing, as Bourke in "Reading a Woman's Death" observes, real anxieties surrounding mother or infant mortality as well as human fertility (570). But as Bourke also comments, "It is hard not to see in such stories a coded aggression against women," with attacks to the physical body being commonplace (571).

The case of Bridget Cleary was not unique, although it was unusual in the ferocity of the violence she suffered. Simon Young outlines that between 1800 and 1900, there were over fifty Irish court cases "where fairy belief caused or informed those involved in an 'outrage' against the state or their neighbours" (181). The cases of MacDonough and Lally from Longford in the 1840s are cases in point. The former involved an attempt by two men to convince relatives of the deceased James Lyons that they were the dead man and a long-lost nephew returned from the otherworld. The deception was planned to exploit the Lyons family economically. In an adjoining parish, Matthew Lally tried to convince a local family that he was their son returned from beyond the grave. He claimed the fairies had taken him for sixteen years but he was now restored to them. Young places these phenomena within the context of the aftermath of famine in Ireland. The Great Famine (1845–52) and the famine of 1879 wreaked devastating consequences on all aspects of Irish society, causing "a sort of moral and intellectual breakdown of the old worldview and a spiritual chaos which encouraged people to desperately cling to new religious truths," especially those of the Catholic church (Young 189). In a society where over half the population had died of starvation, or vanished through emigration, the shadow of a devastating trauma could explain attempts, however irrational, to ward off inexplicable misfortune. As Young observes, the Protestant rhetoric of the time also conflated Catholic belief in purgatory, with the gullibility of certain classes to believe the dead were somehow suspended in limbo. In popular lore, the fairy otherworld was believed to exist in neither heaven nor hell but an in-between place, akin to Catholic purgatory. Ruksar Hussain describes how these traditions date from the medieval period. For example, the poem of Thomas the Rhymer, from the thirteenth century, expresses a belief in "not just fairies [but] all sorts of creatures and spirits believed to roam alongside humans." This otherworld, Hussain observes "was an enchanted universe, where the line between religion and magic was often blurred" but which "provided explanation, meaning and mechanism to cope with what could be a very harsh and frightening world." For women however, as Bourke notes, the fear of being branded a changeling had serious implications. It could lead to physical attack and would have been a cause to alienate, isolate, and other certain women ("Reading a Woman's Death" 571).

Witnesses told of how Bridget Cleary fell ill some days before her death. In *The Burning of Bridget Cleary*, Bourke draws upon court records from the subsequent trial in Clonmel, which provide a timeline of events from key witnesses. Based upon the testimony of her cousin Johanna Burke, Bridget visited the home of Jack Dunne and his wife on Sunday March 3, 1895, to deliver eggs or possibly collect payment of money owed. She walked the two miles to Ballyvadlea bridge and past the fairy fort on the hill of Kylenagranagh. It snowed the previous day, so the weather was cold but clear. Finding nobody home, she waited for some time on the doorstep before eventually walking home. The following day she had a violent headache, was shivering and took to her bed, where she stayed for the week, as family and neighbours, including Dunne and his wife called to visit her. Bourke also notes here that "Dunne's interventions at all stages of this story are crucial. Several witnesses pointed to him as an instigator of Bridget Cleary's torture on the days that followed" (*The Burning* 58).

Articles from the *Cork Examiner*'s coverage of the trial describe Dunne as fairy-ridden, a believer in the lore and superstitions carried in rural folk traditions. Bourke observes that this might have given Dunne a certain prestige within the local community, similar to the role of seanachí, the storyteller of earlier times (*The Burning*). A small man with one leg shorter than the other due to a previous injury, this privileged position would have also protected him from any bullying or maltreatment due to physical disability. It was even believed at the time that lameness and other physical or mental attributes considered irregular or eccentric were signs of being touched by the fairy world. The *Cork Examiner*, at the time as Bourke recounts, went so far as to describe Dunne as a man "learned ... in incantations, charms and spells." No small irony considering it was Bridget who would be burned alive, maligned as a witch or a fairy, largely as a consequence of Dunne's proclamations. As Bourke comments, "His remarks set all the fairy machinery in motion" (*The Burning* 62). This included enforcing the more bizarre forms of ritual enacted, even the final fatal act of banishing her fairy possession by holding Bridget over the open fire. However, before this escalation, when Bridget was not recovering after a week of illness from what was likely a chill, cold, or even pneumonia, on Saturday March 9, Dr. Willian Crean was sent for from the nearby town of Fethard. He did not arrive until Wednesday, March 13, and then only after her father Patrick Boland and husband Michael Cleary had walked numerous times to petition him to visit. At this point the local priest, Fr. Con Ryan was also sent for. As Bourke recounts, during the trial, Dr. Crean stated that Bridget was healthy: "She had a body of good physique and well nourished. The only thing I can say is that she was awfully nervous" but he "could not elicit any explanation" as to why *(The Burning* 66). Dr. Crean who had been Bridget's local physician for at least nine years also stated she had slight bronchitis. When pressed as to what he meant by "awfully nervous," he said, "I always found her a nervous irritable sort of woman" (*The Burning* 66). The comment perhaps reflects an underlying attitude or defensiveness at his delay in attending to her, but also the sociopolitical context within which Bridget lived and died. Had she been from a wealthier class or of higher social standing, maybe he would have called sooner or been more vigilant in ascertaining the root cause of her anxiety. Perhaps Bridget did not conform to the norms of the time, which is how Dr. Crean expected a woman of her station to behave. In casting a shadow over her character, he was excusing his negligence and victim blaming, introducing doubt and potential causes for what was done to her.

Michael Cleary would later state while in prison that it took the intervention of a local Protestant landowner William Simpson and notification of Crean's conduct to the Poor Law Guardian for the district, Mr. Edmond Cummins, before Crean had eventually called to the house to see Bridget. In the contemporary context, it is perhaps also easier to recognize the signs of coercive control: Bridget's silence and inability to disclose the increasingly irrational and dangerous situation she was in and the threatening behaviour of her husband, in-laws and neighbours; the desperation of her appeals to those present, telling how her husband had already attempted to set her alight the previous December; how he was determined to "make a fairy of her"; and her final effort to deflect his accusations by suggesting even his own mother was "taken by the fairies," which only incensed him further. At this point, when Crean did eventually call, it was too late. Her husband, for reasons never fully examined, decided to believe that her true malady was due to supernatural causes.

Witnesses described how she was held down by her male cousins while her husband forced her to ingest an herbal remedy from the local "fairy doctor" Denis Ganey. She was branded with a hot iron, held over the open fire in a seated position, and forced to repeat affirmations that she was indeed herself. Her appeals to her father and others present were ignored, as the collective frenzy to purge her of some feral presence gained momentum. Jack Dunne, as Bourke notes, was "particularly insistent on the rituals of changeling banishment" (The Burning 581). The collective darkness that overcame them, as judge O'Brien would later describe it, seemed to have taken hold to such an extent that Michael Cleary's increasing violence towards his wife, lasting several days and nights, was not halted. This included throwing water, urine, and hen excrement on her, having her physically shaken or slapped, and performing impromptu incantations. The hypnagogic frenzy finally descended into deadly violence. When Bridget would not, or could not, concede any further, he poured lamp oil over her and threw her into the open fire in a final fit of rage. She died on the floor of the cottage from the severity of the burns to her abdomen and legs. Unable to avoid the consequences, all but her husband ran to different corners of the small cottage, with one man fainting in horror. But Cleary had locked the doors and refused to allow them to escape until they swore silence.

Bridget's fate was determined by collective action and conscious or passive collusion. The general outrage at these events reached far beyond the local community, with articles appearing in newspapers in Dublin, London, and New York. The *Dublin Evening Mail* attributed the incident to ignorance, superstition, even Druidical or pagan Danish (Viking) influence. But the judge could not determine what Bridget did to deserve such cruelty. She was a good and faithful wife, pleasant to look at and attended church. She performed her domestic duties, fulfilled her familial obligations and seemed well respected within her community—a fact proven by the number of visitors she received during her illness. Bridget was murdered and her body hidden between March 14 and 15 within two days of the visit of Dr. Crean and the parish priest. Delay, neglect, and indifference from those who could have intervened facilitated an environment where the influence of those with more nefarious intentions managed to convince even Bridget's own father that she was not herself at all but a feral thing undeserving of humane treatment. Estranged and alienated, her body and person became the site of violent erasure. Mary Douglas warns there is a real danger in perceived states of hybridity, where the subject is believed to be in a no-man's land of the betwixt and between. It is precisely because of this that societies the world over devised elaborate forms of ritual to contain transitional or threshold states, where the subject was perceived to be between worlds. A symbolic alteration in Bridget permitted grievous transgression by those who in their right mind should have known better. There was no doubt that Michael Cleary was the main instigator and ringleader. His repeated insistence that "it isn't Bridget we are burning at all" at key moments of escalation assuaged any doubts or attempts to halt events, but he certainly was not alone. Jack Dunne's influence was instrumental in convincing all involved that it was not a woman they were tormenting. He was actively involved in her torture and accompanied Michael Cleary in the ruse of searching for her at the fairy fort of Kylenagranagh in the days following her disappearance. In the 1895 *Folklore* article "The 'Witch-Burning' at Clonmel,"

Michael Cleary is recorded as shouting out, even as Bridget was burning, "She is burned now, but God knows I did not mean to do it. I may thank Jack Dunne for all of it" (376).

Nine people were brought to trial following Bridget's murder. Dunne's involvement was reflected in the sentencing handed down. He was imprisoned for three years and then returned to his community, taking up work as a labourer. His wife died while he was in prison. Patrick, James, William, and Michael Kennedy, Bridget's cousins, were given varying sentences of hard labour. William was sentenced to five years, James and William were sentenced to eighteen months, and Michael Kennedy to only six months. Her father, Patrick Boland, also received six months of hard labour, while charges against William Ahern were dropped. Her mother Mary Kennedy, was not charged due to her age and likely her gender. Johanna Bourke who became the main prosecution witness, though not charged, was not afforded, unlike Dunne, the tolerance of the local community in the years that followed and had to move away from the area. Michael Cleary was convicted of manslaughter and though sentenced to twenty years of penal servitude was released after fifteen in 1910. He moved first to Liverpool and then emigrated to Canada in the same year.

Ironically it had never been Bridget herself who was the true outsider in this community, but Michael Cleary. A man alienated from his own family, he'd followed her to live in her townland, among her people, a reversal of gender roles for the time. Acknowledgement of this outsider status became obvious during his outbursts in court, where his mistrust of his in-laws and the blame he attributed to all but himself erupted. As Bourke notes, a correspondent for *The Irish Times* described him as being "a respectable and good-looking man" but with "a rather wild look about the eyes" ("Reading a Woman's Death" 575). But regardless of his outsider status, the position he held in a conservative patriarchal Irish Catholic society assured him ultimate authority, enabling him to dictate the events and actions leading to her death. It was only when Bridget's body went up in flames and the house was filled "with smoke and smell" that the others involved refused to follow his orders any further. He failed to take a neighbour's gun to compel them to accompany him further. He followed through, however, on his promise to feign madness and search the fort of Kylenagranagh for three nights, claiming Bridget would ride out on a grey horse. The local constabulary had begun the search for

Bridget's body, and she was finally found in a shallow grave, a quarter of a mile from her home.

Taken by the Others

The burning of Bridget Cleary is shocking, as it demonstrates how tenuous the safety of reason, the protection of law and order, the bonds of kinship, and the expectation of fair treatment actually are for women, regardless of the era. For Bridget and far too many women, the collective darkness of mind described by Judge O'Brien in 1895 is not a threat confined to the distant past. From an anthropological perspective, the incident could be interpreted as an example of what C.J. Jung termed "participation mystique," a term derived from Lévy-Bruhl's "Law of Participation": a phenomenon where the prelogical or "primitive" worldview, usually within premodern societies, imbues the world of objects with a spiritual, supernatural, or uncanny presence. Building upon this concept, C.G. Jung later wrote of this as a loss of separation within subject-object relations, involving transference, often of the darker unacknowledged aspects of the psyche upon a particular target. In "Psychological Types,", discussing "primitive psychology," he describes participation mystique as emerging from a worldview where the collective predates any concept of the unique individual: "The collective attitude hinders the recognition and evaluation of a psychology different from the subject's, because the mind that is collectively orientated is quite incapable of thinking and feeling in any other way than by projection" (33). While terminology such as "primitive" to describe a premodern, Indigenous, or native worldview is deeply contentious in the contemporary context, ideas of "status quo" or "collective consensus" are not. For Bridget Cleary, the collective consensus of those in her immediate family and community determined her fate, even superseding the opinion of a local physician. She became for the collective of those involved not a unique human individual but the embodiment of a projected shadow. It was no longer Bridget herself that they were seeing but something so shrouded by superstition and suppression that it had to be destroyed. Warren Coleman describes this as a state of mind in which "we do not experience ourselves as divided from the external world but feel we are in participation with it as an active living force" (236). The inner world of the psyche is transferred onto external objects or other subjects, influencing the formation of shared perceptions, beliefs, and values including shared symbolic forms often inspiring collective actions. Furthermore, these can be "transmitted from one generation to another as the symbolic matrix in which individuals are located" (237). Shared spiritual traditions, customs, mythologies, pishogues, even artistic representations, which signify societal perceptions of reality and contain ideas of the divine or the demonic, exist within this matrix. Michael Cleary did not have to justify himself to those present; they knew the folklore and believed a changeling substitution was possible. As Conrad Arensberg observes, such pishogues are "much more than ignorant superstitions.... They form a symbolic order overlying the values of social life and clothing them in emotional terms in much the same way as do unofficial dogmas and unofficial, non-logical cosmologies among all peoples" (166). Even as Bridget endured the physical torture and the bizarre ritual purging, this did not alter a shared perception, a collective consensus, that it was not a woman they were burning but something other entirely.

Warren Coleman also explains how participation mystique contains impossible states of identity where "things can be themselves and something other than themselves" simultaneously (241). Lévy-Bruhl perceives this as a state where the boundary between humans, animals, elemental forces, spirits, or other unseen presences dissolve. It is also the circumstance where an otherwise rational person can believe in the entirely irrational. This is often presented as revelation, visitation, or encounter in organized religion. Coleman describes how this psychological state is linked to the imaginal, with the imagination becoming a doorway into "a special dimension of reality" (242). Within this psychological state, it was possible to believe the woman Bridget Cleary could be both herself and not herself. She had become both the recognized domestic wife and daughter but also a dangerous feral nonhuman creature that had crept in from the otherworld. Unfortunately for Bridget, this projection, the return of the repressed, held within it centuries of Catholic demonization of all to do with the otherworld. It was not a revelation, awe, or wonder that she inspired but a deadly fear of what had been driven underground into the darkness of the subaltern.

Fear of the Feral

Bridget Cleary's story is ultimately about a primal fear of the feral. That which was once familiar to the domestic Irish psyche and spiritual world-view, driven out into the wilderness of estrangement through centuries of sociopolitical and religious repression. Connelly describes how the fairy, or Sídhe, were demonized during the spiritual colonization of Ireland by the Catholic Church. Drawing upon Peter Burgin's theory of sacred canopy, Connelly describes how organized religions use syncretism to gradually erase and replace pre-existing Indigenous spirituality (1). She describes how it was the Catholic monks who transcribed the previously oral culture of early Ireland into volumes, such as *Lebor na hUidre, The Book of the Dun Cow* (twelfth century CE). Regarded as the earliest manuscript in old Irish, it contains the first recorded references to the otherworld of the Sídhe. What were once the gods and goddesses of the older symbolic order were systematically transformed into malign presences. By the nineteenth century, before the Celtic revival, their names and attributes would have been all but erased, surviving as inverted shadows within superstition and pishogues. The Catholic Church transformed them into vengeful presences, their commune with the mortal world a deception leading to damnation. Through this process of erasure and replacement, all that was once familiar within the domestic cosmology was pushed out into the spiritual and geographical wilderness. The fairy forts as physical remnants of older human inhabitation or spiritual practice became places of danger and taboo. As Bourke notes, these former sites of early medieval dwelling "remain sites of avoidance, overgrown and undisturbed, metaphors for areas of silence and circumvention in the social life of communities.... They are places out of place; their time is out of time" ("Reading a Woman's Death" 569). Like the absences and avoidances in oral, even written narratives, they are sites of the unspoken. From a psychological perspective, to be taken by the fairy to these places could be seen as a metaphor for a return to the repressed, with all of its individual and collective trauma.

Kaitlin Conelly also provides a detailed analysis of how through direct and indirect means, from selective exclusions, re-interpretations and colophons, the "monks in Ireland were purposefully writing books that explicitly demonised paganism and altered the truth to fabricate a story that fit Catholic need at the time" (8). Controversially, she proposes that even *Lebor Gabála, The Book of Invasions*, is "a falsified history of Ireland"

and that archaeological evidence now suggests that the Tuatha Dé Dannan, believed to be the progenitor race of the Sídhe, may also be a fabrication. As the original pagan cosmology and the belief system of the Druids predated written records, it is difficult to be definitive. However, it is certain that in establishing a framework for institutionalized religion, all that was once sacred was cast out through force, fear and violence to the margins, the wild spaces, and the collective subconscious. In the decades directly preceding Bridget Cleary's death, the Irish Celtic revival had also transformed the Sídhe of myth into romanticized diminutive wistful fairies, more reflective of the nostalgic imaginal of an urban upper class, longing for the lost former glory of a Celtic world. We see this in the work of W.B. Yeats, such as *Irish Fairy Tales* (1892) or *The Celtic Twilight* (1893). There is little connection, however, between these reconstructed myths and the darker vengeful fairies of common folklore. In Yeats's poem "The Stolen Bride," later translated as "The Host of the Air" published in 1893, two years before Bridget's death, the Sídhe are little more than voices on the wind, faint echoes lingering on in nature and disconnected from their image among the rural poor, where they are often referred to euphemistically as the "Good People," the "Other Crowd," or not at all for fear of ill fortune. For the rural poor, they haunted the landscape and psyche as feral spectral vestiges, signifying both shadowy presence and absences. What Bessel van der Kolk would describe as disassociations within memory, where the repression of trauma, individual and intergenerational, is signified through ellipse. In the postcolonial context, as Jake Bevan observes, such hauntings can be an "incarnation of the recurrence of the past in the present," representing "the ellipses and lacunae of the national historical memory" (246). Presenting as avoidance, aversion, taboo, irrational terror and violence when triggered, these ellipses or elisions within memory signify a lingering imprint of deep trauma. In over-writing the sacred forms of a pre-existing world view, the new Catholic doctrine recast these as unholy. The old gods were driven under the hills into the mounds, or fairy forts, becoming the Sídhe, the fallen angels of the otherworld. As shapeshifters and tricksters, these archetypal forces now existed within the imaginal as feral presences haunting the thin places. In "The Virtual Reality of Irish Fairy Legend," Bourke describes these sites as nonplaces located on boundaries between, for example, townlands, high and low tide, day and night, dusk and dawn; or they reemerge on significant dates of the older pagan calendar, such as May Eve. Fairies, she observes, are in "no-man's land: they live in no time at all" (12). To be taken by the fairies was to risk damnation and threaten the social, spiritual, and domestic new world order. Bourke also observes how such stories are metaphors for what Richard Breen terms women's "floating" position within the status hierarchy: "Like the cows which accompanied them as dowry, women were regularly bartered and exchanged in marriage contracts. Unmarried they were placeless" ("Reading a Woman's Death" 574).

In a postfamine society, where rootedness to the land was the only financial and psychological guarantee of safety, this state of detachment was frightening. Further, Bourke notes how "In the years following the famine the propertied middle class accumulated land and commercial assets and dictated a repressive morality based on a newly centralized, authoritarian, and misogynist Catholicism which worked hand in hand with the institutions of the state" ("Reading a Woman's Death" 559). However, the right to own land, to even partake in forms of economic bartering associated with it, such as the buying and selling of livestock, was until recently in rural Ireland a strictly male inheritance. English common law, including primogeniture, had been fully imposed in Ireland by the seventeenth century, replacing the earlier Brehon law. As Mary Hederman notes, married women were regarded as chattel within this framework. Barred from having a profession, owning property or financial assets, or seeking refuge in another man's home, a wife was totally at the mercy of her husband. In contrast, under the older Irish Brehon law, based upon the extended familial unit of the Tuath, there was gender equality in inheritance, land usage, ownership of resources, and divorce rights. The limitations placed upon married women and an enforced economic dependency within marriage existed until recently in Ireland. The marriage bar for example, was only lifted in 1973. Before this women were forced by law to resign from their posts in the civil service once married. Survival within this social, political, economic and religious matrix depended upon conforming to a strictly controlled domestication. To transgress risked exile, even incarceration within what James Smith describes as the nation's "architecture of containment." Church-run, state sponsored institutions, such as the Magdalene Laundries and Mother and Baby Homes, were a constant threat for those deemed fallen women. Article 41.2, inserted into the Irish Constitution by the staunchly conservative Catholic-first Irish president Eamon De

Valera, delineated the expected role of women in the new Irish Republic: "In particular, the State recognises that by her life within the home, woman gives to the State a support without which the common good cannot be achieved." This Article within the Irish Constitution remains deeply contentious to the present day in Ireland. In March 2024 a referendum proposing removal of this article and reframing the provision of care within the home, in more gender neutral language was also defeated.

Within Bridget Cleary's lifetime, as Vejvoda observes, to circumvent a patriarchal system that made women so financially dependent on a husband, rural women often kept poultry or used domestic handicrafts, such as weaving, knitting, and sewing to achieve some financial independence. Bridget was part of this evolving suffrage. She earned her own living as a seamstress, sold eggs to supplement her income, and was not financially or physically strained by the worries of bearing many children. The fact that after seven years of marriage she was childless would however, have been cause for comment. No longer a newlywed bride, but not yet a mother, she existed in a socially liminal space. Compared to many women within her community, she was economically self-sufficient and literate, and despite her husband's landlessness, she had secured a good standard of housing. This may have also caused certain resentment and jealousy. She was well on her way to being othered in all these things. In a recent article on Bridget Cleary's story for *The Irish Times*, Millena Williamson comments how people who knew Bridget said she was "a bit queer" and "not like that of every woman in the same social plane." Williamson describes Bridget as "already a threat to the patriarchal order," noting how rumours that she had walked too close to the fairy fort on Kylenagranagh Hill provided a veiled but potent signifier of her difference. There are several indicators that Bridget Cleary in her difference from the traditional expectations of a domestic rural housewife of her time was othered. In his article "Us vs. Them: The Sinister Techniques of Othering," John Powell observes that this process of othering is not about liking or disliking, it is an anxiety based upon perceived threat—a fear that can prompt extremes of dehumanization and violence against what is perceived as different.

Encountering the Feral

A recent short article in *The Irish Sun* tabloid newspaper, "Horror Story, I Heard a Woman Call Out," demonstrates how the vestiges of fear, central to the othering of Bridget Cleary, still haunt the modern Irish psyche. The writer, Sandra Murphy, recounts an uncanny encounter on a lonely forest path. A disembodied voice calls to her and in panic, she reverts to the advice of pishogues. Turning her clothing inside out, she retraces her steps. The linear sequence of temporal time seems distorted. The birdsong of the forest now sounds far away, as if "behind glass." The voice, which is female, darts about. Initially comforted by another woman's voice at a lonely spot in the woods, this modern young woman is overcome by fright when she perceives the voice is laughing at her. The hairs on the back of her legs stand up, and fear of the supernatural takes hold. With nothing more than superstition to interpret her experience, she runs in panic, wondering if she has stepped into the otherworld. Is it by chance that she is wandering close to the Eve of Manon, which in pagan Ireland fell on the autumn equinox? This was when day and night were of equal duration, and the veil between worlds was believed to be at its thinnest. If she knew more of her cultural heritage and the impact of intergenerational memory, or if she had more of a map to refer to beyond prohibitions and superstitions, would her imagination tend less towards horror? Her only reference seems to be the pervasive atmosphere of dread permeating stories such as those gathered from the living memory of rural communities in western Ireland by contemporary folklorists like Eddie Lennihan. In Lennihan's "Meeting the Other Crowd," for example, a sinister undertone of threat attaches to all things otherworldly. The Sídhe, which this modern woman fears she has encountered are considered malevolent, vicious, and vengeful beings, set on destroying those who cross their threshold.

Knowing the symbolic, sacred, and imaginal world of the older Irish myths is an essential counterbalance to this tendency to frame the beliefs of pagan Ireland as malevolent. The diversity, variance, multivalency, hybridity, and transformative capacity, particularly within archetypal forms of the feminine with the older stories and myths, provide a wealth of possibility in reconstituting what has been forgotten, especially in accepting psychological or spiritual experience beyond reductive gendered limitations. Encounters with the otherworld, as they remain in what has been preserved, are common occurrences and rarely treated with mass panic or brutal violence. In the older myths, visitations by the Sídhe often marked moments of initiation or the bestowing of great gifts and attributes. We find this for example in the Ultonian Cycle, *An Rúraíocht*, the conception of Cú Chulainn the prototypical masculine hero, is understood to have happened in the otherworld. His mother Dectera, went with the Sídhe to live with Lugh the God of Light for three years. Like Hercules, Achilles or Perseus in Greek myth, Cú Chulainn received his superhuman abilities because he was of both mortal and immortal origin. In the later Ossianic Cycle, *An Fhiannaíocht*, the story of Niamh and Oisín is preserved by Míchheál Comín (1750) in *The Lay of Oisín and the Land of Youth*. It begins with an encounter on a misty morning near Loch Lena, when Oisín the son of the great warrior Fionn MacCumhaill is visited by Niamh of the Golden Hair, who spirits him away to the land of eternal youth. In T.W. Rolleston's retelling of the myth, he describes how as she spoke, "a dreamy stillness fell on all things, nor did a horse shake his bit, nor a hound bay, nor the least breath of wind stir in the forest trees till she had made an end" (271). We see a familiar trope here: The Sídhe, or fae, are perceived as beings in harmony with the natural world, having deep affinity with its plants, animals, and elements. Distortions within regular linear time are also common, including transcending the limitations of the human lifespan. Niamh describes the otherworld as being one of eternal youth, fairer than anything human eyes have seen—plentiful, rich, and free of all sickness, pain, or death. Niamh arrives as a feral feminine that is golden, radiant and noble. She has fallen in love with Oisín, and he willingly accompanies her to the otherworld. Their children—Oscar, Finn, and Plúr na mBan (Flower of Women)—will all have demigod attributes. This is one of the most famous and oldest popular myths, which tells of a carrying away by the Sídhe. However, Rolleston notes how the prolongation of Oisín's mortal lifespan, through his time spent in the otherworld, is later used to bridge a gap in worldviews between the pagan and the Christian (276). The insertion of a Christian conversion at the end of his saga in more modern versions is both clumsy and unalluring. The magical realm of the otherworld remains far more attractive than Oisín's final transformation into a crippled ancient and feeble old man, when he accidentally topples from his otherworldly horse to find himself in an Ireland where the ancient hunting grounds of the Fianna in Kildare are gone forever and the Christian bell of St. Patrick intrudes upon the air.

In her recent writing on Irish mythology, Lora O'Brien presents another example of the feral feminine in the form of Flidais, a figure almost entirely erased over the centuries. Known as the goddess of both cattle and deer, signifying her ability to move between the domesticated and wild worlds, her hybridity benefited humankind. Traces of this archetype survive in the Ultonian Cycle, notably the *Táin Bó Flidais*, where she is described as a woman of the Sídhe who marries King Ailill Finn, accompanying his army during the great Cattle Raid of Cooley the *Táin Bó Cúailnge*. Flidais has the magical power to feed over three hundred warriors at once from the milking of just one of her cows, signifying her intermediary position as a conduit between the human and suprahuman worlds. In an earlier form, she was the Great Earth Mother, and her sons were the first farmers, BéChuille and Dinand. However, while associated with nurturance and the maternal, Flidais also retains her wild instinctive nature, returning to the otherworld even after her time among men. Artist Judith Shaw finds parallels between Flidais and Arduina, the Lady of the Forest, venerated in parts of England, Luxembourg, Belgium, France, and Germany. A protector of the animals, plants, and woodlands, this feral feminine was both nurturing and fierce. For Shaw, she is the wild woman archetype that Pinkola Estés speaks of; moving between the domesticated and the wilderness. As Lady of the Hunt, she may have also been associated with the Roman goddess Diana and the Greek goddess Artemis. In a society where the symbolic and spiritual worldview recognized such forms as sacred, it is likely that meeting a feral feminine in the forest, even a disembodied voice, would have been perceived as far less frightening, inspiring not terror but the kind of reverence reserved today for places of visitation or miracle. However, with the demonization of these older traditions, the prohibitions against encounters with this otherworld were especially harsh for women. As Bourke notes, it was common belief in Bridget Cleary's time that those who entered a fairy fort would emerge changed, if at all. Gender differences are enforced yet again even here: "Men who return to ordinary life possess new musical or medical abilities, while with the exception of midwives, women who return or are rescued are usually mute, injured, or mutilated" ("Reading a Woman's Death" 569). It demonstrates a centuries-old system of cutting women off through threat, prohibition, and taboo from the roots of their connection to female divinity within older pre-Christian traditions, where the feral aspect of the feminine transcendent was venerated.

Conclusion

It could be said that Bridget Cleary lost her life due to ignorance and superstition at a time when rural communities were less educated and more influenced or repressed by the ideologies of organized patriarchal religion. But her story is ultimately about the struggles between a woman who dared to wander into the transgressive domain of the feral and the violence enacted upon her to contain and curtail this: She wandered too close to the fairy fort and its otherworld of irrepressible feral beings. She drifted out past the expectations of her class and role as a domestic house-wife and strayed into an education, a trade, and financial independence. She roamed with a landless husband, occupied coveted property, rambled on past the acceptable timeline for bearing children, and deviated in her ability to support her aging father, usurping the natural order. There was gossip that she may have even traipsed along the roads to sell her eggs for a tryst with the local egg merchant. As Bourke observes, Bridget may have even been using the idiom of fairy abduction herself as a coded language "to assert her independence and autonomy or protect herself from a violent and impulsive man" ("Reading a Woman's Death" 577–8). Bridget diverged from the dictated script even during her persecution: She dared to speak against the collective will to other her, defying the enforced suppression of her will, her voice, and finally her existence. In the violence of her last moments, we see a desperate attempt by her tor-mentors to restore her to an acceptable form of wife and daughter. This is a theatre macabre of patriarchal enforcement in extremis, down to the last brutal acts of force-feeding, manically insisting she repeat only cer-tain words, or "down she would go." With a knee on her chest, a hand around her throat and the threat of oral rape with a burning stick we see the full force of its enactment. Finally, even the natural physiological reactions of her body—for example, her inability to repeatedly swallow dry bread—were interpreted as resistance, triggering Michael Cleary's fit of rage to extinguish her life completely. Her transgression was her feral state and her ability to shapeshift, to dare to redefine herself in the world. The threat of the feral is here intrinsically linked to prohibitions on what the feminine can be within patriarchal systems of control and enforced submission. It was always a matter of agreeing to a carefully scripted construct, this and only this, on pain of ever-increasing levels of retaliation.

More recent cases involving the murder of women in rural Ireland however, such as those of Imelda Riney (1994), Sophie Toscan du Plantier (1996) and Emer O'Loughlin (2005), demonstrate that the danger of being perceived as feral persists even for women in present-day Ireland. In her controversial novel *In the Forest*, Edna O'Brien reconstructs events leading to the death of Imelda Riney. O'Brien's depiction is unforgiving of a particular rural Irish mindset, where a young, attractive, artistic, single mother, could be othered as a 'blow-in', a traveller and therefore unworthy of respect, even honest testimony when she was abducted by local man Brendan O'Donnell. O'Brien shows how Riney's feral otherness contributed to the events surrounding her murder. As recently as December 2022, in a podcast for the *Irish Independent*, journalist Ralph Riegel describes Imelda as having "this almost bohemian mystique about her, because of the way she dressed, because of her love of art, her love of nature." When she disappeared in May 1994 with her youngest son, Liam, her friends and family began a frantic search around her remote rural cottage in Whitegate, County Clare. Her former partner reported her missing, and suspicions were growing within the local community that a much-feared local man might be involved. Yet, as Riegal describes, the "gardai believed that this was an artistic person, a bohemian person, you know they drift in and out of society. She might have gone off somewhere unexplained. I don't think the importance was attached to it, that had it been a person whose disappearance was totally and utterly out of character." Using witness testimony, O'Brien reveals a conservative attitude of evasion, denial, fear and othering. Imelda was so alienated that when O'Donnell took her into the depths of Cloosh Woods, there would be no timely rescue, no help, no mercy. It was days before her body and that of her young son were eventually found in a shallow grave. Also days before the locals who witnessed her abduction would come forward with testimony that might have saved her. The Irish authorities also failed her by refusing to act in a timely manner.

It was only when it was discovered that O'Donnell had also abducted Fr. Joe Walsh, a local Catholic priest, that a manhunt was finally launched. By then O'Donnell had murdered Imelda, her young son, and the priest. Donal Lynch in his article for the *Irish Independent* in 2014, describes how O'Donnell, with a long and known history of psychiatric illness, including an obsession with good and evil, believed that Imelda was the devil's daughter, and her son, the devil's son. In O'Brien's telling of the story, Imelda wanders into that realm of the feral pagan feminine through her love of nature, her gentle kindness, her freedom from the constraints of traditional domesticity, and her earthy embodiment and sexuality. She imagines Imelda's last night of freedom as a "a Pagan feast on the mountain, an old recitation, old lusts, debauchery and division between men and women amplified to the brazen beat of fiddle and penny whistle" (87), where under the moon she becomes Queen Euvul of the Grey Rock, an allusion to the fairy Queen of the May. Imelda was taken on April 29, 1994, and was believed to have been murdered within the first two days of her abduction. The May eve, as Vejvoda notes was believed in folk traditions to be particularly fraught with danger, especially for those out at night (46). O'Brien brings us into Imelda's last moments, where her death becomes a ritual sacrifice influenced by dark undertows of a struggle within the psyche of O'Donnell, the community and even the Irish state. O'Brien alludes to a symbolic and cultural matrix haunted by both the older mythological archetypes and centuries of institutionalized religious repression. The consequences are brutalization and extreme violence enacted upon the othered woman. O'Donnell's name is rarely mentioned in O'Brien's novel. He is referred to instead as the Kinderschreck, a malign presence from folklore, much like the Irish Pooka, which was believed to prey upon people from the shadows of night.

The recent documentary series *Márú Inár Measc* (*Death in Our Midst*) for TG4, the Irish language TV channel, features the story of Emer O'Loughlin who was murdered in early April (2005). Based upon interviews with family, friends, and individuals within her local community of Ennistymon in County Clare, Emer is remembered for her kindness, her love of nature especially her animals, her creativity and confidence to follow her path in life. Emer's body was discovered incinerated beyond recognition in the burnt-out mobile home of John Griffin, on a plot adjacent to where she was living with her partner in a remote part of County Clare. She was only twenty-three years of age and preparing a portfolio to study art in Dublin when she was murdered. While the love for Emer within both her family and local community is apparent in this program, where friends describe her as very much "one of their own," questions remain about the handling of her death by the Irish authorities. It was not initially treated as a murder case. Her only neighbour, John Griffin, a man with a history of violence and drug abuse, was not arrested, although he was questioned. Only days after her body was found, he barricaded himself into the Dún Aonghasa fort on Inis Mór, pelting stones at passers-by. He was brought to a psychiatric hospital in Ballinasloe and signed himself out within five days. Shaving off his hair and beard, he returned to the fort on Inis Mór. His clothes and shoes were later found on the cliff edge prompting a land and sea search, but he had vanished without a trace. It is believed he attempted to feign his own death to evade further pursuit by the authorities. His repeated return to an ancient fort on the western seaboard, a place linked in cultural memory to the otherworld, and his bizarre actions leading to him being deemed insane bear an unusual resemblance to the behaviour of Michael Cleary in the days following the murder of Bridget. It was only through the persistence of her sister that Emer's body was exhumed and properly examined five years later in 2010. This forensic examination discovered that Emer was violently assaulted and murdered. An Interpol international arrest warrant was issued in 2010, but John Griffin remains at large. Like the family of Sophie Toscan du Plantier, a film producer murdered in rural West Cork in 1996, Emer's family remains without justice or closure.

Like Bridget Cleary, all three contemporary women were creatively independent in their nonconformity with status-quo expectations. They retained something of the feral and the sacred in their wandering and their desire to live close to nature, to pursue dreams of alternative self-determining lives. In the investigations, testimonies, disclosures, speculations, and media coverage that followed their deaths, the overt and latent othering of these women reveals how consciously and subconsciously their lives challenged the domestication of the feminine. To be perceived as feral, as that which transgresses the traditional role prescribed for women, is always to risk everything, even your life. Unfortunately, this threat will remain until the underlying symbolic matrix of our culture— its psychological, religious, and mytho-poetic dimensions—allows for the integrated acceptance of this spectrum of the feminine. The shadow of colonization in the Irish context cannot be overlooked, especially where it impacts and influences the re-enactment of unresolved past traumas, through the othering of those considered outsiders in the present. When the former wealth and diversity of a shared imaginal is twisted by institutionalized violence, the rejected and repressed will always find release through other, often darker means. As in most postcolonial societies, women's bodies become the first, though not last, site of violence in the reconfiguration of hierarchies of othering. As Arensberg has observed, "Those who repudiate the fairies repudiate only the outmoded symbols, the outworn images. They do not deny the necessity of a symbolic order in their own lives... [as] there must always be some socially efficacious organisation of the sentiments of social life in the logic of belief and imagery" (188). The fairy in this context signify the feral as a site of alterity which retains the freedom of not only that which transgresses but also offers the potential of becoming something entirely new and liberated from the strictures of domestic constraint. Their stories as they remain in the oral and written tradition offer connection to a feminine both transcendent and wild. This feral will, however, remain a dangerous zone for women until the predatory shadow of its violent repression is fully understood and questioned.

Works Cited

Arensberg, Conrad. *The Irish Countryman, An Anthropological Study*. The Natural History Press, 1968.

Bevan, Jake. *Trauma, Modernity and Hauntings: The Legacy of Japanese Colonialism in Contemporary South Korean Cinema*. University of Exeter, 2017.

Biagini, Euugenio Federico. "Home Rule for Ireland (1874–1914): the Great Missed Opportunity?" *Études Anglaises*, vol. 71, no. 3, 2018, pp. 257–75.

Bourke, Angela. "Reading a Woman's Death: Colonial Text and Oral Tradition in Nineteenth-Century Ireland." *Feminist Studies*, vol. 21, no. 3, 1995, pp. 553–86.

Bourke, Angela. *The Burning of Bridget Cleary*. The Random House Group, 2006.

Bourke, Angela. "The Virtual Reality of Irish Fairy Legend." *Éire-Ireland*, vol. 31, no. 1&2, 1996, pp. 7–25.

Coleman, Warren. *Act and Image: The Emergence of Symbolic Imagination*. Routledge, 2020.

Conelly, Kaitlin. *Demonic Sidhe: The Fabrication of Catholic Hell in Medieval Pagan Irish Texts*. 2022. Texas State University, PhD dissertation., https://digital.library.txst.edu/items/f932465f-deld-444c-9177-042de05c0613/full. Accessed 27 Jan. 2025.

Douglas, Mary. *Purity and Danger.* Routledge, 2005.

Hederman, Mary. "Irish Women and Irish Law." *The Crane Bag*, vol. 4, no. 1, 1980, pp. 55–59.

Hussain, Ruksar. "Fairy Belief and Fairy Tales in Scotland." *Museums and Galleries Scotland*, 6 June 2022, https://www.edinburghmuseums. org.uk/stories/fairy-belief-fairy-tales-scotland. Accessed 5 Feb. 2024.

Jung, C.J. *The Collected Works of C.G. Jung.* Princeton University Press, 1971.

Kolk, Bessel van der. *The Body Keeps the Score.* Allen Lane, 2014.

Lennihan, Edmund. *Meeting The Other Crowd, The Fairy Stories of Hidden Ireland.* Gill Books, 2003.

Lévy-Bruhl, L. *How Natives Think.* Knopf, 1925.

Lynch, Donal. "The Landscape of a Nightmare." *The Irish Independent*, https://www.independent.ie/life/the-landscape-of-a-nightmare/ 30135907.html. Accessed 27 Jan. 2025.

"Emer O'Loughlin". *Márú Inár Measc*, S2 E2, *TG4*, Dublin, 25 May. 2022.

Murphy, Sandra. "Horror Story, I Heard a Woman Call Out on Walk in Wood." *The Irish Sun*, 6 Sept. 2022, https://www.thesun.ie/news/ 9363676/never-felt-such-fear-woman-fairies-ghost-walk-terrified/. Accessed 27 Jan. 2025.

O'Brien, Edna. *In the Forest.* Weidenfeld & Nicholson, 2002.

O'Brien, Lora. "Flidhais, Who's Who of Irish Mythology Blog Series." *Lora O'Brien Irish Author and Guide*, 14 Jan 2018, https://loraobrien. ie/who8/. Accessed 14 May. 2024.

Pinkola Estés, Clarissa. *Women Who Run with The Wolves: Contacting the Power of the Wild Woman.* Ebury Publishing, 2008.

Powell, John. "Us vs. Them: The Sinister Techniques of 'Othering'—and How to Avoid Them." *The Guardian*, 8 Nov 2017, https://www. theguardian.com/inequality/2017/nov/08/us-vs-them-the-sinister- techniques-of-othering-and-how-to-avoid-them. Accessed 27 Jan. 2025.

Riegal, Sheahan. "Murder, Mayhem & The Manhunt—The Shocking Story of Imelda Riney." *Irish Independent*, 19 Dec 2022, https://www. independent.ie/podcasts/the-indo-daily/the-indo-daily-murder-mayhem-and-the-manhunt-the-shocking-story-of-imelda-riney/ 42225406.html. Accessed 12 June. 2024.

Rolleston, T. W. *Myths and Legends Series, Celtic*. Bracken Books, 1985.

Sexton, D., and M. Fitzgerald. "Autism and Changelings," https://www. researchgate.net/publication/276059373_Autism_and_Changelings. Accessed 27 Jan. 2025.

Shaw, Judith. "Arduinna, Gaulish Goddess of Forests and Hunting." *Feminism and Religion*, 24 Feb 2016, https://feminismandreligion. com/2016/02/24/arduinna-gaulish-goddess-of-forests-and-hunting/. Accessed 27 Jan. 2025.

Smith, James. *Ireland's Magdalen Laundries and the Nation's Architecture of Containment*. University of Notre Dame Press, 2007.

"The 'Witch-Burning' at Clonmel." *Folklore*, vol. 6, no. 4, 1895, pp. 373–84.

Young, Simon. "Fairy Imposters in County Longford in the Great Famine." *Studia Hibernica*, no. 38, 2012, pp. 181–99.

Vejvoda, Kathleen. "Too Much Knowledge of the Other World: Women and Nineteenth-Century Folktales." *Victorian Literature and Culture*, vol. 32, no. 1, 2004, pp. 41–61.

Williamson, Millena. "Bridget Cleary and a Poetry Journey." *The Irish Times*, 24 Mar. 2022, https://www.irishtimes.com/culture/books/ bridget-cleary-and-a-poetry-journey-1.4834164. Accessed 27 Jan. 2025.

2.

From Harlots to Irresponsible Economic Citizens: Shifting Discourses on Sole Mothers

Emily Wolfinger

Introduction

The *Oxford Dictionary of English* defines the word "feral" as "(especially of an animal) in a wild state, especially after escape from captivity or domestication" and "resembling or characteristic of a wild animal" (Stevenson). "Feral women" by implication exist on the figurative outskirts of society as regards normative femininity. Similarly, "feral mothers" contravene normative prescriptions of motherhood and thus are positioned as bad mothers who require intervention and reform, if not control and punitive action (Martínez Guillem and Barnes). Understandings of what constitutes "feral" or "bad" mothers are culturally and historically specific but almost always include the figure of the sole or single mother,[1] and, consequently, so too have the interventions designed to "tame" or reform them.

This chapter draws upon scholarly literature to highlight these shifting discourses across politics, media, and academia. Accordingly, it argues that in Australia (as in other anglophone nations), sole mothers have been constructed as "feral" or "bad" mothers within three primary discourses over time. In the first section, this chapter locates the discourse of unmarried motherhood within moral-Christian theology, whereby "good" and "bad" motherhood was historically defined according to marital status. During this discursive period, feral mothers produced offspring outside the confines of marriage, which ensured women's sexual domestication or taming, and were labelled "harlots." However, this construction of sole mothers began to shift in the late 1950s, with the problematization of unmarried teenage mothers taking precedence within institutional discourses. In the second section, this chapter reflects on how discursive emphasis shifted further away from sexual immorality to poor timing, as norms governing sexuality and the family changed from the 1970s, resulting in greater visibility of ex-nuptial teenage pregnancy. "Kids having kids"[2] became a household catchphrase as moral panic about teenage pregnancy ensued. As outlined in the third section, this problematization of sole mothers peaked in the late twentieth century with the construction of the welfare mother, whereby, increasingly, the economic irresponsibility of sole mothers—regardless of age or marital status—was emphasized in institutional discourse and maternal ferality became associated with welfare use.

Finally, this chapter asks the question: "Is the deficit discourse on sole mothers finally shifting?" In doing so, it examines recent research and policy changes in Australia that point to further discursive shifts, namely greater emphasis on the lived experiences of sole mothers and the structural inequities that hinder their lives. As dominant forms of discourse, politics, the media, and academia can influence—for better or worse—public perceptions of marginalized groups and the policies that affect them (Wolfinger, "Welfare Debate"). These discursive spaces are, thus, important sites of examination.

Harlots, Strumpets, and Unmarried Mothers: Early Discourses on Sole Mothers

Until at least the second half of the twentieth century, normative and deviant motherhood was generally defined according to marital status (May). While married motherhood was seen as virtuous and integral to moral and social order, unmarried motherhood was deemed illegitimate, a source of social decay, and a threat to established norms. Marriage therefore represented a contained (and God-ordained) domestic space in which to practice sexuality and produce offspring, particularly for women whose impropriety could be more readily detected through pregnancy. Mothering outside this context, unmarried mothers were the ultimate "bad girls," viewed with suspicion, and labelled "whores" (Summers, "Damned Whores"). Although unmarried mothers transgressed normative femininity by forgoing marriage, they conformed to another part of it by being mothers. Like feral beings, they existed on the boundary between civilization and the untamed hither as they straddled the identities of mother and transgressor.

In Australia, the denigration of sole mothers as immoral harkens back to pre-Federation (Summers, "Damned Whores"). Shurlee Swain and Renate Howe show how the stigma associated with sole motherhood has been reinforced through language over time: "'Harlots' and 'strumpets' became 'fallen women,' 'unmarried mothers,' and more recently 'single parents'" (2). They explain that the term "single mother," adopted by self-groups in the 1960s as a replacement for "unmarried mother," continued to assume many of the negative connotations it sought to overcome, thus the sense of deviance or otherness associated with sole motherhood remained (2). While understandings of sole motherhood now include married and never-married women, sole motherhood was once a label (and status) exclusively reserved for unmarried mothers by virtue of their failure to adhere to social customs (Quirk). Their children were in turn branded "bastards" and, later, "illegitimate" (Swain and Howe 2). Today, the negative connotations of this terminology "live on" in the vernacular of demographers, policymakers, and social scientists, among others, who refer to the births of unmarried women as "ex-nuptial."

The social stigma associated with unmarried motherhood (and the deprivation, coercion, and cruelty that frequently accompanied it) was a key means by which patriarchal societies enforced community morality and the behaviour of heterosexual women in particular (Swain and Howe). To use the metaphor of the loyal domesticated dog, stigma had the effect of directing the gaze of women inwards rather than outwards toward the oppressor, thereby maintaining their pliancy. When women had erred, stigma worked to retame or reorient them through fear of punishment or ostracization, leaving single pregnant women with two primary options: a hasty marriage where possible or confinement and segregation during pregnancy (May; Quirk; Summers, "Damned Whores"; Swain and Howe).

In nineteenth-century Australia, and during the interwar years, women largely made their own arrangements to conceal their pregnancy, often moving out of town for board and employment or relying upon the discretion of family or employers rather than maternity homes (Swain and Howe). As ex-nuptial and nuptial births increased in the postwar years, maternity homes expanded, and single pregnant women increasingly "chose" the institutional route. The primary aim of maternity homes that housed unmarried pregnant women during this period was "conversion or, at the very least, reformation" and infants were routinely separated from residents following their birth (Swain and Howe 74). This aim can be likened to the desexing and sterilization of animals in the process of domestication as it worked to reduce the risk of future impropriety.

Aside from social stigma, unmarried mothers faced almost certain economic hardship up until the late twentieth century as their access to government income support was restricted due to perceived undeservingness (May; Quirk; Summers, "Damned Whores"). Thus, economic hardship in combination with the social stigma associated with unwed motherhood made it difficult for unmarried women to keep and raise their children. The denial of government income support to unmarried mothers was arguably designed to prevent or discourage out-of-wedlock pregnancy, as well as to reduce its economic and social costs—just as denial of food to feral animals might decrease the possibility of their encroachment or return with yet more offspring.

In Australia, unmarried or divorced mothers could only access minimal government assistance as compared to their widowed or deserted peers, and even then, the meagre benefits available to them were often denied due to administrative bias (Blaxland, "Mothers"; Swain and Howe). Meanwhile, non-British migrants, Indigenous peoples descended from Africa, New Zealand and the Pacific Islands, and Indigenous Australians were altogether excluded from entitlement (Blaxland, "Everyday Negotiations"). It was not until 1973 that the Labor Whitlam government introduced the supporting mothers benefit (SMB), allowing all sole mothers, regardless of social status, access to an equal amount of income support (Blaxland, "Everyday Negotiations"; Daniels). Thus, during the period of the White Australia policy,[3] unmarried mothers were counted among those groups deemed outsiders in so far as they were denied a reliable source of income that would allow them to meet their basic needs.

This denial of subsistence to unmarried mothers and other groups can be likened to the treatment of feral creatures who are forced to rely on scraps (charity)—or perhaps their own ingenuity—to survive.

The historical treatment of Australian unmarried mothers can be traced to seventeenth-century Britain (Swain and Howe). As such, it had a "moral and economic basis", specifically one rooted in Christian morality and the "very particular British experience of poor relief," instituted in the form of the Poor Law and its various iterations (Swain and Howe 3). Writing about this unholy union of morality and economics in the treatment of unmarried mothers, Swain and Howe elaborate as follows:

> The sanctity of marriage was central to Christianity, offering a space within which sexuality, and particularly female sexuality, could be both expressed and controlled. The single pregnant woman provided a highly visible challenge to such control, yet the concomitant belief in the sanctity of human life meant that her punishment had to be carried out alongside a duty of care. (3)

Accordingly, separation of children from their mothers, corporal punishment, and mandatory labour formed part of the "Poor Law repertoire," introduced in 1601, even as single pregnant women were offered shelter and food during their confinement where they lacked protectors of means (Swain and Howe 3). However, the new Poor Law—introduced in 1834 in response to a rise in ex-nuptial birthrates preceding and following the Industrial Revolution—further restricted unmarried mothers' options by removing their right to force marriage or sue the father of their child for maintenance.

From the 1950s, the morality discourse on sole mothers began to shift towards a medicalized discourse recasting unmarried mothers as feeble minded and in need of treatment rather than punitive redemption (Quirk). Writing of this change in narrative in the twentieth century, Swain and Howe argue that the sole mother "the victim of seduction became in turn the product of poor heredity, poor social conditions or neurotic tendencies" (15). Comparison can be made here to differential understandings of the process by which previously domesticated animals are made feral. Although humans might be inclined towards sin and domesticated animals towards wildness in the absence of control, genetics or breeding could also explain a propensity towards ferality.

In Australia, the clinical and medical management of unmarried pregnant women became entrenched throughout hospitals in the 1950s and 1960s—a period in which forced adoption practices were endemic (Quirk 212). The rise of social work as a profession occurred within this context, playing a pivotal role in these practices, which occurred across the anglophone world (Quirk). In fact, Australian social workers were heavily influenced by British and North American texts that maintained a view of ex-nuptial pregnancy as the result of dysfunctional or troubled upbringings.

In the United States (US), the discourse surrounding unmarried mothers during this period differentiated according to race and class, with unmarried motherhood among white women being attributed to difficult home lives or poor decision-making that could be rectified. However, just as some animal species are known to be more difficult to domesticate than others, unwed motherhood among Black women was attributed to failures of communities as a whole rather than individual disadvantages (Geronimus; Solinger). This racist double- standard set the tone in US political discourse for decades (Solinger), particularly in the 1980s and 1990s when sole mothers became the targets of vitriolic political discourse, state intervention, and punitive and paternalistic welfare reform (Thane and Evans).

In contrast, in Australia, Black Indigenous motherhood had long been denied. Between 1910 and 1969, "half-caste" Indigenous children were systematically removed from their mothers and families through the so-called Protection Acts (Manne; Quirk). It was believed at the time that "the Aboriginal problem" could be bred out of existence through forced assimilation of stolen children into White society (Manne)—a notion that can be likened to the breeding and training of animals to promote certain so-called favourable traits, such as compliance. Thus, Indigenous mothers were seen as entirely improper in their embodiment of Black motherhood and denied parental rights altogether, whereas white Australian mothers were targeted based on marital status and, later, age through discriminatory welfare policies and practices (Quirk).

It was in the 1950s that the discourse on sole mothers also began to shift towards an age-based, though still marriage-oriented, narrative. The beginnings of this narrative can be traced to the mother and baby homes that housed unwed pregnant women in London for much of the twentieth century. These homes began to separate older and teenage expectant mothers in 1959 in response to anxieties about ex-nuptial adolescent pregnancies (Koffman). Ofra Koffman points out that, previously, teenage residents were not distinguished from older residents because it was the character of a woman and not her age or mental maturity that was emphasized within moral-Christian discourse (123). In contrast, the work of the homes that housed pregnant adolescents was shaped by psychological knowledge whereby a woman's immaturity rather than her character was highlighted (Koffman).

These homes marked a turning point in the discourse on sole mothers (Koffman). In contrast to the unmarried mother of the moral-Christian discourse, the teenage mother of the scientific discourse was rendered "inherently problematic" and assumed to be incapable of proper motherhood (Koffman 129). According to this view, the teenage mother blurred the boundaries between adulthood and childhood and mother and daughter, thereby defying normative girlhood. At the same time, she contravened normative womanhood by rejecting marriage, complicating set expectations and definitions. The unwed teenage mother of this period therefore existed outside cultural norms entirely on account of her youth as well as her marital status. This problematization of teenage mothers only intensified with the decline of early marriage across anglophone countries from the 1970s. Writing of the period that preceded this decline, Frank Furstenburg notes: "Few observers today appreciate how common this pattern [of early marriage] was in the past century (and in earlier times as well). As many sociologists in the 1950s and 1960s noted, early marriage was a way of managing the risks associated with premarital sexual activity" (10). Thus, with cultural change, influenced by scientific discourse, teenage mothers became outcasts, although young motherhood had been commonplace. As the new objects of control and taming or reform, they straddled multiple conflicting identities at once ("mother," "girl," and "whore") but were never fully embraced within any of them.

Perhaps it is no coincidence then that unmarried teenage women and girls were the primary targets of forced adoption practices during the second half of last century. In Australia, the majority of mothers who relinquished their child for adoption between 1951 and 1985 were aged between fifteen and nineteen years (Commonwealth of Australia). Overall, sixty-eight percent of never-married Australian mothers were separated from their babies between 1945 and 1975 (Quirk). It is important to note that while young unmarried mothers were deemed incompetent and unable to provide a "normal environment and upbringing" for their child, adoptive parents were cast as "benevolent and sympathetic" (Quirk 212). However, the reality was that adoption was a consumer-driven market that often resulted in the institutionalization of infants deemed less than perfect by a market that "preferred above all others ... healthy fair baby girl[s]" (Quirk 212).

"Kids Having Kids": The Construction of The Teenage Mother

During the second half of the twentieth century, economic, social, and technological processes began to promote changes to family forms and roles (Parke). Pat Thane and Tanya Evans write: "The changes became dramatic from the later 1960s, and gathered pace through the 1970s and, particularly, the 1980s and 1990s, as divorce, cohabitation, and births out of wedlock reached unprecedented levels" (3). Increasingly, women entered the paid workforce and higher education while the introduction of the pill gave women more control of their fertility (Parke). At the same time, reducing the legal and moral restrictions against divorce— accompanied in part by "a shift in the focus of family life from economic dependence to emotional fulfillment" (Parke 209)—gradually resulted in greater social acceptance of nontraditional family forms, including unmarried couple families and sole-parent families (Parke 209).

Despite increased tolerance of diverse family forms, teenage motherhood was increasingly problematized in institutional discourse from the 1970s even as it trended downwards from this time (Simic). This intensification emerged in part from a relaxation of gendered and sexual norms, a decline in early marriage, and a concomitant increase in the visibility of unwed adolescent pregnancies rather than the presupposed "epidemic" of teenage pregnancy (Furstenburg; Koffman; May; Nathanson; Quirk; Simic). At the same time, a new understanding of adolescence was gaining traction while changing economic conditions made early parenthood increasingly difficult (Simic).

In Australia, births to teenage mothers peaked in the postwar decades of the 1950s and 1960s when "the stigma, poverty and social exclusion associated with illegitimacy ... accounted for the high rates of adoption and 'shot-gun' weddings among the increasing numbers of pregnant teenagers" (Simic 434). Zora Simic explains that up until the 1970s, "the legitimacy of the child was of greater concern than the age of the mother or father" (434); however, as nonmarital births became more common from the 1970s, the stigma "of keeping a child out of wedlock was transferred disproportionately to the teenage single mother" (434). This period signalled "the beginning of the collapse of Christian morality in an increasingly secular Australian society" (Thompson 140) even as a new morality around age and maternity was forming.

As the visibility of teenage pregnancy increased in the 1970s, alarm grew in Australia and other anglophone countries over its links to poor outcomes and social ills (Simic; SmithBattle). Specifically, teenage pregnancy was associated with such factors as low socioeconomic status, premature exit from school, unemployment, and dependence on the public purse (Simic). This narrative of teenage pregnancy characterized teenage mothers as feral, poor, and undereducated young women who make poor choices including "miscalculating the natural sequence of life events, and within this, the appropriate time to bear children," thus perpetuating poverty and other social ills (Harris; May 78). However, early evidence often overlooked the downward trend in early marriage (Furstenburg) and "the systemic inequities and discrimination that contribute to teen births, in effect blaming young parents for their circumstances and broader social problems" (SmithBattle 323).

The discourse on teenage mothers was further elaborated on ethnic-racial grounds. In the US, for example, teenage pregnancy was depicted as predominantly, though not exclusively, a problem for the Black population, thus "ferality" was associated with youthful maternity and race, whereas in Australia the reverse was true. Teenage pregnancy was predominantly considered a white problem. Simic explains: "This is sometimes represented as a demographic effect, with the Indigenous population described as too numerically insignificant to influence overall statistics, or explained by specific migrant communities exhibiting different fertility patterns" (437).

The problematization of teenage motherhood further intensified in the 1980s and continued into the 2000s as successive governments across the anglophone world and beyond consistently represented young motherhood as a social problem requiring intervention and containment (Simic) should it encroach further and destabilize society. This intensification occurred alongside growing concerns regarding the social "problem" of welfare dependency that positioned teenage mothers as "irresponsible, incompetent parents who were looking for handouts" (SmithBattle 323). Simic argues that in Australia, "it was primarily in concert with anxieties about welfare dependency, youth unemployment and single parent families, that teenage pregnancy and lone motherhood came to be understood as synonymous with poverty and systemic features of lower socio-economic communities" (435).

As the twentieth century closed, rates of teenage pregnancy began to decline in Western industrialized countries, although they remained relatively high in the US (Chase; Simic; Swain and Howe). In Australia, rates fell from 25 per cent of all women giving birth in 1971 to ten per cent in the mid-1990s (Swain and Howe). Today, only two per cent of births are to teenage women and girls (Australian Institute of Health and Welfare). This decline followed increased availability of contraception and abortion, an overall trend towards delayed childbirth—which "invariably shifted the parameters of normative and deviant fertility and motherhood" (May 74)—and, critically, teen parent prevention campaigns and sex education programs (May; Vinson). It also coincided with sweeping welfare reforms targeting sole mothers. In this so-called postfeminist age of free-market capitalism, women were free to work; thus, sole mothers on welfare contravened the new moral order by burdening society with their dependency. Their decisions around family and work formed the new object of social control. Today, normative, socially accepted motherhood is associated with delayed childbirth, emotional and physical maturity, planned pregnancy, education, and financial security (Neiterman). Constructions of teenage motherhood continue to shape understandings of ideal motherhood even as they reflect contemporary preoccupations with self-sufficiency. It is towards this neoliberal fixation that the discussion now turns.

The Welfare Mother: Contemporary Depictions of Sole Mothers

In the 1980s, Western industrialized countries began to move away from a view of government income support as an unconditional, though limited, social right. This transition followed twenty years of welfare state expansion following World War Two (Dwyer; Hamilton Raven). Market and family were once more deemed the favoured institutions for social support, as new welfare rules required everyone on welfare to be actively engaged in looking for work (Caragata and Alcalde; Considine et al.; Dwyer; Green; Shaver). These programs have been called workfare or welfare to work (WTW) and were most hardline in the liberal democracies of anglophone countries such as the US, United Kingdom, Canada, Australia, and New Zealand (Caragata and Alcalde).

In the 1990s and 2000s, WTW reforms were made with respect to sole parents who were transitioned "from mothers entitled to welfare assistance as caretakers of children to a group to be reintegrated into the job market" (Derbst-Debby 304). Where once caregiving was seen as the appropriate role of women, and sole mothers (first, those deemed deserving and, later, all sole parents, regardless of marital status and gender) were supported by the state in exercising this role, by the early twenty-first century, that view had drastically changed (Blaxland, "Mothers"). Sole mothers were deemed workers first and caregivers second in the context of welfare reform and, as such, were targeted for "correction" and "containment" (Blaxland, "Mothers"). In Australia, following years of parliamentary and media debate, the Employment and Workplace Relations Legislation Amendment (Welfare to Work and Other Measures) Act 2005 was passed by the federal parliament, and new recipients of parenting payment single (PPS) (those who began receiving PPS after July 1, 2006) were moved to the unemployment payment, newstart allowance (NSA), once their youngest child turned eight years; previously, it was sixteen years of age (Grahame and Marston). It also introduced mandatory participation requirements of fifteen hours of paid employment per week or job search activities (Winter).

Discourse problematizing sole mothers' welfare use played a pivotal role in the transformation of the welfare state and in influencing discourses on sole mothers generally (Atkinson et al; Bullock et al.; Derbst-Debby; Hancock; Kelly). While Western industrialized societies have entered an age of liberal sexual attitudes and changing family structures, where explicit moral judgments are less tolerated, the denigration of sole mothers persists via a construction that sees them as flawed economic citizens (Wolfinger, 'Welfare Discourse"), although undertones of sexual immorality and ageism persist. Consequently, both deserving (primarily widowed) and undeserving (divorced and young or never married) sole mothers are lumped together via their welfare use and likened to "drug addicts, criminals, and other socially-defined 'degenerates'" (Fineman 283) who exist on the fringes of society. Martha Fineman argues that the undeserving status of welfare-using sole mothers is "established partly by their lack of relationship to the work force (either through their own jobs or through their attachment to a male breadwinner) and partly by their asserted role as mothers in the perpetuation of poverty" (283).

Constructing sole mothers as nonworking has its basis in neoliberal discourse. This discourse conflates productivity with market participation, thereby excluding mothering as a socially productive endeavour. Neoliberalism emerged as a set of ideas guiding public policy as second-wave feminism was beginning to make inroads into politics in the late 1970s, resulting in women's increased participation in paid work (Fraser and Bedford). As neoliberal and feminist ideologies converged, mothers who participated in paid work became good parents, while sole mothers on welfare were deemed incompetent, lazy, and in need of intervention to end their dependency on handouts. Writing of this shift in the context of Australian welfare reform in the 1990s and 2000s, Megan Blaxland argues that "parental obligation to employment as an element of good and 'normal' mothering" was a key rhetorical element of welfare discourse of this period" ("Mothers" 143). As such, sole mothers on welfare were not only assumed to be unproductive but bad mothers by virtue of their welfare dependency.

In Australia, it was during parliamentary debate that sole parents were first associated with the label "welfare dependency" (Engels) with its connotations of irresponsible parenthood and bad economic citizenship (Blaxland, "Mothers"). This debate followed the election of the Liberal Howard government in 1996 and preceded the establishment of the Reference Group on Welfare Reform in 1999, which led to the introduction of WTW policy. Of particular concern to the Howard government was the so-called culture of dependency and intergenerational welfare dependency wrought by a lax welfare system that was parasitically exploited by welfare recipients who had reproduced this undesirable characteristic in their offspring. Sole parents—or more to the point, sole mothers, though not explicitly named—were the primary targets of the discourse of intergenerational welfare dependency, which drew on old (as well as new) stereotypes of bad sole mothers, thereby resonating with the Australian public (Blaxland, "Mothers"). As implied in the following statement by former minister for employment and workplace relations, Kevin Andrews, sole mothers were more than unproductive and exploitative—they were bad parents for failing to set an example of work to their children. Like feral cats, they needed to be managed or culled to contain successive generations of welfare users:

At a time of sustained economic growth and unemployment at twenty-nine-year lows, it is unacceptable to have 2.5 million or 20 per cent of working age Australians on income support. Of these, more than 1.3 million people are in receipt of Parenting Payment or the Disability Support Pension and have few, if any, participation requirements. It is also unacceptable to have seven hundred thousand children growing up in jobless households, in which two or three generations of Australians may not know what it is like to have a job, let alone steady employment and regular income (qtd. in Blaxland, "Mothers" 136).

Welfare debate intensified again under the Labor Gillard government in 2012 when the coalition government transferred grandfathered recipients of PPS onto the lower-paying NSA. According to a study on welfare discourse and news from this time, sole mothers are depicted as being an economic burden, irresponsible for not setting an example of work to their children, and dishonest in claims of welfare fraud by labor politicians and bureaucrats who were interviewed by the media studied in this research (Wolfinger, "Welfare Discourse"). In all these depictions of sole mothers, sole motherhood, bad parenting, poor character, and welfare use are conflated and are at times difficult to disentangle.

Nevertheless, the literature points to signs of further discursive shifts on the horizon, even as neoliberalism has reframed notions of good and deviant motherhood via the construction of the welfare mother. It is to discussion of these shifts—largely the result of the tireless advocacy of sole mothers—that this chapter now turns.

Listening to Sole Parents: Is the Deficit Discourse Finally Shifting?

The growth in sole-parent families over the last half-a-century represents one of the most significant changes to family life in contemporary societies (Yorks). In Australia, the proportion of sole-parent families with one or more dependents increased from less than seven percent in 1976 to nearly sixteen percent in 2021 (Australian Bureau of Statistics; Qu). Similar patterns can be observed in other anglophone countries (Statistics Canada; Yorks).

The sociodemographics of sole-parent families have also diversified since the 1970s. Once typically headed by widowed or young unmarried women, sole-parent families are now most likely to be headed by older and divorced or separated women (Bergnehr and Wahlström Henriksson). Moreover, they include, increasingly, male-headed families, sole mothers by choice, families formed through nontraditional means, such as through in-vitro fertilization, as well as multigenerational households (Yorks).

The growth and diversification of sole-parent families can be understood as a form of resistance to patriarchy when considering the social stigma associated with sole motherhood, which has prevailed via various discourses through time. That is, sole-parent families have increased despite institutional attempts at deterring their proliferation by problematizing, punishing, and reforming, or "taming" them. Moreover, despite their marginalized status, sole mothers and their advocates—often sole mothers themselves—have tirelessly pushed back against discriminatory attitudes, laws, and policies, resulting in social and political change (Swain and Howe). This advocacy was especially evident from the second half of last century—a period of rapid social change. Writing of this time, Swain and Howe argue, "Where single mothers in the past had avoided the harshest impact of stigmatisation by 'passing' and denial, their sisters in the late 1960s and 1970s contested that stigma, appropriated it, and redefined the outcast state" (196). In Australia, Melbourne-based Council for the Single Mother and Her Child (CSMC), formed by a group of sole mothers in 1970, was pivotal in affecting policy and social change, including in eliminating the legal status of illegitimacy (Swain and Howe). The CSMC later became the basis of a national council that lobbies the government to this day.

Perhaps in part a result of this resistance, the discourse on sole mothers may be finally shifting—away from homogenizing or problematizing discourses towards narratives that reflect the diversity and complexities of sole mothers' lives. This shift is largely evident in the recent growth of social science literature that examines the lived experiences of sole mothers and in recent policy changes in Australia. Sole mothers and their longstanding lobby group, Single Mothers Australia (formerly, The National Council of Single Mothers and Their Children), have been at the forefront of these changes.

Social science research on sole-parent families emerged alongside the growth of this family form from the 1970s (Yorks). According to Yorks, it has largely examined the causes and consequences of sole parenthood and has often compared sole-parent families with the idealized nuclear family form, framing them as deficit from the outset. With respect to causes, this research has focussed on the relationship between socioeconomic status and sole parenthood, whereas the literature on consequences of sole parenthood has focussed on poor outcomes for children (Yorks). Such research suggests that like other degenerates who exist on the fringes of society proper, sole-parent families are deviant and harmful to children. It further implies that sole-parent families pose a threat to social stability considering their growth in the last fifty years and, as such, must be carefully managed.

As a result of such critiques, social science research has recently moved away from a focus on harms to children towards examining the multifaceted lives of sole parents, "document[ing their] challenges and struggles, such as their lack of economic support and the stigmatization they face, as well as their adaptive characteristics, such as their resiliency and fortitude" (Yorks 2). Crucially, Yorks shows how this emerging body of research has its roots in feminist methodology and is reflective of a broad trend in social science research of centring the voices of research participants. She argues that the rise of research focussed on sole parents in multigenerational households, sole fathers, and sole parents by choice is further indicative of this trend and the growing emphasis on complexity and diversity in research on sole parents.

At the same time, there is some evidence of growing recognition in policy of the complexities of sole mothers' lives, including the prevalence of domestic violence and poverty among this group. In Australia, the Howard and Gillard governments' harsh welfare reforms were all but reversed by the Labor Albanese government in September 2023 when it passed legislation to allow sole parent recipients to continue claiming PPS until their youngest child turns fourteen years (previously, it was eight years). This legislative change followed years of feminist advocacy and campaigning—headed by Terese Edwards of Single Mothers Australia—which culminated in the publication of a powerful report by Anne Summers, titled *The Choice: Violence or Poverty*. This report drew on national data to show a clear link between domestic violence, sole motherhood, and poverty and was used to drive a campaign to restore the sole mothers on JobSeeker Payment (formerly NSA) to PPS (Summers, "The Choice"). In May 2023, Prime Minister Albanese acknowledged the work of Summers and others in identifying sole mothers as a group in need of greater support when he announced the restoration of PPS for sole parents with children under fourteen years:

> This morning, I have an important announcement, one I'm very proud to be giving. That for some time, sole parents have been identified as one of the groups who are particularly struggling, as identified by the work of people like Dr. Anne Summers, as well as the Women's Economic Taskforce led by Sam Mostyn, to identify this group as particularly needing support. So we want to extend the financial safety net for single parent families by raising the age in which it is cut off for the youngest child of a single parent, for single parenting payment, from eight years to fourteen years. (1)

Alongside increased recognition of the prevalence of domestic violence among sole mothers, there has been greater emphasis on the actions of perpetrators rather than the choices of victim-survivors whose experiences of violence have been historically minimalized and rationalized (for example, see Hill). For example, it has been reasoned that like other fringe beings who are vulnerable to violence, victim-survivors of domestic violence are susceptible to mistreatment due to wilfully or knowingly putting themselves in harm's way. "Why doesn't she leave?" is a retort that persists to this day (O'Brien). Through such rationalizations, society proper can distance itself from its own complicity in creating or enabling conditions of poverty that make it untenable for many mothers to survive outside of violent relationships. Comparison can be made here to justifications for the culling or maiming of feral animals despite the role of human activities in disturbing the ecosystem on which we all depend.

Conclusion

Institutional discourses on sole mothers have shifted over time and while problematizations have changed, the "encroachment" of sole mothers and their children has been consistently portrayed as a threat to the integrity of society proper, whether by virtue of the mothers' marital status, age, welfare use, or any combination of these factors. Through instilling fear, their management and punishment became justifiable and in fact necessary.

Discursive trends surrounding sole mothers are noted across the anglophonic literature, although the focus of this chapter was primarily on Australian histories and case studies. As discussed, the marital status of unmarried mothers was highlighted in institutional discourses prior to the 1960s due to the influence of Christianity, which guided social norms and policy. Whereas unmarried mothers were "proper" in their embodiment of motherhood, they contravened Christian morality by rejecting marriage and were condemned to live between worlds. During this time, the social stigma associated with unmarried motherhood frequently resulted in early marriage or confinement, and unmarried mothers were virtually excluded from the social security system. Unmarried pregnant women increasingly spent their confinement in institutions from the 1950s as ex-nuptial births increased and maternity homes expanded across Australia. Institutionalization frequently resulted in forced adoption—the ultimate punishment. Following women's liberation in the 1960s, the discursive emphasis shifted towards the age of the mother as the trend of early marriage declined, and scientific discourse came to replace Christian morality in an increasingly secular Australia. In this era, young sole mothers were deemed entirely improper in their embodiment of motherhood by virtue of their age and the socioeconomic conditions that they were likely to experience. By the time the twentieth century ended, neoliberal logic guided political decision-making, and the economic unproductivity and parental irresponsibility of "welfare mothers" were highlighted in political discourse.

While shifts in discourse have occurred over time, and the social stigma associated with sole motherhood has lessened, the cost of becoming and being feral has always been high for single-parent women. Indeed, the economic penalty historically attached to sole motherhood persists despite recent discursive shifts whereby the diversity and complexities of sole mothers' lives are increasingly highlighted in discourse. Just over one-third of sole-parent households—the majority of whom are women—live in poverty in Australia today, making sole-parent households the poorest household type (Uni. of NSW and Aust. Council of Soc. Services). However, as sole-parent families increase and diversify, and their voices are heard through research and advocacy, hopeful possibilities emerge.

These possibilities lie in broader recognition of caregiving work and include universal income payments for mothers, superannuation for mothers who are not in paid work, and unconditional entitlement to sole parents.

Endnotes

1. This chapter uses the terminology "sole mother" rather than "single mother" to highlight the caregiving responsibilities of sole mothers and not their marital status. However, the terms "unmarried mother" and "teenage mother" are also used where appropriate.

2. The oft-used phrase "kids having kids" comes from a *Time Magazine* cover story published in 1985 but has been used in successive government campaigns, academic research, and reports published by non-government organizations (Koffman).

3. The White Australia policy, as it is colloquially referred to, is the policy by which nonwhite people were excluded from immigration to Australia until 1973 when the Whitlam Government abolished it (Jupp). In the decades since this time, Australia has become known as one of the most multicultural societies in the world.

Works Cited

Atkinson, Karen, et al. "'Happy Families?': Single Mothers, the Press and the Politicians." *Capital & Class*, vol. 22, no. 1, 1998, pp. 1–11.

Stevenson, Angus, editor. *Oxford Dictionary of English*. Oxford University Press, 2015.

Australian Institute of Health and Welfare. "Australia's Children." *Australian Institute of Health and Welfare*, Government of Australia, 2022, https://www.aihw.gov.au/reports/children-youth/australias-children/contents/health/health-australias-children. Accessed 11 Jan. 2025.

Albanese, Anthony. "Press Conference–Perth." *Prime Minister of Australia*, 2023, https://www.pm.gov.au/media/press-conference-perth-5. Accessed 11 Jan. 2025.

Australian Bureau of Statistics. "Household and Families: Census." 2022, *Australian Bureau of Statistics*, https://www.abs.gov.au/statistics/people/people-and-communities/household-and-families-census/latest-release. Accessed 11 Jan. 2025.

Bergnehr, Disa, and Helena Wahlström Henriksson. "Hardworking Women: Representations of Lone Mothers in the Swedish Daily Press." *Feminist Media Studies*, vol. 21, no. 1, 2021, pp. 132–46.

Blaxland, Megan. "Everyday Negotiations for Care and Autonomy in the World of Welfare-to-Work." *NSW: University of Sydney*, 2008, https://ses.library.usyd.edu.au/bitstream/handle/2123/4134/ Blaxland-2008-thesis.pdf?sequence=1. Accessed 11 Jan. 2025.

Blaxland, Megan. "Mothers and Mutual Obligation: Policy Reforming the Good Mother." *The Good Mother: Contemporary Motherhoods in Australia*. Edited by Susan Goodwin and Kate Huppatz. Sydney University Press, 2010, pp. 131–52.

Bullock, Heather E., et al. "Media Images of the Poor." *Journal of Social Issues*, vol. 57, no. 2, 2001, pp. 229–46.

Caragata, Lea, and Judit Alcalde, editors. *Not the Whole Story: Challenging the Single Mother Narrative*. Wilfrid Laurier Press, 2014.

Chase, Elizabeth. "Rethinking the Marginalizing Discourses around Teenage Pregnancy." *Discourse: Studies in the Cultural Politics of Education*, vol. 40, no. 4, 2019, pp. 560–72.

Commonwealth of Australia. "Commonwealth Contribution to Former Forced Adoption Policies and Practices." Parliament of Australia, 2012, https://www.aph.gov.au/parliamentary_business/committees/ senate/community_affairs/completed_inquiries/2010-13/commcon-tribformerforcedadoption/report/index. Accessed 11 Jan. 2025.

Considine, Mark, et al. *Getting Welfare to Work: Street-Level Governance in Australia, the UK, and the Netherlands*. Oxford University Press, 2015.

Daniels, Dale. "Social Security Payments for People Caring for Children, 1912 to 2008: A Chronology." Department of Parliamentary Services, Parliament of Australia, 2009, https://parlinfo.aph.gov.au/parlInfo/ search/display/display.w3p;query=Id%3A%22library%2Fprspub%2F5 428620%22;srcl=sml. Accessed 25 Jan. 2025.

Dwyer, Peter. "Creeping Conditionality in the UK: From Welfare Rights to Conditional Entitlements?" *The Canadian Journal of Sociology*, vol. 29, no. 2, 2004, pp. 265–87.

Engels, Brenno. "Old Problem, New Label: Reconstructing the Problem of Welfare Dependency in Australian Social Policy Discourse." *Just Policy: A Journal of Australian Social Policy*, vol. 41, 2006, pp. 5–14.

Fineman, Martha A. "Images of Mothers in Poverty Discourses." *Duke Law Journal*, vol. 2, 1991, pp. 274–95.

Fraser, Nancy, and Kate Bedford. "Social Rights and Gender Justice in the Neoliberal Moment." *Feminist Theory*, vol. 9, no. 2, 2008, pp. 225–45.

Furstenburg, Frank. "The History of Teenage Childbearing as a Social Problem." *Destinies of the Disadvantaged*. Edited by Frank Furstenburg. Russell Sage Foundation, 2007, pp. 1–23.

Geronimus, Arline T. "Damned if You Do: Culture, Identity, Privilege, and Teenage Childbearing in the United States." *Social Science and Medicine*, vol. 57, 2003, pp. 881–93.

Grahame, Teresa, and Greg Marston. "Welfare-to-Work Policies and the Experience of Employed Single Mothers on Income Support in Australia: Where are the Benefits?" *Australian Social Work*, vol. 65, no. 1, 2012, pp. 73–86.

Green, Kate. "Welfare Reform in Australia and the United States: Tracing the Emergence and Critiques of the New Paternalism and Mutual Obligation." *The Drawing Board: An Australian Review of Public Affairs*, vol. 3, no. 1, 2002, pp. 15–32.

Herbst-Debby, Anna. "(De)legitimization of Single Mothers' Welfare Rights: United States, Britain and Israel." *Journal of European Social Policy*, vol. 32, no. 3, 2002, pp. 302–16.

Hamilton, Myra. "The 'New Social Contract' and the Individualisation of Risk in Policy." *Journal of Risk Research*, vol. 17, no. 4, 2014, pp. 453–67.

Hancock, Ange-Marie. "Contemporary Welfare Reform and the Public Identity of the 'Welfare queen.'" *Race, Gender and Class*, vol. 10, no. 1, 2003, pp. 31–59.

Harris, Anita. *Future Girl: Young Women in the 21st Century*. Routledge, 2004.

Kelly, Maura. "Regulating the Reproduction and Mothering of Poor Women: The Controlling Image of the Welfare Mother in Television News Coverage of Welfare Reform." *Journal of Poverty*, vol. 14, no. 1, 2010, pp. 76–96.

Jupp, James. *From White Australia to Woomera: The Story of Australian Immigration*. Cambridge University Press, 2003.

Koffman, Ofra. "Children Having Children? Religion, Psychology and the Birth of the Teenage Pregnancy Problem." *History of the Human Sciences*, vol. 25, no. 1, 2012, pp. 119–34.

Manne, Robert. "The Stolen Generations." *Quadrant*, vol. 42, no. 1–2, 1998, pp. 53–63.

May, Sandy M. "Teenage Pregnancy and Mothering in the Face of Social Exclusion: Discourse, Phenomenology, and an Affirmation of Positive Maternal Identity." *Memorial University of Newfoundland*, 2014, https://research.library.mun.ca/15580/1/thesis.pdf. Accessed 12 Jan. 2025.

Martínez Guillem, Susana, and Christopher C. Barnes. "'Am I a Good (White) Mother?' Mad Men, Bad Mothers, and Post(Racial) Feminism." *Critical Studies in Media Communication*, vol. 35, no. 3, 2018, pp. 286–99.

Nathanson, Constance A. *Dangerous Passage: The Social Control of Sexuality in Women's Adolescence*. Temple University Press, 1991.

Neiterman, Elena. "Constructing and Deconstructing Teen Pregnancy as a Social Problem." *Qualitative Sociology Review*, vol. 8, no. 3, 2012, pp. 24–47.

O'Brien, Carmel. *Blame Changer: Understanding Domestic Violence*. Threekookaburras, 2016.

Parke, Ross D. "Changing Family Forms: The Implications for Children's Development." *Children in Changing Worlds: Sociocultural and Temporal Perspectives*. Edited by Ross D. Parke and Glen H. Elder, Jr., Cambridge University Press, 2019, pp. 192–234.

Qu, Lixia. "Families Then and Now: 1980–2010." *Australian Institute of Family Studies*, 2010, https://aifs.gov.au/research/research-snapshots/families-then-and-now-1980-2010. Accessed 12 Jan. 2025.

Quirk, Christin. "Historicizing the Marginalization of Single Mothers: An Australian Perspective." *Motherhood and Single-Lone Parenting: A Twenty-First Century Perspective*. Edited by Maki Motapanyane, Demeter Press, 2016, pp. 207–24.

Raven, Judith. "Popular Support for Welfare State Reforms: On Welfare State Preferences and Welfare State Reforms in the Netherlands." Erasmus University, 2012, https://repub.eur.nl/pub/32005/Proefschrift%20Raven%20definitieve%20pdf%20versie%20(A4).pdf. Accessed 12 Jan. 2025.

Shaver, Sheila. "Australian Welfare Reform: From Citizenship to Supervision." *Social Policy and Administration*, vol. 36, no. 4, 2002, pp. 331–45.

Simic, Zora. "Fallen Girls? Plumpton High and the 'Problem' of Teenage Pregnancy." *Journal of Australian Studies,* vol. 34, no. 4, 2010, pp. 429–45.

Solinger, Rickie. *Wake Up Little Susie: Single Pregnancy and Race Before Roe v. Wade.* Routledge, 2000.

SmithBattle, Lee. "Walking on Eggshells: An Update on the Stigmatization of Teenage Mothers." *MCN: The American Journal of Maternal/Child Nursing*, vol. 45, no. 6, 2020, pp. 322–27.

Statistics Canada. "Portrait of Children's Family Life in Canada in 2016." 2017, *Statistics Canada*, https://www12.statcan.gc.ca/census-recensement/2016/as-sa/98-200-x/2016006/98-200-x2016006-eng.pdf. Accessed 12 Jan. 2025.

Summers, Anne. *Damned Whores and God's Police.* NewSouth Publishing, University of New South Wales, 2016.

Summers, Anne. "The Choice: Violence or Poverty." *Labour and Industry*, vol. 32, no. 4, 2022, pp. 349–57.

Swain, Shurlee, and Renate Howe. *Single Mothers and Their Children: Disposal, Punishment and Survival in Australia.* Cambridge University Press, 1995.

Thane, Pat, and Tanya Evans. *Sinners? Scroungers? Saints? Unmarried Motherhood in Twentieth-Century England.* Oxford University Press, 2012.

Thomson, Roger C. *Religion in Australia: A History.* Oxford University Press, 1995.

University of New South Wales and Australian Council of Social Services. "Poverty in Australia 2020," 2020, https://povertyandinequality. acoss.org.au/wp-content/uploads/2020/02/Poverty-in-Australia-2020_Part-1_Overview.pdf. Accessed 20 Jan. 2025.

Vinson, Jenna. *Embodying the Problem: The Persuasive Power of the Teenage Mother.* Rutgers University Press, 2018.

Winter, Myjenta E. "Silent Voices, Invisible Violence: Welfare to Work and the Exploitation of Single Mothers Who Have Experienced Domestic Violence." Southern Cross University, 2014, https://www.

semanticscholar.org/paper/Silent-voices%2C-invisible-violence-%3A-welfare-to-work-Winter/305af1c77bb2bddb8b84c92ad7aaa7916a5c7a52#:~:text=This%20research%20applied%20Bourdieusian%20field%20theory%20to%20explain,cultural%20and%20economic%20dom. Accessed 20 Jan. 2025.

Wolfinger, Emily. "Australia's Welfare Discourse and News: Presenting Single Mothers." *Global Media Journal: Australian Edition*, vol. 8, no. 2, 2014, pp. 1–16.

Wolfinger, Emily. "Welfare Debate in the Comments Section: Perceptions of Sole Mother Poverty and Welfare in an Age of Neoliberalism." *Southern Cross University*, 2020, https://www.researchgate.net/publication/371874704_Australia's_Welfare_Discourse_and_News_Presenting_Single_Mothers. Accessed 20 Jan. 2025.

Yorks, Jessica. "Singled Out No Longer: The Changing Narratives and Types of Single-Parent Families." *Sociology Compass*, vol. 16, no. 2, 2022, pp. 1–15.

3

Gone Spielreinian: Maternal Ferality and the Suprahumanities

Jessica Spring Weappa

> Perhaps our field has built a canonical story, as many empires do, upon the disappearance of indigenous people— many, though not all of them, women.
>
> —Adrienne Harris

Sabina Nikolayevna Spielrein (1885–1942) was a prominent twentieth-century thinker whose transdisciplinary contributions—rooted in biological, relational, and evolutionary perspectives—continue to shape and inform contemporary research and scholarship. Spielrein's writings disappeared from the historical record for three decades following the horrifying murder of her and her daughters, enacted by a Nazi firing squad. But her writings are now in the complex process of retrieval and revival. The scope and breadth of Spielrein's beneficence, however, have only recently been recognized by scholars. Spielrein is now appropriately acknowledged as the originator of some of the most well-known concepts and theories in psychoanalysis and developmental psychology. Many of her contributions remain relevant today. Until very recently, however, her ideas were historically attributed to colleagues and acquaintances once privy to her innermost thoughts and extraordinary mind. Carl Jung, Sigmund Freud, Jean Piaget, Anna Freud, Melanie Klein, and several other notable thinkers were informed and inspired by Spielrein's writing, lectures, and psychoanalytic processes. Despite a renewal of Spielreinian inquiry and appreciation, attention to the maternal specificity in Spielrein's work remains lacking. This chapter positions Spielrein's thinking and theory as primarily relational, maternal, and belonging to a transdisciplinary field of study that has yet to come into being in scholarly discourse.

This chapter weaves two narratives to explore maternal and evolutionary themes rediscovered in Sabina Spielrein's work, situating her contributions within an emergent mother-centring field of inquiry that strives to evolve beyond androcentric philosophy and matriphobic psychoanalysis. Using a reflexive scholarly personal narrative, I examine gatekeeping, silencing, and the century-long appropriation and disaffirmation of Spielrein's theories alongside my experiences of marginalization as a developing scholar-practitioner. I argue the forces obstructing Spielrein's true legacy extend through and beyond historical misogyny, reflecting a deeper "missing mother" dysfunction that continues to be pervasive in society, especially in elite academic, psychoanalytic, and medical fields. I map Spielrein's work onto my conception of (r)evolutionary matrisophy, focussing on her maternal biological approach to psychoanalysis, reproduction, death-instinct theory, species-psyche theory, somatic expression, and psychic representation in the development of speech and thought. Spielrein's legacy informs a biopsychosocial-spiritual field of humanities grounded in the mother-baby dyad and its relational continuum. This emerging field strives to restore the symbolic order of maternal love, and love for mothering, to philosophical and religio-historical meaning making, and could be known as the "supra-humanities."

Although comprehensive biographies have been written on Sabina Spielrein, her story has most often been overshadowed by her relationships with Carl Jung and Sigmund Freud, reducing her to a patient, a protégé, and supporting character in their narratives. In particular, the myth of Sabina Spielrein and Carl Jung revolves around their complex personal and professional connection, which has been the subject of romanticization, speculation, fantasy, and reinterpretation since her papers and diaries have been rediscovered and translated. The relationship offers a complex case study in the dynamics of power and sexual consent; broad agreement exists about a clear power imbalance between the two due to Jung's dual roles as her analyst and mentor. What I attempt to highlight in this writing are the complexities of mutual agency in psychological consent, drawing attention to Sabina Spielrein's resistance to androcentric analysis and her engagement in and healing through self-analysis. I foreground her resiliency and her innate brilliance, which is ever present in her collaboration and creative efforts towards human dignity, human potential, maternal nurturance, and relational transformation. This exploration of Sabina Spielrein's life and work reveals a woman who resisted the constraints of domesticated narratives, enacting a feral prowess—wild, untamed, and flourishing in her natural state of intellectual curiosity and creative autonomy.

Collins Dictionary defines "feral" is "existing in a natural state, as animals or plants; not domesticated or cultivated; wild." The Latin ferā-lis means "bestial, wild." Sabina Spielrein's focus on biological specificity and her lived experience as a woman embodied a feral love—untamed and authentic—challenging the male-dominated narratives that dismissed women's unique contributions to psychoanalysis. Despite recent recognition of Spielrein's visionary contributions to many fields, including evolutionary biology, there remains a strong drive in contemporary discourse to dismiss or eradicate any ideas that could potentially be labeled as essentialist, a trend political theorist Carole Pateman and psychotherapist Petra Bueskens refer to as "essentialism hunting" (Pateman in Bueskens par. 17). This "hunting" distorts important discussions on sexual difference, particularly evolutionary biological maternal specificity in scholarship, including Spielrein's work. Elaborating on the defense mechanism of what John Wellwood names "spiritual bypassing," I recently coined the term "maternal bypassing" to refer to the neglect or sidestepping of key questions about maternal subjectivity and the biopsychosocial-spiritual development and wellbeing of mothers throughout their caregiving lives, both in theory and practice (Wellwood in Weappa, "(R)evolutionary" 9). I view Sabina Spielrein as the first maternal psychologist of record. She explores the relational depths of love, empathy, and evolutionary humanity while consistently referencing her standpoint as a woman. Spielrein insists her lived female experiences offer unique insights. Her psychoanalytic explorations centre on the role of love and nurturance in questions about what it means to be human. While studying science and psychoanalysis, she dared to continue asking the question, "What is this for?" (Launer). Spielrein's psychoanalytic inquiry is concerned with understanding and connection between individuals. Eventually seeing child and human development through a maternal lens, she names the foundational role of love between mother and child and how it shapes human potential, cocreating meaning. She wished to be remembered, perhaps above all else, as a *human being* (my emphasis; Launer 51).

The Realm of the Mothers

Setting out on a doctoral journey, my original aim differed significantly from going feral; instead, it stemmed from a genuine desire for continued professional growth and the betterment of my family in American society. As a first-generation college student endeavouring to overcome childhood adversities including adoption trauma, I strove tenaciously to succeed in my conservatory-like undergraduate theatre arts program. I fell into a deep relationship with philosophy during a theatre historiography course. When studying Johann Wolfgang von Goethe's tragic play, *Faust*, I was drawn towards "das ewig-weibliche" (the eternal feminine) and "the realm of the mothers" (von Goethe). Imagining ancestral maternal powers with the capacity to balance supernatural paternal forces controlling the universe, a door opened within me to a path I continue to explore. Sabina Spielrein elaborates on the concept of an archaic mother that resides timelessly within the psyche. She uses "The Mothers" from Faust as a reference to explain her view of them as representations of the unconscious symbolic maternal, illustrating the connection between death and rebirth through the relational symbolism of the physiologic womb (Sells).

As a young, lone-single mother and artist, I navigated matrescence while exploring the archetype of Sophia as a goddess and as wisdom in philosophy and through various religiohistorical lenses. When I became a mother, I moved on from my theatre career to teach, creatively integrating women's wisdom teachings, ecological literacy, and the arts into education. I was invited to train as an Indigenous-centring birth doula, often volunteering to attend births of low-income women, and became an integral part of a cross-cultural maternal underclass in my inner-city community. Basic mother-child needs and bonds were embedded in personal growth and spiritual inquiry. This experience led me to continuously question meanings of the divine feminine and note how abstractly defined the term "feminine" often is, perhaps increasingly so. While keeping this question in the back of my mind, my concern shifted to maternal specificity and the needs of mothers over what kind of femininity was equal to divinity. My aim was to support the dignity of mothers and honour diverse mothering practices, especially as I witnessed and experienced shocking disregard for underclass mothers in various social, legal, and medical systems in my life. As my academic career continued, I remained rooted as an organic intellectual connected to my social class.

During late nights while my children slept, I earned a master's in human development, focussing on distinctly maternal development. Although I considered formally studying psychoanalysis, I consistently bumped up against my class-based, organic, and maternal ethics and how my worldview aligned better with a different path. Like Spielrein, I aim to be "deliberately un-intrusive" (Harris) as well as transdisciplinary in supporting others. I was raised by feral grandmothers, who were elder care and hospice nurses. Their role model, Elizabeth Kübler-Ross, "changed the *context* of clinical ethics" with her lived understanding of peace and "enriched the *process of doing* clinical ethics" with human dignity in heart and mind (Dougan par. 1). Despite her dignity focused impact, it is rare to see Kübler-Ross positioned as a care ethicist. I became a narrative therapist, centering on the inherent and learned strengths and dignity of my clients—most of whom are mothers—rather than engaging with mother erasing and mother-blaming psychoanalytic frameworks and popular psychology. Before carefully choosing my doctoral program in somatic and depth psychologies at a Jungian institute, I had already navigated a multifaceted maternal existence on the margins, which raised my matristic consciousness (Weappa, "(R)evolutionary").[1] I recognized that for mothers to thrive, we require familial, cultural, and social support. We need warmth, welcoming, and love to provide warmth, welcoming, and love. For most mothers who cannot afford to outsource care, maternal resilience in the United States (US) requires resistance to myriad societal systems that exhaust, devalue, and blame us. As Spielrein noted in her diary in 1905, "How stupid that I am not a man: men have it easier with everything. I do not want to be a slave!" (qtd. in Kelcourse).

Psyche, Soma, and Matribodiment

"I feel like I'm going to hurl right now!" exclaimed a female classmate, and her words seemed to escape almost involuntarily. I had noticed her hands gripping the edges of her chair for several minutes as discomfort built, and our eyes briefly met. The male lecturer, a declared expert in Freudian psychoanalysis, maintained an air of superiority. He was seemingly oblivious to the fact that he was addressing a predominantly female cohort researching soma and psyche. He had been delivering a lesson that centered on Sigmund Freud's "castration complex" and suggested that women's sexual development was affected by the lack of a penis, highlighting how Freud claimed women's sexuality took an aborted trajectory due to this perceived deficiency. He discussed Carl Jung's "Electra complex," which suggests that very young girls blame their mothers for their penis envy and are unconsciously sexually attached to their fathers (Jung and Kerenyi). The instructor responded to the disruption by asking my colleague if she needed to excuse herself to the restroom. She sat speechless and wide-eyed for a moment before responding quietly with embarrassment, "Sorry."

When I enrolled in the program, I expected to join a progressive cohort in updating outdated, sexist ideas in depth psychology. Freud's infamous reference to female sexuality as a "dark continent," borrowed from colonialist language, had been critiqued by many feminist and postcolonial scholars, and I assumed critiques would have been integrated into the curriculum (Khanna). Jungian influence on the feminine remains pervasive today, although early women analysts, including Spielrein, found his ideas insufficient in addressing female psychological realities (Crowley). While Jungian feminists have tried to revise his theories, they face challenges due to the deep reverence for Jung and the entrenched value placed on the feminine within his framework (Wehr 125). Psychotherapist Demaris S. Wehr explains, "With his unexamined acceptance of male-generated gender-related images, Jung has dealt primarily with the inner world of the male and its projections (126).

In the depth psychology meets somatic studies program, students were asked to place their depth psychological thesis inquiries on a somatic studies family tree, provided by the program director, who was then emerging as a leader in academic somatic and social justice circles, particularly where they intersect with queer theory (Johnson). The tree's roots were labelled shared principles and premises with the idea that the body is an essential component of being human, but the trunk was left blank, despite supporting eleven branches: philosophy, psychology, anthropology, and others. Of the thirty-nine thinkers listed in the branches, most were men, and none focussed on maternal subjectivity, intersubjectivity, or embodiment. Unable to place my work on this tree, I added the terms "the absent mother" to the trunk of the tree, "placental relationships" at the roots, and "mitochondrial DNA" in the earth's strata in red ink. The concept of the "missing mother" can be examined and applied in many ways and has been identified academically to "address spaces of scholarly and creative enquiry from which the figure of the mother has, historically speaking, been missing" (Missing Mother, par. 1).

As a somatic exercise, the class was asked to first visualize the tree shape on the floor and then physically move to stand on their chosen branch to see which member of the cohort might be on a similar research path. I stood frozen for a moment before moving my body to the space between the branches of neuroscience and traumatology, wondering about interpersonal neurobiology which I was engaged with as a narrative therapist. I then moved squarely into traumatology and gazed at the space in the room where the placental beginnings of this family tree were invisible.

Including Maternal Beingness

I began to realize how my success in this academic program might require that I participate in the negation of the maternal body and research that would suppress the inquiries I arrived to explore (Vissing). I wished to further explore physiologic birth as a somatic and depth psychological experience and wanted to formally research maternal embodiment through a deep retrieval and reclaiming of excluded maternal meaning-making in the historical underpinnings of depth psychology and somatic studies. When I tactfully brought my concerns to instructors and the program director, it became clear that my hunch was spot on. A focus on mothering as transformative or empowering was immediately assumed or judged to be promoting biological determinism or essentialism. In nearly every case, my inquiries regarding empowered maternal embodiment were taboo and provoked disaffirming or hostile attention from peers and professors. This judgment was palpable even as I took care to make clear my inclusive intentions, highlighted my lived experience as a lone-single mother, and framed my work within biopsychosocial-spiritual inquiry. I expressed how I should not need to be apologetic in daring to consider that we have yet to fully understand how evolutionary biological maternal specificity can point towards revolutionary human potential more than devolutionary human limitations. The exclusion of biological women from a majority of clinical research until the 1990s and since should consistently remind researchers about what we have yet to learn about female embodiment and call forth continued critical analysis. To date, the female body has scarcely been studied.

I discussed my inquiry somewhat freely in one course in the somatic studies program, which was about healing practices in Ancient Greece taught by elder mythologist Christine Downing. It seemed to me that the wandering womb, with its origins in ancient Greek medical texts, in which the prenatal home of every human being is perceived as a site of mischief and danger, might still be perversely shaping attitudes and beliefs about maternal embodiment. One outcome of the wandering womb theory was the catch-all diagnosis of hysteria, a dismissive victim-blaming label projected primarily onto women, including Sabina Spielrein. Spielrein proposed anchoring Freud's talking cure in human biology and evolution, leveraging her unique perspective on the precarious and dark aspects of reproduction as a woman and her comprehensive understanding of scientific evolution in her time (Launer). This emphasis on archaic maternal materiality remains mostly in the background of elaborations on her work a century on, even in the recent swell of scholarly discourse on Spielrein's writings and life.

Confronting the Freudian lecturer for dismissively responding to a cohort member's somatic reaction to his course content was met with great resistance by the lecturer and the director of the program. I realized I had crossed an unspoken boundary. After that, powerful figures in the administration at the institution turned against me. My perspectives, as a lone-single mother and caring birth attendant from the maternal underclass, theorizing from sacred experiences with birth and mothering, were not welcome or even tolerated. The message was clear: Stay silent or face consequences. I received a formal letter from the program director warning me to curb my tendency to take active, directive, or leadership roles. Any further behaviour deemed challenging by faculty or administration would result in probation. Given how this warning came from a rising public figure within the somatic activism and embodied social justice movements, the exclusion of and aversion to maternal embodiment in these movements could not have been clearer to me. As I watched these movements grow and influence culture over a decade, I witnessed an increasing intolerance and aversion to subjective, and intersubjective, maternal experience and expression in somatic training, some social justice spaces, and academic settings.

In the face of this academic intimidation and other disturbing experiences, I knew I had to leave the institute to protect my wellbeing. Still grappling with the stress of lone-single motherhood and the long consequences of abuse because of womanhood, I consulted my support system and decided to remain quiet and finish the year. It was a painful decision. I completed a fieldwork project on maternal embodiment and mother goddess mythology, but it was censored. I was never offered an opportunity to present it to my cohort or to receive constructive faculty feedback.

I had entered the program as a seasoned forty-year-old maternal somatician and departed feeling silenced and scarred. Despite this, I transferred my credits to another graduate institute that promised greater academic freedom and diversity and carried on with my studies. I continue to unearth the missing mother and make meaning in various realms of matribodiment, distinctly maternal embodiment in which mothering, materiality, matter, māter, spirit, soul, and mind are inextricable.

Letting Beauty Linger

Matrescence, coined by anthropologist Dana Raphael in the 1975, refers to the critical transition into motherhood, where physiology, identity, relationships, and daily life undergo profound changes (Raphael). Raphael introduced the term to challenge historical male bias in anthropology by redefining how women's power and leadership roles were examined. Clinical psychologist Aurélie Athan endeavours to build upon and definitively outline the concept of matrescence, emphasizing psychological, social, and political changes in the transition to motherhood. In my view, her greatest contribution to Athan's project, appearing earlier in her matrescence scholarship, highlights how the spiritual awakenings of motherhood remain underexplored (Athan and Miller, "Motherhood").

In her current research, however, Athan moves in the direction of reproductive identity as an overarching concept to examine how everyone has a relationship to reproductive potential (Athan, "Reproductive"). Though an important topic and one of interest to me, I caution against subsuming research on bionatal genetic birth mother-child relationships into overarching reproductive identity studies, as this risks overshadowing significant distinctions. It is crucial to recognize that diversity emphasizes difference, and more research has long been needed to fully understand the bionatal mother-child bond, the impact of its disruption, and the importance of continued study that centres (rather than bypasses or negates) maternal experience and development. We are just beginning to hear the voices of adoptees and adults conceived through various reproductive technologies. There is often an expressed loss that is difficult to even name much less speak about, and there is too little acknowledgment of how these losses affect people's lives and generations to follow.

One outcome of Spielrein's matrescence is that her approach shifts from analyzing adults with apparent psychosis to mother-child bonds and child development (Spielrein; Launer, "Sex vs."). It has come to light that Spielrein was the first child psychologist, although Melanie Klein and Anna Freud have historically been credited as such. Both Klein and Freud were inspired by Spielrein's ideas while attending a psychoanalytic conference and presentation by Spielrein (Naszowska). Both later incorporated Spielrein's ideas into their own theories. When reading Spielrein's work on the bliss of breastfeeding, I was struck by how the spirit of it aligned with what semiotician Genevieve Vaughan calls "the secret gift in the heart of language" (Kindle Loc. 144). Vaughan envisions language as inseparable from the hidden maternal gift paradigm, which she sees as restoring maternal practice to language and to the symbolic order (Kindle Loc. 470). The following is part of Spielrein's elaboration on the transition from magical speech to social speech:

> The word "Mama" (in baby pronunciation "mö-mö-mö") reproduces sucking. The world "Papa" (= "pö-pö") stems from the phase when the satisfied child is playing with the breast. Both words owe their origins to sucking. Like no other, the act of sucking is fundamental to the most important of the child's life experiences: here it learns the bliss of knowing its feelings of hunger satisfied, but it also learns that this bliss has an end and has to be won again. The infant has its first experience that there

is an external world; its contact with the mother's body plays a part in this by offering resistance to the movements of the tiny mouth. And finally the little creature learns that there is a refuge in this external world, which is attractive not only because its hunger is satisfied there, but because it is warm, soft, and safe from all dangers. If we have felt once in our lives "Let this moment linger, it is so beautiful," it was surely at this time. Here the child learns for the first time to love, in the widest sense of the word, that is, to perceive contact with another being, independent of nourishment, as the highest bliss. (qtd. in Launer 258)

In her 2020 presentation, "The Language of the Mother and the Language of the Father: Sabina Spielrein's Anticipation of the Concepts of Jacques Lacan, Hélène Cixous, and Luce Irigaray," cultural historian Klara Naszowska compares Spielrein's ideas on language development with those of those notable scholars (Naszowska). While Naszowska's enlightening presentation highlights Spielrein's far-reaching insights and observations, I believe she undermines Spielrein's emphasis on the beauty and potential in the breastfeeding relationship by suggesting her linguistic observations equally apply to bottle-feeding. Although I understand the need to approach breastfeeding discussions with sensitivity—avoiding any implication of judgment towards mothers who cannot or choose not to breastfeed—it is essential to include diverse maternal perspectives on experiences like breastfeeding. More maternal voices are needed to challenge academic interpretations of mothering practices and to illuminate how resistances to patriarchal capitalist pressures on motherhood are enacted. As scholars, I believe we should avoid layering assumptions over biological specifications when they do not align with our political views or agendas. We must broaden and update our knowledge, recognizing that breastfeeding can offer benefits to both mothers and infants, serving as a form of "personalized medicine" (Jackson and Felder).

Genevieve Vaughan sees Hélène Cixous as a "radical groundbreaker," with her écriture féminine creating an opening to the maternal gift paradigm via writing. Vaughan's goal, however, is to reconfigure the symbolic order, defining it as the primacy of the maternal gift outside of or beyond exchange, from within reconceived language and communication that equals unilateral gifting. This illuminates human beings as a maternal gift giving species, or, as Vaughan describes, "homo donans" (Kindle Loc. 1074).

Scholar-midwife Nané Jordan introduced the term "placental thinking" as related to the maternal gift economy concept developed by Vaughan. She describes the placenta as a relational interface and a unilateral gift from mother to baby, noting its unique role as the only organ that willingly exits the body once its life-giving purpose is fulfilled. Jordan vividly portrays the placenta's rich life blood and the baby's nourishment through a network of veins yet observes how it is often discarded, treated as refuse, or used for research purposes—some that raise ethical concerns. While feminist philosopher Sarah Ruddick's concept of "maternal thinking" emphasizes intellectual skills developed in maternal practice beyond biological ties, Jordan highlights the placenta's distinct biological-relational significance. She argues that the placenta embodies a "gift morphology" that extends to the breasts, drawing parallels to treelike structures and extending mother-child centred reality in all directions (Jordan 148, 149).

Rosi Braidotti names her materialist feminist biopolitics "placenta politics" and argues that the placenta "is the perfect figuration for thinking both unity and diversity, specificity and difference within a monistic frame" (316). She explores the placenta as a metaphor and biological reality to examine the relationship between identity, embodiment, and interconnection. Critiquing the binary thinking that separates self and other, Braidotti uses the placenta as a symbol of relationality and continuity. Braidotti highlights the placenta as representing a nonhierarchical, interdependent connection while also referring to "toxic pharmacological aspects of contemporary reproduction" and "high level of technological mediation" surrounding reproduction today. Discussions about the sacrality of the mother-child relationship in an affirmation of "life as radical immanence" (318) to disrupt certain transhumanist agendas exceed the scope of this chapter but are of crucial importance.

Lifecourse Matrescence

In 2023, journalist Lucy Jones wrote a rich and complex poetic inquiry on matrescence and its inherent "radical metamorphosis" (263), which bridges matrescence scholarship with mainstream audiences. In this work, she extends the ideas of psychologist Gina Wong-Wylie and her cultural feminist practice of "matroreform," defined as an "act, desire, and process of claiming motherhood power" that creates "new mothering rules and practices" (Wong-Wylie). Matroreform is elaborated on while untangling the meaning of "phobia" in Adrienne Rich's term "matrophobia." Matrophobia was initially articulated by Rich as a fear of becoming one's mother; a "desire to become purged ... of our mother's bondage" (Rich qtd. in Wong-Wylie). A more compassionate process is outlined by Wong-Wiley, which strives to depersonalize and restory the sociocultural and historical suffering in one's maternal lineage while tending to a new kind of self-agency in mothering. It is an empathetic and fear-facing turn to understand that self-agency was scarcely attainable to mothers in previous generations and to reflect empathetically on the rippling of this generational loss and what it means for us personally and collectively. Matroreform offers a path to transform matrophobia— shifting from a fear of inheriting maternal suffering to a compassionate reckoning with its origins—by reclaiming maternal power and imagining new possibilities for flourishing beyond generational and cultural constraints. In 1912, Sabina Spielrein wrote, "The depth of our psyche knows no 'I' but only its summation, the 'We'..." and "I have arrived at the conclusion that the main characteristic of an individual is that it is 'dividual'" (qtd in Cooper-White).

Jones brings several mother-centring authors into relationships with matroreform in her book, ending with some brilliant instructions for making necessary sociological changes to enhance maternal wellbeing (Jones). Jones's writing on matrescence is beautifully imaginative, yet I long for more living images of the feral joy that is available within and through mothering throughout the lifespan, under socially nourishing conditions most mothers can only imagine. Critique is vital, as is poetry. Envisioning flourishing mothers, well beyond oppressive contexts and normative constructs, is needed to further inspire us towards changemaking.

Matristic Time and Matrisophy

Diving deeply into an excavation of lost maternal knowledge and meaning led me to "revolvere," a Latin word that means "to turn over, roll back, reflect upon." Sankofa, from a Ghanaian Akan proverb, means "It is not taboo to go back for what you forgot (or left behind)" and is more loosely defined as "go back and get it." (Stockton) The focus becomes what will be retrieved in our efforts to (re)create societies that begin with loving the mother in a mother-thriving world. My imaginary tends mothering futures on the other side of the struggle against patriarchal motherhood and the institution of motherhood in a necessary retrieval process that heals and invokes (though not without grief) a return not only of empowerment but of bliss in and through mothering (Rich).

In Spielrein's most famous paper, "Destruction as the Cause of Coming into Being," she presents a matrifocal view of time to elucidate transformation: "Mother is also simultaneously the image of the depths of the unconscious that exists out of time…, In the unconscious, all places merge with one another" (Spielrein qtd. in Sells).

Philosopher Fanny Söderbäck explores time and sexual difference by engaging in a dialogue between the writings of Julia Kristeva and Luce Irigaray in her book *Revolutionary Time*. Like Spielrein, these thinkers focus on reproduction, embodiment, and species survival. Söderbäck highlights how women have historically been associated with the cyclical time of nature, marked by repetition, while men are seen as representing linear time, with greater potential for change and progress. She argues that rites or rituals can disrupt both cyclical and linear time, creating a "revolutionary time"—a process that neither repeats nor forgets the past but stays open to transformation. My concept of (r)evolutionary matrisophy, which I explore in my dissertation, aligns with this idea of combining revolutionary and evolutionary processes. It is crucial to revisit and reauthor evolutionary narratives, particularly in understanding human relationships and how patriarchy undermines these. Evolution, defined as a gradual process of transformation into a more complex form, whether socially or economically, is central to this method (Weappa, "Evolution"). While philosophy traditionally means the love of wisdom, I replace "philo-" with "matri-" to return Sophia (wisdom) to a knowledge-loving process that reintegrates maternal wisdom and ethics into the continuum of human evolution (Weappa, (R)evolutionary).

Intergenerational Maternal Love Power

My background in child and human development and birthwork and my life experience as a marginalized single mother and adoptee complicates my relationship with equality feminism and the contemporary view of gender as merely a social construct. In academic gender studies, equality is often framed within an egalitarian model that overlooks the unique aspects of mothering, reducing it to generalized parenting or caregiving. This narrow vision of inclusion reinforces outdated and reductionist ideas about maternal norms. Sexual difference is frequently dismissed, and the distinctiveness of mothering is sidelined. Maternal theory is often ignored, unless it aligns with antinatal queer theory, or queering motherhood, which sometimes promotes the erasure of natal maternal identities. As discussed above, matrophobia is understood as a fear of becoming one's mother (Rich). I suggest matriphobia (with an "i" not an "o") as an unconscious or conscious fear of the distinct love power available to mothers and motherers through matrescence and self-determined mothering, which have the potential to move humanity towards postpatriarchal futures (Weappa, *(R)evolutionary*).

Queer theorists often dismiss concerns about maternal erasure as unfounded, yet in the US, suicide is the leading cause of death for new mothers (Hemstad). This silent crisis remains largely overlooked. While I aim to include all individuals who identify as parents in my vision for the future of mothering, I advocate for a mother-centring approach to parenthood that values parents equally while equalizing the distribution of parenting responsibilities. It is unhelpful to create new taboos around female biology and maternal specificity or to assume that generalized parenting or caregiving can replace the unique bond between mother and child. We still lack sufficient scientific and social understanding of the long-term effects of disrupting these bonds. My perspective on matrescence stems from the recognition that we are only beginning to grasp the far-reaching societal impacts of acknowledging—or neglecting—sexual difference, maternal materiality, maternal identity, and birth giving as an existential experience. This stance does not seek to diminish the importance of studying reproductive identity, patrescence, queerness, or the transformative nature of caregiving and parenting more broadly. Ignoring the preventable suffering and death of mothers in our studies on motherhood, fatherhood, or parenthood is unacceptable.

My academic contribution of "lifecourse matrescence" recognizes that while motherhood begins with an initial transformative shift, women experience multiple maternal rites of passage as they develop relational skills and gain experience throughout the mother-child relationship—from postpartum to the empty nest and beyond (Weappa, *(R)evolutionary*). This lifecourse matrescence perspective highlights the unique opportunities to notice and name the cultivation of relational maturity and wisdom (sophy). Despite a strong focus on child development and a comprehensive understanding of the human life course, there is still a lack of language to describe the various stages of maternal development, which continue well beyond childbirth and the postpartum period, evolving as mothers age, and as they transition into roles such as grandmothers and invaluable community elders.

Remembering

In 1977, two years after Dana Raphael introduced the concept of matrescence in the anthropological collection *Being Female*, psychologist Carol Gilligan published *In a Different Voice*, a groundbreaking work recognizing the distinctiveness of female experiences and perspectives in human growth and development. In a recent interview, Gilligan credited writer Cynthia Ozick as an inspiration ("In a"). Ozick, now in her late nineties, asks a crucial question: "What was lost?" Initially referencing the profound loss experienced by the first generation of Jews after the Holocaust, Ozick extends this question to the historical exclusion of women from meaning-making in traditions and religions, linking it to dehumanization. She argues that recognizing this exclusion should first evoke grief, followed by a collective mission to uncover the religious and philosophical origins of such dehumanization. Gilligan's recent work suggests that patriarchy persists partly because it undermines our relational capacities. She explains that patriarchy frames the loss of relationships as irreparable, turning the sacrifice of connection—a psychological harm—into a psychological gain. This dynamic leads us to avoid love to escape vulnerability to further loss, which has come to feel inevitable and unbearable (Gilligan and Snider).

From Being Analyzed to Being Who We Are

I was a teen under extreme duress, perched on the edge of a metal folding chair near the door of a therapist's office, staring at the luminous tears splashing like stars onto my salmon pink flats. A tissue box sat behind him, untouched, never offered. I wiped my face with my sleeves, avoiding his gaze. Across the room, the therapist gestured to a black leather sofa, assuring me I'd be more comfortable there, leaning in with breath that reeked of stale coffee and halitosis. I trembled, arms crossed, open to help but knowing instinctively this man was not it.

Amid the typical struggles of adolescence in the 1980s, I had discovered I was adopted, mourned the loss of a grandmother, endured assaults by an older female peer, and suffered a toxic relationship with a popular male athlete who had groomed me with promises of eternal love. These traumas destabilized me, and I found myself alone in a room with a middle-aged man eager to pathologize me.

At the end of the unbearable session, the therapist handed me a psychological questionnaire—hundreds of true/false questions, many of them offensive. I gave up halfway through, randomly filling in answers to escape the ordeal. On the way to the next session, I admitted this to my parents. My dad laughed darkly, and my mother shook her head with a knowing smirk. I was not sure if I was in more trouble or less.

Back in the office, I again sat in the metal chair by the door. My dad unfolded two extra chairs for him and my mom, refusing the black couch. The therapist scratched his head, launching into a cold, clinical evaluation of me. My mother chewed her gum harder, her face revealing the same expression she wore when she knew she was being bullshitted. My father's steady breathing was the only sign of his simmering anger.

Then, after just a few minutes, my dad interrupted. "That's enough," he said firmly. He would settle the bill but refused to pay the therapist another cent. "You don't know our daughter," he added. My mother nodded in agreement, scoffing a quick "nope" as they stood to leave. I noticed my father did not offer his usual handshake—a gesture he never withheld, even in disagreement. On the way home, my anger towards my parents softened. I felt a deep sense of relief and started forgiving them for not responding to my needs sooner. We talked about finding a new school, a fresh start. In the weeks and months that followed, those changes helped me begin to heal.

Like my own resistance to an androcentric therapeutic model that sought to define me through its limited gaze, Sabina Spielrein resisted the reductive labels and biases imposed upon her, choosing instead to engage with her trauma on her own terms and transform her experiences into groundbreaking contributions that continue to inspire those who seek to challenge oppressive norms and reclaim agency in the face of adversity. Despite widespread interpretations of Spielrein as an "everpatient" of Carl Jung, she was assigned to his caseload for a very short time (Sells). Admitted to the Burghölzi hospital by her parents, Spielrein was a nineteen-year-old young woman grieving the death of her younger sister who tragically died of typhoid. She showed symptoms typical of someone who has suffered abuse. She creatively resisted analysis during her time at Burghölzi hospital and throughout her life. Psychotherapist John Launer, who has written a comprehensive biography of Spielrein, discovered that Carl Jung, then a married man in his thirties, went on a leave from the Burghölzi not long after Spielrein was admitted. Although Spielrein and Jung were engaged in a longstanding relationship, I agree with Felicity Brock Kelcourse that Spielrein was an "analyst to her analyst" from beginning to end. In a letter to her mother dated 1909, Spielrein writes, "I fell in love with a psychopath" and would later refer to herself as Jung's "little mother" in her diary (qtd. in Lothane 203). Spielrein spent about nine months at the Burghölzi hospital, which was a progressive community, rare in its time. Eugen Bleuler, its director, wanted to create a community environment where patients participated in enriching activities (Launer). The latter half of Spielrein's time at the hospital served as a kind of internship for Spielrein in which she "engaged in scientific studies, assisting in research, including some of Jung's work on word associations" with Eugen Bleuler declaring Spielrein as "not mentally ill" and recommending that she depart from the Burghölzi to attend medical school, where she earned qualifications as a doctor (Harris). Sabina Spielrein was a sane and bright polymath who substantially influenced many. She spoke several languages, studied the history of art, and was a talented pianist.

When I first heard of Spielrein alongside epithets such as "hysteric", "mistress" and "seductress" I intuitively knew that living in time periods a hundred years apart hadn't prevented us from having some things in common, as women disrupting the status quo by nature of simply being who we are.

Transformative Love Drive

Spielrein's concept of the death instinct diverges significantly from Sigmund Freud's later formulation, despite his attempts to integrate her ideas into his own framework. Freud acknowledged Spielrein's early work on the subject, although he minimized her contribution by suggesting she had only anticipated his theory of the death drive. However, Spielrein's death instinct, as interpreted by several scholars including Julie Reshe, is distinct from Freud's understanding entirely. Spielrein's notion of the death instinct is closely linked to love, motherhood, and the dissolution of the self, offering a perspective that directly challenges Freud's male-centric and ego-driven view of human nature (Reshe, "Negative").

Spielrein saw destruction not as a purely negative force but as a transformative process tied to renunciation and the interconnectedness of subjects. Her framework, rooted in intersubjectivity, focusses on the blurring of individual boundaries, particularly in acts of love and motherhood, whereas Freud's death drive is fundamentally dualistic and individualistic, centred on self-preservation. Spielrein's death instinct, therefore, challenges the very foundations of Freudian psychoanalysis by proposing a nondualistic, relational model that emphasizes difference, connection, and the erasure of distinct subjectivity in love. This represents a profound departure from Freud's theories, signalling a radically different, and arguably more nuanced, understanding of human drives (Reshe, "The Death Drive").

I see Spielrein's thoughts on love continued in the emergent field of feminist love studies, which builds on Anna G. Jónasdóttir's concept of "love power," which is the fundamental human ability through which we empower one another as valuable individuals (Jónasdótter). Operating within a historical-materialist framework, she bases her ideas on the existence of basic human capacities and needs, which serve as the foundation for understanding specific power structures. She distinguishes between two forms of power: a positive form, as an inherent psycho-organic capacity, and a negative form, as oppressive or exploitative power (Ferguson and Toye).

Humanities That Love the Mother

Italian feminist philosopher Luisa Muraro's *The Symbolic Order of the Mother*, originally published in 1991 in Italian and only translated into English in 2018, details a journey towards developing her concept of creative sexual difference. Muraro reflects on the difficulties she faced in beginning to write and think through these ideas, eventually drawing inspiration from various thinkers, including Luce Irigaray and Adrienne Rich, while navigating the intersection of feminism and psychoanalysis. Eventually, she arrives at the concept of the "symbolic order of the mother." Muraro addresses motherhood both literally and symbolically, blending the personal and metaphysical. She views language as the result of our postnatal negotiation with our mothers, positioning the mother as the primary civilizing force in early life. Like Sabina Spielrein, Muraro's work focuses on reconnecting thought with this childhood love for the mother experienced through embodiment, relationality, and language acquisition. Her understanding is that "knowing how to love the mother creates symbolic order" (Muraro).

In my 2022 dissertation, *(R)evolutionary Matrisophy: Motherlines, Matricultures, and Maternal Ethics for Mothering Futures*, I argue that humans are fundamentally a mothering species, but we have lost touch with this identity by neglecting the core elements of our evolutionary nest—our biological heritage, in which mothering plays a central role (Narvaez). If we accept that mothering is essential to our species, then sustaining human futures may require a form of remembering that involves cultivating resilient frameworks rooted in "nested mothering" principles (Weappa, "Nested"). My proposal is not about asserting supremacy—whether anthropocentric, racial, or gendered—but about reconnecting with the relational foundations of human existence.

Although some postmaternal[2] and posthumanist feminists and thinkers aim to move beyond the nature vs. nurture debate or bypass it entirely in transhumanist fantasies, leading the way to motherless planets, we have only begun to explore our evolutionary human potential in nurturance. I envision freedom for our species through the love power of mothering, which depends heavily on the role of attuned motherers.[3] This vision calls for a renewed understanding of our interconnectedness, returning to a sense of belonging within nonhierarchical matricultural (and ecocultural) contexts. Through this, the pervasive delusion of motherlessness might dissolve.

Inspired by a conversation with a coresearcher from my doctoral program in transformative studies, which is grounded in creative inquiry and transdisciplinary research, I contemplated the term "supra" alongside the humanities. After reading philosopher Jeffrey Kripal's book *The Superhumanities*, I was struck by his Nietzschean inspiration from the coming of the Superman (Übermensch) (Kripal). When juxtaposed with the Nietzschean positions Spielrein argues with and elaborates on, from a standpoint of sexual difference in love and mothering, destruction and creation are regenerative aspects of earthly existence. Kripal is not "writing on the posthuman or the transhuman" (583). I appreciated his creative leaps and was entertained by the content in every chapter. Although Kripal is clear that he is "against spiritual and moral bypassing," his view of the superhumanities does not (yet) invite the missing mother or her love power (Kripal 583). The mother of Superman was imagined by two men and a fictional character dwelling on another planet. I suggest the suprahumanities are a next step for the superhumanities in a matrignosis[4] that calls the missing mother forth into modern discourse.

From Latin, "supra" translates to "above, beyond, before in time," which can be compared with (r)evolutionary time discussions in relationship with my articulation of matrisophy (Weappa (R)evolutionary). Matrisophy retrieves and reintegrates the missing mother historically excluded from philosophy. It includes full human experience and encourages expanded ways of perceiving the self, other, world, past, and future. Recovering the symbolic order of the mother offers a lens that, as I see it, holds the potential to transmute and dissolve any existing definition of "suprahuman" or "suprahumanity"[5] presently defined as any person or group of people "having powers above and beyond" another person or group of people (Collins Dictionary). Rather, it is supra because it reemplaces the mother-baby in the human story, from the beginning and throughout. It is about being fully human and becoming ever more relationally and earthly human.

Psychotherapist Adrienne Harris describes how Spielrein's "deep interests ... take her into waters we are still exploring and into ways of thinking that we continue to evolve and practice." John Launer comments on the breadth of Spielrein's work: "At different points it leaves the reader astounded at the breadth of her knowledge or frustrated at her precocious efforts to construct a psychological 'theory of everything,' or both at the same time" (Launer 9). Indeed, there is an essence of "supra" in the "higher calling" of Spielrein's legacy and possibility for a transdisciplinary field of study rooted in the original organic love power of ordinary human mothering.

Endnotes

1. The term "matristic," coined by Marija Gimbutas, refers to mother-centred societies featuring a cosmology that includes both male and female deities; the veneration of female deities is linked to a mother-

kinship system and ancestor worship. In such societies, women, especially as mothers, are honoured as representatives of the sacred original mother, the culture's progenitor.

2. Julie Stephens defines "postmaternal thinking" as a tool to explore the cultural anxiety surrounding nurture, caregiving, and human dependency, which stems from a dominant societal trend she calls "the postmaternal," characterized by forgetting of key historical narratives.

3. See Genevieve Vaughan's *Gift in the Heart of Language: The Maternal Source of Meaning* for an explanation of the term motherers as including all sexes and genders, depending specifically on typical maternal behaviour.

4. See my 2022 dissertation for a discussion of matrignosis. The prefix "matri-" applies to both mother and matter. Matrignosis can be taken to simply mean "mother knowledge" or material knowledge and mother knowledge simultaneously. As knowledge is relationally constructed, gnosis can be considered as knowledge with.

5. The vision of suprahumanities outlined in this chapter has no theoretical relationship to problematic ideas in Daniel S. Forrest's book *Suprahumanism: European Man and the Regeneration of History.*

Works Cited

Athan, Aurélie, and Lisa Miller. "Motherhood as Opportunity to Learn Spiritual Values: Experiences and Insights of New Mothers." *Journal of Prenatal and Perinatal Psychology and Health,* vol. 27, no. 4, Summer 2013, pp. 220–53.

Athan, Aurélie. "Reproductive Identity: An Emerging Concept." *American Psychologist,* vol. 75, no. 4, 2020, pp. 445–56.

Bueskens, Petra. *Academia,* 10 July 2019, www.academia.edu/40361026/ Wollstonecrafts_Dilemma_Identity_Politics_and_Feminism. Accessed 12 Jan. 2025.

Braidotti, Rosi. "Placenta Politics." Posthuman Glossary edited by Rosi Braidotti and Maria Hlavajova. Bloomsbury, 2018, pp. 315–18.

Collins Dictionary. "Feral." www.collinsdictionary.com/us/dictionary/ english/feral. Accessed 13 Jan. 2025.

Crowley, Vivianne. "Jungian Feminists." *Encyclopedia of Psychology and Religion*. Edited by David A. Leeming, Springer, 2017, pp. 1–4.

Dougan, Daniel O. "Appreciating the Legacy of Kübler-Ross: One Clinical Ethicist's Perspective." *American Journal of Bioethics*, vol. 19, no. 12, 2019, pp. 5–9.

"Evolution, N." *The Free Dictionary*. https://www.thefreedictionary.com/evolution. Accessed 13 Jan. 2025.

Ferguson, Ann, and Margaret E. Toye. "Feminist Love Studies—Editors' Introduction." *Hypatia*, vol. 32, no. 1, 2017, pp. 5–18.

Freud, Sigmund. "Analysis of a Phobia of a Five-Year-Old Boy." *The Pelican Freud Library*, vol 8, Case Histories 1, 1977, pp. 169–306.

Gilligan, Carol. *In a Human Voice*. 2023.

Gilligan, Carol, and Naomi Snider. *Why Does Patriarchy Persist?* Polity, 2018.

Goethe, Johann Wolfgang von. *Faust*. Translated by Charles Timothy Brooks. Tredition Classics, 2011.

Harris, Adrienne. "Language Is There to Bewilder Itself and Others." *Sabina Spielrein and the Beginnings of Psychoanalysis*. Edited by Pamela Cooper-White and Felicity Brock-Kelcourse. Routledge, 2019. Kindle edition.

Hemstad, Mia. "Suicide and Overdose Are the Leading Causes of Death for New Mothers; Screening Could Change This." *Maternal Mental Health Leadership Alliance: MMHLA*, 2023, www.mmhla.org/articles/suicide-and-overdose-are-the-leading-causes-of-death-for-new-mothers-screening-could-change-this. Accessed 13 Jan. 2025.

Jackson, Joynelle, and Tisha Felder. "Breastfeeding Benefits Mothers as Much as Babies, but Public Health Messaging Often Only Tells Half of the Story." *The Conversation*, 11 Feb. 22024, theconversation.com/breastfeeding-benefits-mothers-as-much-as-babies-but-public-health-messaging-often-only-tells-half-of-the-story-214543. Accessed 13 Jan. 2025.

Johnson, Rae. "Specialization in Somatic Studies." *Pacifica Graduate Institute*, www.pacifica.edu/degree-program/somatic-studies/. Accessed 13 Jan. 2025.

Jónasdóttir, Anna G. "The Difference That Love (Power) Makes." *Feminism and the Power of Love*. Routledge, 2018, pp. 14–35.

Jones, Lucy. *Matrescence*. Penguin Books Ltd., 2023.

Jordan, Nané. "Placental Thinking: The Gift of Maternal Roots." *Placenta Wit: Mother Stories, Rituals, and Research*. Edited by Nané Jordan. Demeter Press, 2017, pp. 142–56.

Jung, C., and C. Kerenyi. "Science of Mythology." *Essays on the Myth of the Divine Child and the Mysteries of Eleusis*. Edited and translated by R.F.C. Hull, 1963, pp. 156–183.

Kelcourse, Felicity Brock. "Sabina Spielrein from Rostov to Zürich." *Sabina Spielrein and the Beginnings of Psychoanalysis*. Edited by Pamela Cooper-White and Felicity Brock Kelcourse. Routledge, 2019, pp. 36–72.

Khanna, Ranjana. *Dark Continents: Psychoanalysis and Colonialism (Post-Contemporary Interventions)*. Duke University Press, 2003.

Kripal, Jeffrey J. *The Superhumanities*. 4th ed. University of Chicago Press, 2022.

Launer, John. *Sex Versus Survival: The Life and Ideas of Sabina Spielrein*. Gerald Duckworth & Co Ltd., 2014.

Lothane, Zvi. "Tender Love and Transference: Unpublished Letters of C.G. Jung and Sabina Spielrein (with an Addendum/Discussion)." *Sabina Spielrein: Forgotten Pioneer of Psychoanalysis*. Edited by Coline Covington and Barbara Wharton. Routledge, 2003, pp. 89–222.

Missing Mother Conference. The University of Bolton, UK, 2021 Apr. 22, https://themissingmother.wordpress.com. Accessed 23 Apr. 2021.

Muraro, Luisa. *Symbolic Order of the Mother, the (Suny Series in Contemporary Italian Philosophy)*. State University of New York Press, 2019.

Narvaez, Darcia. "Our Mission, Vision, and Team." *The Evolved Nest*, https://evolvednest.org/mission%2C-vision%2C-our-team. Accessed 13 Jan. 2025.

Narvaez, Darcia. "The Indigenous Worldview: Original Practices for Becoming and Being Human." *YouTube*, 5 Oct. 2016, https://www.youtube.com/watch?v=wmQ3CkUkhuw. Accessed 13 Jan. 2025.

Naszowska, Klara. *The Language of the Mother and the Language of the Father: Sabina Spielrein's Anticipation of the Concepts of Jacques Lacan, Hélène Cixous and Luce Irigaray*. Academia.edu, drive.google.com/

file/d/1YOevF2iRmQgW_kPqb_Ms0sVZtxIXTmTJ/view. Accessed 10 Sept. 2023.

Ozick, Cynthia. "Notes Toward Finding the Right Question (A Vindication of the Rights of Jewish Women)." *Lilith*, vol. 6, 1979, pp. 121–151.

Raphael, Dana, editor. *Being Female*. Mouton, 1975.

Rich, Adrienne. *Of Woman Born: Motherhood as Experience and Institution*. W. W. Norton, 1986.

Reshe, Julie. "Sabina Spielrein–The Death Drive, Love, and Motherhood." 19 Mar. 2023, www.youtube.com/watch?v=t4lUxfwqUqA. Accessed 13 Jan. 2025.

Reshe, Julie. "Sabina Spielrein's Negative Psychoanalysis." *YouTube*, 31 Mar. 2024, www.youtube.com/watch?v=RBeifWW-ssg. Accessed 13 Jan. 2025.

Stockton. https://www.stockton.edu/sankofa/about.html

Sells, Angela M. *Sabina Spielrein: The Woman and the Myth*. Reprint ed., SUNY Press, 2017.

Söderbäck, Fanny. *Revolutionary Time: On Time and Difference in Kristeva and Irigaray*. Suny Press, 2019.

Spielrein, Sabina. *The Essential Writings of Sabina Spielrein*. 1st ed., Taylor & Francis, 2018.

Spielrein. "Destruction as the Cause of Becoming." *The Essential Writings of Sabina Spielrein*. Edited by Ruth I. Cape and Raymond Burt, Routledge, 2019, pp. 97–134.

Vaughan, Genevieve. *The Gift in the Heart of Language: The Maternal Source of Meaning (Sociology)*. Mimesis International, 2015.

Vissing, Helena. "The Impact of Negation of the Maternal Body on Embodiment and Subjectivity in Modernity." *Psychoanalytic Perspectives*, vol. 21, no. 3, 2024, pp. 306–29.

Weappa, Jessica Spring. *(R)evolutionary Matrisophy: Motherlines, Matricultures, and Maternal Ethics for Mothering Futures: A Portfolio of Three Papers*. 2022. California Institute of Integral Studies, dissertation. *ProQuest*, www.proquest.com/openview/ef42ea81f19c888a-6f387a17ecb879be/1?pq-origsite=gscholar&cbl=18750&diss=y. Accessed 13 Jan. 2025.

Weappa, Jessica Spring. "Nested Mothering: Transdisciplinary Considerations for Mothering Futures." *International Association for Maternal Action and Scholarship (IAMAS) Conference.* Chicago, IL. October 2–4, 2020.

Wong-Wylie, G. "Images and Echoes in Matroreform: A Cultural Feminist Perspective." *Journal of the Motherhood Initiative for Research and Community Involvement,* vol. 8, no. 1, 2006, https://jarm.journals. yorku.ca/index.php/jarm/article/view/5020. Accessed 13 Jan. 2025.

4

Three Little Witches

Hillary Di Menna

Three little witches form a circle around the fire, a cauldron resting atop the flames. Inside the cauldron are tomatoes, garlic, and sewing buttons. The tomatoes represent the rich soil from which the little witches draw their roots; the garlic keeps the witches sharp of mind and edge; and the sewing buttons are used to mend generational curses. This circle is where spells are cast, and trouble is born.

The magick dawned in a small village where church bells rang with promise as if fastened to a kitten's collar, chiming alongside families' whispered secrets of sand and clay. Hydrated vines twisted from the ground as omens of beautiful riots to come. Witchlets hatched from fruits. Curly vines sprouted dreams from the witchlets' minds before popping out of the tops of their heads. Crooked-toothed smiles formed to the rhythm of hearts that would continue to beat in tandem with those bells even when broken. These ancient recipes promised naughty little girls, the kind that would make Lilith's red lips smile.

The trinity's crone kept her fingers dancing as she dug dirt and kneaded dough. This work appeared effortless to the mother and maiden, but the crone worked hard to hone these skills. She moved under the careful direction of ghosts and kept her wavy hair short. Although she was always working, her eyes remained playful. She loved nothing more than caring for her family—although food and fashion were close seconds. Her plants towered over her, and her heart could fill any room lucky enough to have the smells of her pizza and parmesan wafting through.

Years before, when the crone was a new mother to a boy who played the accordion on the village's dirt roads, the winds were especially strong.

The full moon screamed against a velvet dark sky and frightened the stars enough to stand back but not so much that they didn't remain curious, sparkling a little extra shine in anticipation of what was to come. The crone-then-mother ran to the fields without question, her nightgown billowing; lace trim sweeping the earth her bare feet caressed.

Nosy Little Owl watched from above, knowing the news was too big even for them to share before the time was right. "Be quiet and don't be a fool," Owl told Open-Mouthed Tree Snake. Snake, caught off guard by being seen so quickly, bit down on some strange fruit, trying to save face by pretending this was their plan all along. A Seven-Spotted Lady Beetle giggled as Barrel Jellyfish sang encouragement through light beneath the Adriatic Sea.

The crone-then-mother fell to her knees, out of breath, her eyes both wild and calm. She pressed her left hand's palm against the ground. Thump, thump, thump: Roots pulsed through the ground like the grass snakes that frightened her so. Listening to the beat's spirit-like whispers, the crone-then-mother knew she had to follow these slithering roots so that a new witchlet could sprout. The family would have to move.

Two cats—named collectively as Freyja—pulled the gondola towards the family's new home, hissing at the waves. They stopped only when they met a large turtle. The crone-then-mother, her husband, and their accordion-playing boy stepped out of the vessel and carried their suitcases across Turtle's large shell. Their spirits knew where to go. They soon saw the tomato vines sprouting from the roots that pulsed from all the way back home. The crone-then-mother placed her suitcase carefully on the ground and popped the lock open. The suitcase opened like a book, flat against the dirt, before evolving into a little brown house made of paper and wood. The roof came to a point, reminding the family to never stop looking at the sky.

The earth quaked out an announcement. Someone magical was arriving. A new witchlet sprouted from the tomato plants. The crone-then-mother was met with a set of dark and knowing eyes, lifted by cheeks round like the moon, and lips plump with a soft-spokenness enveloping an edge, like a red fox playing Scopa.

As moons passed, the witchlet grew long, dark hair. She learned to speak in tongues, devouring scholarship over languages like fruit jam. She learned to walk Turtle's shell and climb among the vines. With so many spirits living within her, she couldn't help but be drawn to her elders, asking questions, their wisdom an apothecary. Taking notes, she created grimoires of the stories, adventures, and histories of townspeople who followed pulsing roots, on boats pulled by cats, to grow intertwined with fruits and climbing plants.

Like many women, the crone-then-mother would be visited by a hateful presence. Misogynistic violence was a strong force employed by weak beings void of magick in their souls. A dangerous byproduct of this toxic presence was witch hunters—those jealous and scared of a witch's magick. Witch hunters sought to destroy magick rather than celebrate it. Sensing this poison moving towards her home, the crone-then-mother tried to save her family by returning to their old farm, across Turtle's shell, and through hissing waves. They fled by cat-drawn gondola.

They unpacked their wooden house with a pointed roof honouring the sky, tended to the earth, and listened to the church bells chime. This escape lasted for a little bit before the sounds of bells were drowned out by pulsing roots calling out, beckoning for the family's return. The maiden confided in her mother: "I hear a man's voice. He threatens, 'I will capture you.'" The crone-then-mother felt uneasy returning to a place where these threats hid within the wind, but she knew her magick was needed to break the curse. The crone-then-mother and her witchlet called upon the feline collective once more and returned to the land where the crone-then-mother first unpacked her house of wood and paper. The crone's husband and accordion-playing son stayed back on the farm to water the plants.

By the light of a screaming moon and its adoring stars against that plush sky, the mother-then-crone tended to her garden's soil. She called upon her daughter, who hydrated the soon-to-be-twisty vines. Knowing the witch hunter would place a curse on the newest witchlet, the crone-then-mother kissed the earth with the cure, just as her mother had taught her.

Three little witches with dark brown eyes, shorter than the plants they tended to, with hair of twists and turns. All unafraid of the shadow work needing to be done. The baby born from that tomato was born into so much love that although the witch hunter tried to squash her, a deep-rooted resiliency got her through.

Seeing the strength of the trinity, the hunter attempted to destroy their power by kidnapping the new mother and baby to somewhere he hoped the crone would not find them. He took the mother and witchlet as they slept and locked them in a red truck. The truck reluctantly served to drive them far away, its apologies heard through its rumbles.

When the crone awoke the next day to find her family gone, she climbed to the top of her house and cried for help. The earth growled in unison with the sway of the tomato plants, perfectly timed to the crone's cries, which went uninterrupted until she heard the faint sound of a puppy's bark. Catching her breath and wiping her tears away, she called down to the pup, "Are you here to help me?"

The black-and-white spotted pup nodded. "You're very small," said the crone, as she climbed down from atop the roof. Little Spotted Dog shrugged, "Yes, like you and your coven, I am smaller than the beautiful plants that you grow." Appreciating the compliment to her gardening, the crone smiled, "You will fit right in. Let's go!"

The crone and Spotted Dog asked the two water-crossing cats if they could help them on their voyage. "Climb aboard," Freyja yowled. The elder felines enlisted a couple of their own kittens—Nemi and Triora—to stay with the crone and her pup on their journey.

As they waited for the crone to join them, the mother and her witchlet built a barricade against the witch hunter. Every time the mother finished reading a book to her witchlet, they would lay it like a brick to create the barricade's walls. The curious mother knew that knowledge shared by witches past could act as present-day guides. Insulation was created by using the witchlet's princess costumes, which she always carried in a pouch just in case.

The witchlet would cackle every time she tried a new costume dress on. With each new frock, the witchlet would twirl three times, generating a cloud of stars. The stardust would guide the dress to fly off the witchlet's frame. The garment would give a curtsy before tucking itself away to keep the fractured coven warm. The dresses reminded the mother of the crone and how they shared a love of fashion, which was so obviously passed down to the twirling witchlet, dancing within the walls built of knowledge.

The mother showered her witchlet with so much love that Fireflies appeared, making sure the mother and daughter had light. The witch hunter's presence could be sensed outside the walls at times, lurking, pouting, but the witchlet was never scared: She had her mother's magick to protect her. Her mother's heart was safe indoors.

Witchlets may believe their mothers always know what to do.

Mothering is a powerful magick, but even mothers yearn for protection. The mother missed the crone. As her witchlet danced and Fireflies laughed, the mother allowed a tear to fall down her face and onto the floor. Fireflies were putting the witchlet to bed when a mole popped up from beneath the ground. Mole's nose twitched in the air and found their way into the cross-legged lap of the mother. "How can I help?" The mother whispered, as to not wake the witchlet, telling Mole all about the crone, the house with a pointed roof, and the cowardly witch hunter jealous of their magick. Nodding with understanding, Mole vowed to help the mother.

Mole returned to the ground in three nose twitches. Hearing the beat of the roots' pulse, Mole knew where to go. Burrowing with precision, Mole's whiskers sized the space and brushed against the tunnel's walls until it felt something strong and warm. Pausing, Mole allowed this new finding to move and breathe around them—Mole found the roots. The beating began to get louder, shaking the tunnel so that dirt fell lightly on Mole like the stardust they deserved to be anointed in for their kindness. Knowing what to do, Mole tunneled upwards until their head met the bottom of a puppy's paw. Mole looked up, and Spotted Dog looked down. The two familiars knew they had much to catch up on.

Nemi and Triora arched their backs and puffed themselves out, their kitten magick allowing them to grow to the size of two large horses. The crone, Spotted Dog, and kind-hearted Mole climbed upon the kittens' backs, clutching their fur as they galloped towards the mother and her witchlet.

The power of kittens should never be underestimated. Even those who have been pampered are not naïve. Kittens recharge each night as they sleep above their mothers' heads and travel from shadow to shadow within the apron pockets of their crones.

Hearing the gallops of kitten paws, the witch hunter began to run away, but he was not fast enough. Shrinking from their horselike sizes back to their small and nimble forms, the kittens flew above the witch hunter's head, leaping from the bare branches of the trees like shooting stars. Triora floated to the ground, hair on end. The kitten tripped the witch hunter while letting out a hiss, her tongue like a snake sliding through the spikes of their sharp teeth. As the hunter fell to the ground, Nemi descended from the celestial body above. The same paws that would knead alongside the crone's as they made pizza dough curled back to expose sharp claws. With the grace of an autumn leaf, Nemi positioned herself to lunge at the hunter's face, like a synchronized dancer, Triora pounced at the same time. Domesticated dogs could be heard unleashing their wild barking in the distance from behind living room windows. Coyotes yowled encouragement like a choir, harmonized by the howls of the crone's brave spotted pup.

The kittens slashed the hunter's right eye and smiled as a bloody scratch formed across his sclera in the shape of a cross. A spell was cast, leaving the witch hunter to live in total isolation for the rest of his life, his only company the consequence of his cruelty.

Reunited, the crone, the mother, and the witchlet created magick never seen before. The kittens played with the spotted pup among the sunbeams, and every Sunday, Mole would visit them all for dinner. The crone used their finest plates. The trinity's new home was near the water and bordered by mountains, just like the village where the magick that started it all shone. The trinity twirled in dresses made of lace and sparkle, cackled over otherworldly meals, and sang songs to the ghosts of all the mothers that came before them.

As the witchlet became a maiden, the crone taught her how to make her fingers dance while kneading the dough, feeding her the products of ancient spells. The mother continued to nourish the maiden by fostering a curiosity and drive to quench the thirst for knowledge and rituals of the past. The three little witches formed a circle around the fire. They danced around the cauldron which rested atop the flames containing food, fashion, and fun. As the moon cycles passed, those three little dancing witches became two and then only one.

The maiden wept as the moon shapeshifted with each passing night. She had her own little witchlet now, but she did not feel all-knowing in the way she thought her mothers had been. Her fingers were not ready to dance on their own, and her mind was so twisty and curly that the thoughts did not come to her as clearly as her mother was able to summon.

She could not see the point of these spells. If their coven's magick was not powerful enough to prevent death, to prevent the call of crossing the veil, were they nothing more than glamours?

Who was she without her mothers? Why was she so slow to learn?

The kittens rubbed their heads against the maiden's cheeks with affection, to wipe away the tears. Fireflies watched over the new witchlet as she fell asleep to the notes of Mole's lullabies.

"Did you watch the crone as she gardened?" asked Spotted Dog, whose snout began to look a little gray. The loyal canine had been sleeping by the fire, body curled to mirror a crescent moon:

"Sometimes the roots would grow strong without effort; other times they were tangled and needed more time. And when the crone knew that there was too much for one plant to carry, she collected cuttings and planted them to expand somewhere new. But they always came from those same roots, roots that go so deep and pulse loudly from our foundations, so that no matter where we end up, we know they are there."

Pausing, the maiden sighed deeply, nodding, and gave Spotted Dog a kiss. She allowed herself to drift to sleep, hoping to find more clarity within dreams.

"Plant dandelion seeds in the backyard to surprise your mom with what will grow," the kittens whispered in unison into the maiden's ear as she slept. "Tufts of white hair are not weeds; they are wisdom. Recipes for cures are passed down for centuries, but so are curses. You are not fighting them alone. No one on earth, or other realms, is ever done learning."

Walking through the pastels of her dreams, hopscotching through the lyrics of kittens' purring wisdom, the maiden realized: She was not meant to know it all. In fact, the ghosts of her mothers were watching and learning alongside their daughters still on earth.

Self-forgiveness washed over the maiden as kittens smiled in approval, exposing tiny fangs. She was not failing her mothers. Kneading dough, learning languages, and creating chaos through femininity were all the same magicks cast in different ways—ways that complement each other through growth and wisdom. The magick flowed; it never stood still.

Although her mothers had joined the choirs of ghosts, in hymn with all the mothers before them, she knew that she would be able to take their roots and grow something new with her own witchlet—something new, but something with a history to guide it. The ups and downs are how life moves through love, troublemaking, and grief.

Three little witches form a circle around the fire. In a cauldron resting atop the flames are tomatoes, garlic, and sewing buttons. The tomatoes represent the rich soil from which the little witches draw their roots; the garlic keeps the witches sharp of mind and edge; and the sewing buttons mend generational curses. This circle is where spells are cast, and trouble is born. The mother, the maiden, and the ghosts of all the crones before them. Their blood, a potion of something both rooted and feral.

5

Selected Poetry

Joy Domingo

A Dangerous Game

Let's pretend I'm your mental patient
And I'll pretend you're my nurse
Pretend you don't resent it

Let's pretend you like who I am
I'll pretend I like your TV shows
Let's pretend we know each other

I'll pretend I'm honest with you
Let's pretend we share our thoughts
Let's pretend we need each other

Let's pretend that love is enough
Let's pretend celibacy is okay
Let's pretend we're close

Pretend I sit in judgment of you
And I'll pretend you don't judge me
Pretend a pill can fix it all

I'll pretend I didn't spend all the money
Pretend I'm the root of all your problems
Pretend to share your emotional needs

We'll make believe we're living a life
Let's pretend we can comfort each other
Let's pretend we're not lonely

We can pretend dog voices are human
You can pretend to respect me
I'll pretend I don't know you don't

Let's pretend we have no choice
Pretend we're not bleeding
From biting our tongues

Let's pretend we need each other
We'll make believe we can do this forever
Pretend we're not dying inside
Let's pretend we are married

Fixing a Whole

Am I a slut? Where did my body go
when it was taken so often
from childhood up? What happened to
it during the fondling, the rape,
exposure, a dick in my face every
time I turned around? Or was it
inside me?

What does it mean to consent?
What if I made the first move?
Did that make it my choice?
Because it was going to happen
one way or another; I will
fuck or be fucked.

Whose body is this here in pieces?
What will it take to reclaim it? And who
wants it anyway? It's dirty, it's used,
it's damaged goods. It's made of
shame, of terror, and of filth.

How will I ever get it back?
Make it mine, keep it whole?
I've tried celibacy; hermitized,
stayed inside, keeping quiet,
keeping safe. Isolated, but still
dirty, terrorized, shattered.

Where have all those little parts
gone? When will I ever be clean?
Where does it go from here?
Cobble together the whole thing,
start from nothing and rebuild it,
piece by piece.

Internal Family System

fire in the kitchen
better put it out

run around in circles
chaos all about

where's the fucking water
hidden underground

no communication
stumbling around

mother always crying
seeking peace of mind

children whisper secrets
a little at a time

she can barely hear them
fire crackle low

holding them so tightly
never let them go

picking up the pieces
she didn't know were there

covered in a blanket
they never want to share

keeping it together
stumbling and blind

creeping forward inches
leave no child behind

Distanced between Two Hands

Rough and thorny every hour
Trying to escape the tower
Cut the cherry from the flour

Closed-up doors and shut-up faces
Horses straining at the traces
Pulling hard for different places

Measuring distance with her hands
In between the other lands
Somewhere far from where she stands

Finds herself in wretched spaces
No room here for homeostasis
Footprints small the only traces

Isn't this a pretty scene
Littered room of sickly green
Painted thick with words obscene

Lift the bucket, let it drop
Filled with blood and guts and slop
Find a way to make it stop

Getting darker by the minute
Moving slowly up and in it
Finding newer ways to spin it

Not alone for once and all
Stuttered words to pitch and squall
Padded ground to break the fall

Never felt this safe before
Tucking up her pinafore
Sifting sands for something more

Call of Consent

Unwrite the book, unlearn the pages
Here's a lesson learned in stages
Never mind about the sages
Me instead I'll rock your ages

Study hard and learn your courses
I got answers, I got sources
Time to hold on to your horses
You'll be beaten by my forces

Take a week to pull the sheets out
Gonna toss your ass about
Rolling thunder, never shout
I will reign upon your drought

Asking you to fucking listen
Make your eyes well up and glisten
Find a lake to float dead fish in
Hold on tight, nuclear fission

Me and you we're both consenting
Unreserved and unrelenting
Never sorry, unrepenting
This is love we're representing

6.

Feral Itch

Caroline Carey

Something itched beneath my skin, something trying to get out, to be free of the conformity label of this family name.

We lived in the Midlands, a house near Birmingham, quite middle class and substantial. Our life was suburban. We went to good schools and were raised to be polite and modest. We had a wonderful big garden with tall poplar trees at the end of it. At least it looked big to me at that little age.

Still, a visit to the local park was a highlight. If we were to walk across the park to go anywhere, then I was willing. I was easily bribed. Whether to shopping centres, parties, or school, it would give me a reprieve from the itch for a short while. Walks in the other direction to ladies' coffee mornings or the dreaded make-up, wigs, or Tupperware parties often ended in complete meltdowns, particularly on one occasion when it had been promised we would feed the ducks in the park on the way home.

It rained, heavily, so we were offered a lift in a car. This did not serve a much-troubled child, having put up with the party surrounded by ladies' nylon stockings, fallen plastic bowls, and a few other obnoxious children who insisted on offering me their sandwiches with demands that I play with the Tupperware!

Having to sit in the back seat of a car next to a child who frowned at me and not feeding the ducks was deplorable; hence, the itch rampaged around my body causing the most blood-curdling of screams that our nice new friend had never heard the like of. There were embarrassed glares, which I knew meant trouble, but the itch got more profuse, and I screamed louder.

The ducks went hungry.

I think back to Birmingham, in the centre of England, and the Black Country area, where my father worked. The old and dark factories and the loud machinery that smelled of industry and hard labour. Black Country was rough and coarse in its nature and this appealed to me. The people were loud and swore a lot, but they cherished me, the little red-haired girl who made them cups of coffee by putting threepenny bits in the coffee machine, carrying to them the hot mugs on the red tin tray, which always got sticky with sugar and coffee granules as the cups splashed their contents over the rims. They would smile at me, talking in that rough dialect that my elocution lessons had wrung out of me.

They felt so real, so funny, and so down to earth. I knew that they knew hardship and in some ways, I envied them—their freedom, laughter, and joy at the simple ways of living. I watched them working with the huge machines, each making rhythmic sounds as metal pieces were punched into shapes and then packaged up in sacking. Those smells of sacks, grease, hot sweaty bodies, and black coffee would be other scents to add to the repertoire of primal instincts, a gathering of natural aromas that fed my fascination with real life, interesting smells that filled the air—until Mother's perfume would shut them down as I held my breath so as not to take in its vile, bottled-up scent.

I would help in the factories, feeling the oiliness of each piece of metal filling sack after sack, tying each top with string so nothing would fall out. I might be given some pennies at the end of the day, just enough to buy the loose sweets from the big jars in the corner shop I was forbidden to enter.

My father would take us to the factories during the school holidays, for a different experience, and then my grandparents would pick us up and take us to Beatties, the very posh department store not far away, where we would ride the escalators and the lifts that felt like cages as we were taken to the top floor restaurant, given tea and scones as we sat looking out at the view over the tops of the city with all its roofs, big chimneys, and factory smog. That is why it was called the Black Country, because of the smoke and fog of industry, the iron making, and use of so many coal-fuelled furnaces that had filled the air. So, there we were, on occasion, with lunches at Beatties, with its plush purple carpets, the velvet chairs with tassels, and the infuriating white tablecloths that nothing must ever be spilled on.

I did my best to be patient as I waited for the trip back to the factory where I could get my hands dirty again. Yes, this was Birmingham, the centre of the country, the place of my ancestors, the city of my birth.

And now, moving away from suburbia, returning to the countryside that my father had always wanted, much to my delight, I would inhabit it well, with occasional visits back to the harbours of Birmingham's docks and river ways to get that occasional taste of something old, yet raw and vibrant.

I began my life living in polarity, from a nurturing existence in a country home to visits to the darkest part of our culture, a metal-processing town since the fourteenth century, full of heavy buildings, canals, and, in those days, the possibility of great prosperity. It was a hardened part of the world.

I rarely contemplated what was expected of me. It was hard to fathom what propelled the notions that insisted upon the usage of tableware being in certain positions, the correct socks to go with which shoes, and why white shoes were superior to the red glossy ones that sat on show in the shop window, the ones that matched the same coloured coat with fur borders and inner linings I hungered for. I thought it matched well with my rabbit friends. But she insisted upon the camel-coloured two-piece, with brown socks that covered the bruises on my roughened knees. Shopping was never fun, even if it was in the finest department store that Birmingham could offer.

I tried to refuse all the nice dresses she tried to insist upon, preferring my brother's hand-me-downs, by far my favourite way to dress; they were tatty, stained with engine oil, and had a feel of being worn to the bone that meant they were loose and less rigid than the clothing meant for school and church and other occasions far less important than clambering across meadows, climbing stone fortresses, and riding horses.

Rolling up the legs of my old jeans under my boring church dress was another challenge, endlessly hoisting them up during the service so no one would notice. This was my attempt to make the quick change after the scriptures were read aloud. I would not then have to go through the unpleasant changing of clothes in our cold house for every occasion that she deemed extremely necessary for every day, meal, and activity. Thus, rolled-up jeans would make my escape outdoors quick, painless, and less time consuming.

She was my mother. A rather beautiful yet firmly put-in-place lady grown up in the forties, when her family had aspired to be seen to do things correctly. I knew there were undercurrents of dysfunction, but we did not talk about that. I just felt it in my bones and did my best to activate the deeper anxieties that would one day help her to realize she wasn't perfect.

I'm not sure she ever took the bait, so I turned my attention elsewhere, mostly to my animal companions and the rural landscapes I found fascination with.

Still that sensation under my skin prevailed.

Whatever the itch was, it was uncomfortable. I did my best to ignore it, but try as I might to deny it or scratch it from me, it would never go away. Layers upon layers surrounded my psyche. I did my best to break free.

As a younger child, one born in the sixties, it was different from Mother's upbringing. We aimed for more freedom, and there I was, many times, stealing away from my home environment with my little black case—on one day full of hats—marching out up the road away from our suburban house. I would pass trees and hedgerows as the sounds of traffic diminished and the parkland lay ahead, opening its arms for me, welcoming me into its woodlands and grasses. Until Father took my hand, steering my four-year-old body, kindly but firmly back to where I belonged—for now.

And now that we had moved away from suburbia, into the deeper rural landscapes, I could run away as if it was the most obvious and natural thing to do, and nobody ever seemed to want to bring me back. And there was more freedom and plenty of places to hide away, to cross to the other side of rivers, to meet with more of nature's furred and feathered beings—digging into the soil to meet with the dead and aging and communicating with every beastie that was willing to stick its nose over a fence and receive the crumbs and oddments of the "for-later" snacks I had pocketed for emergencies. These adventures would take place at the best times of day, as I ventured beyond the radar of Mother's glare.

I would often be gone, only to arrive home again with a hungry stomach or a need for a thicker jumper, to sit within the confines of the gates, the brick walls and the borders of the kind of society that made the itch even more intolerable. Still, I loved having my room that I didn't have to share, with my small record player that began its journey into rock and roll once it had been superseded by the new gramophone that the parents had acquired for their collections of classical and jazz. I could move with the rhythm here, and no one needed to know once the door was closed.

I attended a new school, so now there were boys, too; it wasn't so far from home, and clearly the previous institution hadn't had the desired effect on me. Still, I was not like many of the other schoolkids who puffed on cigarettes and thought a choice in fashion to be their birthright. They talked of boyfriends, not horses.

To make a mild attempt at having a friend, which seemed the normal thing to do, I joined in. I veered towards the ones who blended in with the playground corners rather than the ones who thought it more productive to study at playtimes, the ones who brought mountains of papers and pencils into the school grounds, keen to finish the latest project or assignment for the day, chatting about science, mathematics, and the meanings of English literature that I could never grasp.

I had known some of this gang's language before, when they talked about the touch of a boy, a different entity to us. Kisses, touch of hands, fingers in places that they giggled about. Ghastly, I would think, mainly because I had an experience of "it" that overshadowed my life, but they did not know about that. The talk of music enthralled me however, as that leant itself to another kind of freedom, one where the gods of the TV screen, which I was rarely allowed to watch, came alive and excited the beat of my own heart, the breaking free of my voice as it found the notes of passion and beguiling me into territories of rocking hips, stomping feet, and rebelling beyond the trappings of eternal platitudes.

The cigarettes made me cough, but if coughing meant I would not be ridiculed from across playgrounds or bumped carelessly-but-on-purpose in corridors, then cough I would, for I deemed it better than standing alone, looking like a wallflower gone wrong. I never really found that friend, as others did, but the gods of the music sufficed in my imagination as I moved my body to the rhythm that told me I belonged to no one.

I made a few attempts at inviting friends home, but there was always something wrong with them, or my choices, or me. My mother's insistence was that only certain young people could dine at our table, with the right kind of manners and attire, and that they would have to be of her choosing.

Conversations were stifled. I didn't know what to say, with what politeness to discuss how school had been that day. The teacups tottering on saucers, spilling their contents onto the tablecloth, I would laugh, finding it funny, much to Mother's annoyance.

And so my greatest friends remained the animals, which included every kind of pet and all that I could rescue, including borrowing the occasional pony from the neighbourhood and riding bareback across the fields, which felt like an average thing to do. The ponies loved it and seemed excited whenever I approached. It would give me that reprieve from the itch for a while.

Galloping hoofs cutting into mowed lawns, brushing over hedgerows, as flaxen mane and tail mingled with the flowing locks of my wild hair, riding towards the edge of nightfall as starry skies lit our way and the mists of dawn would begin to greet us. Saying goodbye as I took them home to graze in the silence, snorting nostrils, them and me, as gentle kisses on soft dappled noses breathing hot air met with my lips. Ah, the smell and taste of horse!

Clambering through dilapidated ruins and sailing on a borrowed boat across a private lake, I was becoming the feral child that Mother dreaded I would become. It all helped to alleviate the discomfort that others imposed upon me. My rebel lifestyle prepared me for the greater things I knew somewhere I was here to create.

Living the rural life at least connected me to the wild and to an old rambling house where I could dream of ghosts and magical things. Along with the undercurrents of family stuff that we didn't talk about, I held the secrets well, every skeleton in the cupboard that the family name would not endure. So be it. They wanted it hidden, but one day I knew I would tell the world and there would be nothing they could say or do about it. I was angry, and although I would hide this for many decades, it would add to the problem itch that was waiting—what seemed like an eternity—to be free.

Sending me to the perfect schools had seemed an option that would change me, that would turn me into the creature so desired for the public face, for her face, to look at society with pride as if she was the one who had created this adorable child with rosy, red cheeks and the prettiest of smiles and so clever with her studies.

I had become none of this: unbrushed was my wild hair, subdued was my nature in the company of others, grubby fingernails that had scuffled horse's manes, old clothes I had refused to change, still hungry for some acknowledgment that told me I was OK, that I was not a pawn in the workings of the aspiring upper middle class. Education merely aggravated the scorn and contempt I never really deserved.

I had been sent to a school for young ladies, where they taught me about elocution and posture. I did love ballet lessons, which gave me freedom of movement. I was allowed to get the steps wrong and follow my kind of dance, one of free expression, especially when the rhythm was louder, and the piano felt like a roaring river or the wind in the treetops. How I loved to dance, to meet with the inner landscapes that felt real and not stuffy like some old book lying dusty on a shelf, full of stories that no one was ever going to read.

I wanted to read myself, through the dance, through the expression of creativity that was mine, the hunger from deep within becoming the free dancing spirit of my birthright. Here I could imagine the greatest ride, the deepest of dives into mighty oceans. I could be a flying eagle or a swooping owl. I could meet the earth like a snake recoiling as I shed each skin that was now too tight to enclose me and my quest for freedom.

I had such wealth of spirit in my life, so as the wealth that others considered wealthy crossed my path, I knew it was not for me, but still he bought his way into my favours, grooming me for the pleasures of a twisted old man who gained his satisfaction from my innocence.

My itch growing stronger, as I held every breath, not daring to move. He told me it was our secret, and he paid me well but not well enough. What of my freedom to live a joyous life? Maybe the itch sufficed for some time, to enable me to react with scorn and move out into the more open, less claustrophobic spaces.

They lived over the hill, camping out in the fields beyond our house and tidy gardens. We became aware of the smoky fires, dogs that barked, tin homes, and what my family judged as raggedy clothing. Their existence was nothing like the existence I had grown to hate. Another he, this one wearing an earring in his right ear, his hair dark, curly and rough looking, a beautiful face though dirty, with yellowed teeth. He rode a bike as well as the horses, bareback like me. He smelled of smoke and the sweat of hard labour.

Then they were gone, as quickly as they had arrived, but the smell never left my nostrils, the firelight glow in my eyes as the sparks that flew among his wild black hair, the cigarette loose in the corner of his mouth as he sang. I never touched him, he never touched me, our eyes just met across the heat. He held something for me, something I would never forget, so far removed from my own family's curse.

And so I hunted for him, seeking out the outlandish communities, the bikers, the junkies, and for a while the peace lovers, although they never fitted the bill. I didn't like their niceness. It reminded me too much of my upbringing; be nice, smile, say the right things, be pleasant, mind your manners! It didn't feel real. I preferred the leather-clad motor bike riding rogues, but they were hardened, and I was still caught in the trappings of soul searching and needing something familiar to break away from. And if I needed to break away, then I needed to go back to the familiar nest so I could once more cut the thread and run.

Run to where? It seems I fit in nowhere. I abandoned myself to feral landscapes, wild in my nature and wild in my heart. I would not change for anyone, fixed in my ways, refusing the attire of those who would uniform the innocent.

I needed to be different, always needing the difference. And if it meant that I would go without to meet the worthlessness of my being, with the worth of a monetary system gone wrong, then so be it: I would survive anyway. I knew how to live and live I would, without the trappings of prosperity.

I would begin to live as the lost souls did, and it would not matter because I could play the downtrodden martyr, and no one would ever suspect where I had come from, that inhabitance that had shamed me so deeply. It was hard not to scream it out to the heavens.

I would deepen this dark exterior to find what was lost, to go beyond the sore flesh from trying to scratch the itch away. But no amount of journeying with undesirables was going to break me free from this chain. I would have to seek out the undercurrents and swim with their changing tides to uncover the depths of shame and betrayal.

As I aged, the fireside embers called me to explore what lived on the outer edges of my middle-class existence.

Searching beyond its scope, I continued to hunt for the dark and mysterious, the outlandish communities that refused the conformity and the conditioning bestowed upon us. As my own sacred and creative fire was stirred, I felt the embers begin to sparkle until the sound of crackling was heard.

Or was it cackling as I coughed and spluttered in the fire-lit glow, as I became that part of me struggling to awaken? I often couldn't be bothered to share what I knew, and why should I?

Still, it was beginning to stir, the memories flooding back as time and time again something would remind me that it had happened before. What was it that tried to awaken me? I had to remember, and I had to tell the tale.

I wasn't interested in the obvious, only what was hidden. And there was plenty hiding away. I didn't let myself be distracted from this.

I knew I had carried many a burden on my shoulders and within my belly—too much some would say. I was tired. Yet here I am, at the fireside's heat, the heat of age that grants me the freedom to impart my wisdom because I have aged and because I know this journey so well. Not the pretty pink, rosy and trippy journey of self-adoration and the meaningless task of being alive. I have long suffered the grit and disharmony of tales from the dark and what others might choose to forget.

There was the remembering, a story so old, so woven together with wealth and stability, and again I would run, so far into the distance.

To be free of the shame the guilt, of not fitting in, of being held within the constraints of being a good girl when I knew all too well I was not. I would search, and I would seek into the terrible lands of dysfunction to find the part of me before it all began.

Still hunting his smile, his eyes from the fireside glow, I would try yet fail to find that one, each time getting burnt by the dishonesty of their lies. I would go so far as to walk down the aisle after the hunt had worn off. Then I would grow dissatisfied because he was not the one, nor would he ever be, but it would be too late to flee and the itch would grow stronger, and I would again recoil from the nest and the demanding wishes of his sex.

I made my commitment to life and to the living. I hunted and gathered the knowledge that would make me whole, that would guide me to stand up, to be tall, to love myself and hopefully another. I related to many, and I married a few. I would wear their ring. Still hunting the wild-eyed beauty, who could not be found. He was gone, so I inhabited him myself, embodying my masculine fire, a meeting of the two within me: my feminine spirit and whoever he was. I would soften our lips in a passionate kiss and sit within the flames of being united as one.

I did not care about the family name. I did not care for the worlds of fortune. All it meant to me was privilege and disconnection from what was real in the world.

Yet she, that mother one, had seen much too, what had turned her head from the crimes of war, to the witnessing of her neighbour's home, demolished by a bomb, sitting in dark holes in the back garden wearing a gas mask, claustrophobia and the fear of not knowing what she would see when she entered the garden once more.

Moving above it all, to be the daughter her mother wanted her to be, to marry into the life where she would not have to share breakfast eggs with her little brother.

What had she come from that had moulded her into the one she was today? The man who forced himself upon her in the car, the refusal of her father that she should follow her passion and head to the art college to fulfill her scholarship. No, a proper job was in order, real money and a career must be the making of her and her family. Heaven forbid she would go down the road of the poor artist and live in misery forever more.

And me, determined to live my life, to grow through the veils of conformity, to carry what was mine to hold onto, to be the tale of growing up, releasing the skins of time and illusion, to manifest some understanding about it all.

The deep itch would insist I share every part of that story, that I would not leave any stone unturned, that each part of my tale would speak a language of heartbreak, of trauma, of the conditioning that forces the soul inward. The itch in the bones and the muscles where it contorts the body into shapes unspeakable, yet feeling the dance of it, it breaks free, bit by bit, piece by piece. Until it dances wildly to make sense of the discomfort as the rage embarks on a willingness, to shout the victory of each fragment of soul that finds its way into the light.

Like the artistry of recovery, the voice becomes the artist's brush, full of all the colours and shapes, destined for truth.

I do not paint it as a beautiful painting, but it is beautiful.

It includes the face of the trauma-filled adolescent maiden, and it breaks through the heart of the fragile mother, for each passage holds a memory destined for forgetfulness yet contemplated and known deeply from the core of who I am. There is medicine in the grief, and for the betrayal of what is lost, there is anger carefully germinated as it feeds the fire of protection for the innocent.

My feral crone makes her way forth, and I am encouraged to share that cackle without the shame those unfortunate ones might hold onto.

A grandmother's tale I tell. I have birthed three sons and three daughters, now a grandmother to many. To protect yet honour would be my aim, yet even in trying to protect and doing my best to honour their individuality, I fail so many times. I leave them to their journeys, to find the wildness within, to be the outspoken, free-spirited adults I would want them to be and not be tied to any dogma or conditioning that manipulates them into a person they are not.

My mothering could weave many tales, how to allow the feral nature within each one find its way to the surface and live in the world of normality for moments at a time, so they did not fall into the trappings of the law as it laid down the boundaries I could not enforce. And why should I?

For those boundaries hurt my soul, and I did not wish to hurt the spirit or soul of my dear cubs. I would encourage their wild natures, their roaming animal qualities, and free-spirited dreaming of all that could be achieved. I allowed them to run wild.

Watching and knowing their gifts, as I trusted them to be guided into the life that was already chosen for them, and that was not my doing but the sacred contract designed long before I gave birth to them, just as mine had been masterfully conceived without my mother's knowing.

I knew that my job was to let go, to surrender to the will of their spirit and allow them to find the dream that unfolded their wisdom, to live the life that was destined for them. And if that meant they would be feral too, then so be it, despite my knowing it was not an easy life to live. To be free of conformity, to be true to themselves, to grow into good people, principled and sound within their bodies, to follow the instinctual rather than what society dominated them with, to make their own choices.

Yet wouldn't that youngest one be so determined and try as she might to shock her mother, to be the rebel that her teenage years needed to be? She would fail, as my horror at her antics was hidden from view, even as the heavy gold jewellery and the green luminous nylon shell-suit and corporate branded sneakers were donned. I knew it had to pass, for she was her mother's daughter, and this could never last. Still if she needed the bling-status for a while, then so be it.

My younglings and I, creating a new story of parenting, one that does not fit within the trap of today's society, not wanting to follow the curriculum set out for them, not wanting the structure of a collar-and-tie-informed education. The mothering they would receive would be focussed on their creative and nature-bound talents, sometimes going unseen because they hadn't been stamped high enough up the financial ladder of pay cheques.

This was not the story that I would share with the world, for their stories would be their own and not ones designed to keep their mother proud and feeling like she had done her duty.

Her duty to whom?

I continue to share my history like it's the only history worth telling and the only one that is truly mine to tell. I tell it from my heart of gold and my storytelling lips and eyes that light up and sparkle with every dancing flame of that fire that rages inside. So much ease in telling it how it is, not to make it into a script corrected in the King's, or is it still the Queen's, English? Either way, it is my voice, my landscape of the heart, my ferocious yearnings that touch others to awaken.

I laugh with its untimeliness as it wrings out the sodden leftovers of meals untouched, clearing the tabletop of debris and fluff to make a space for a feast so rich with the recipes of tales untold throughout our existence, that many will dine—only to be repelled by the idea that they are feral, too.

I'll shock if I must, for the world will awaken at my bravery to tell it as it is, without the need for a white tablecloth and the correct serving manner.

Mother tried to tame me, unbearably she tried. But if being born a certain way, with a certain existence deemed necessary for her life, who was she to try and change me? Mother, in this case, did not know best.

How could she? She had never felt the growth of claws emerging. She had never given a growl of protection for her young. She might have felt the original itch that would have become the fur-lined corset deep beneath her skin if she had allowed it, but she had certainly never left the certainty of an existence labelled with politeness.

I was on my own with this one—and knew I always would be.

7

Mothers Born Feral: An Exploration of Birth Trauma

Teela Tomassetti

As I sat down to begin this chapter on birth trauma, my mind wandered to an unexpected place as I reflected on what it means to have "gone feral." It led me to my three-and-a-half-year-old daughter. Mind you, if you have a toddler, that was not as far-fetched as I initially thought. The other night, I was at the dinner table admiring her ability to yell, laugh, say silly things, and be anything but ladylike as we enjoyed supper. I hoped she would never change this part of herself and said the same to my partner, who thankfully agreed. We spoke of how she is already different from what one typically thinks a little girl is supposed to act like. She is not a huge fan of big bows, sitting still, or quiet. She fills the entire space with her personality, warmth, loud voice, sense of humour, and stubbornness. I hope this unruly and unkept version of how she can be as she is, with no apologies, sticks around.

As I write this, I find myself appreciating her wild ways, I wonder when we first begin apologizing as women. When do we start to learn that we are supposed to stay small? This has been often on my mind as I complete my doctoral work and focus on traumatic births and the fawn trauma response. More on this response a bit later. Back at the dinner table, my husband laughs as we reflect on her, and he points out that she got it from me. Sometimes, when that phrase is used towards women and their daughters, it is meant to hurt, make fun of, or cast doubt on the existence and state of these two women. But as my partner shares this, I know it is because he was proud. As I glanced at her again, my mind began to tumble down a rabbit hole of thinking of myself, where I had lost that feral essence, the domestication that had taken place, and how I found myself relearning and embracing that wild side these last few years after surviving a little thing called birth trauma.

When I was young, my nickname was "Teela, the terrible two-year-old terror." I wonder what I did to earn this name, what act had created its existence. It continued throughout my childhood. Even at twenty-two, my cake still read this cute running joke with my family, alongside the appropriate number of candles: "Teela, the terrible terror turns twenty-two." Imprinted on the cake was a childhood photo of me, in a white long-sleeved pyjama shirt, my hair still wet from a bath and in low pigtails. I have this relatively relaxed look as I stick my tongue out to the camera. Was I the same terror at twenty-two years of age that I was at two? Or had I changed my ability to be feral over the years to suit and adapt to my circumstances to survive? I think that is how and why domestication occurs: It becomes an act of survival in a world that keeps women small and silent. Once the cuteness wears off, and the wild ways become well-versed arguments, a problem arises. It is no longer cute but dangerous. But waiting inside each of us is a time to return to that wild state, and for me, I think it was becoming a mother that led me there, and birth trauma pushed me over the edge of no return.

There were moments in my childhood when this spicy energy was celebrated. My mom encouraged me to take up as much space as I needed. But other people around me began to discourage it, or I would get in trouble. From a young age, I noticed that I was not great at being the "good girl" and that something in me felt caged the moment I even pretended to engage in this. I wanted to use my voice; it only felt natural to do so when I was young. But then I was told I was being "too loud," "unladylike," or even "dramatic" because I had raised my tone an octave or two higher or louder. I think that being called "dramatic" was one of the most damaging things that was done—how dramatic is that statement? Oh, the irony, but truthfully it hurt. I remember not wanting to express emotion because I was worried it would not be taken seriously. When we want a young lady to behave herself, we do so by letting her know that stepping outside of that will land her the name of "crazy," "unstable," or "dramatic." So, we begin to blend in, even though the deepest parts of us wonder what it might feel like not to. How often do women fantasize about that later in life, about being rebellious, saying how they think. Or going after that career they dreamed of or in a direction that is less predictable or accessible? When I entered my mid-twenties, I was not sure I wanted to be a mother. I had always loved babies and children, but there was a part of me that feared repeating patterns my parents had created. I have always been one of "those women"—the kind that are ambitious, driven and focused on their careers and education. Laurel Thatcher Ulrich coined the expression "well-behaved women seldom make history" (1). She speaks about how good behaviour is typically defined as playing by the rules, even the unspoken rules that society does not clearly define but that women should all know. When I was a little girl, rules were a weapon used to abuse my mother, my siblings, and me. As I aged, I noticed how things did not change; only the person using the rules to their advantage to harm others changed.

Safety is why domestication takes place for some. It becomes safer to engage in that small state than to make ourselves known and risk harm— whether that is physical, emotional, financial, or mental. I also had this striking ability to understand when I needed to make situations safer. This may even be a part of the wild side's adaptability, like an animal's instinct to perceive danger and channel what it needs to survive. I could sense when power dynamics were at play, when people in power were abusing it, and I found this inner desire to fight against it but also knew that if I did, punishment in one form or another was waiting for me. The connection to my childhood? My father was emotionally and physically abusive. He would make you feel small with just one comment, look, or hit to get his point across. The psychologist in me knows now that my nervous system engaged in a fight trauma response in these other moments with strangers or teachers because then it was much safer to do so compared to my father. Looking for the feral side later in life became an act of rebellion connected to my past. I could not do it then but watch me do it now. I never knew or could have guessed that one of the most significant areas of my life—where people would label me as unruly, wild, and feral—was becoming a specialist in the birth trauma field.

Women are sold an exceptional story about childbirth; from a young age, we are told that it is beautiful from the moment of conception to that moment we hear our little one cry. We are shown through television, film, and media what this looks like; sometimes, the woman is hysteri-cal but always in a comical way. Time moves so fast in those scenes; her water breaks, and in the next moment, she holds a perfect baby in her perfect robe with her perfect hair. It looks relatively easy—just a couple of grunts, screams, and pushes, and there it is, motherhood in all its glory. Social media has replaced the TLC "A Baby Story" with magazine -worthy first photos of mother and child. The message is clear: You are meant to be a mom, and your body was made for this. The destiny of women everywhere.

This was not my experience. Despite my best efforts, I was left with debilitating birth trauma. After hours of midwifery violence in my home, parts of me are still unrepairable to this day. An excessive hemorrhage threatened my life, requiring blood transfusions and a week in the hospital. This was followed by months of trauma symptoms and short- and long-term physical and emotional impacts. Birth trauma is anything that exceeds the ability of the nervous system to cope before, during, and after childbirth. Traumatic births occur in 34 to 45 per cent of women (Beck and Watson). Birth trauma is a subjective experience defined by the woman's experience; it can include symptoms such as avoidance, negative affect, re-reexperiencing, hyper-arousal flashbacks, anxiety, depression-like symptoms, and nightmares (Wetherell). Part of domes-tication involves not talking about this trauma. Up until the last decade or so, birth trauma was a debilitating issue women had faced alone for centuries because they did not want the love of their child to be put into question and they were told that this is just how it was. We were taught this is a struggle we must bear on our own.

I began my journey into motherhood in broken pieces and a cloak of darkness, one I never knew would exist during what was meant to be the brightest time. It felt as though I was such a misfit in this perfect postpartum world, as I managed flashbacks, nightmares, intrusive thoughts, and anxiety those first few months. This is where the true unravelling began, where domestication could no longer reign. The feral side became more present, not necessarily by choice at the beginning but because this wild, untamed side could no longer hide within the symp-toms and under the pressure and expectations to parent perfectly. The feral side helped me to survive that time in my life. This deep instinct was to fight and scream I am not okay in a world wanting me to be.

I began an Instagram page, @theteaonbirthtrauma, at twelve-weeks postpartum sitting on my recliner, snuggling my daughter, and not know-ing what else to do. All I knew was that I felt isolated. I did not want others to feel so alone in the cascade of trauma symptoms following a traumatic birth. I ventured out into the social media world, naïve, without experience building an Instagram account. The name "@theteaonbirthtrauma" just came to me. I have always been a fan of Ru Paul's television show *Drag Race*, where you will often hear the phrase "the tea." This phrase was coined by Black and queer communities. They explain that "the tea" is the truth—no sugar coating or sweetener, just the truth regardless of how uncomfortable it may be. I suppose deep within I knew just how scandalous my page would be in the postpartum world. I wanted it to be the truth because as a trauma therapist, I know that for people to heal, they need to see honest depictions of the difficult situations they face and to know they are not alone.

Some of you may be wondering, if you are unfamiliar with birth trauma and my page, what exactly am I up to? Social media is bizarre and has become a news source to many; it can build a person up or break them down within seconds of a scroll. Social media can be dangerous. Many influencers advertise cures and tell tall tales that result in people leaving their pages, receiving more harm than healing. Wanting fame drives many pages; people race for more likes and followers and disregard what happens along the way. As the number of followers began to climb on my page, I often felt a deep sadness because sometimes I wanted to be wrong about how many people the research stated were being harmed by childbirth. My page was always meant to be a soft place for people to land around a real issue deemed taboo by many in the postpartum world. I believed back then, and I still do now, that social media can be a healing place, especially for mothers who feel alone in their experience. It has become an act of rebellion for many to jump on the page and see the truth that others are also falling apart, do not have all the answers, are sick and tired of carrying the mental load, and do not always like their role as women and mothers.

James Roberts and Meredith David state that social media can open multiple avenues for connecting with others who share their experiences. Isolation keeps women stuck in their symptoms, as they grow exasperated feeling like they are the only ones experiencing them. I think that society wants that and the norms that exist around motherhood, they bank on that. They know that for most, the shame, self-blame, and profound guilt that comes from hating their birth experience is enough to silence women into submission. When I first began my Instagram page, I started believing that every person would see my intentions of creating a safe space for people like me to share and receive well-researched and evidence-based information in a world hellbent on selling people absolute nonsense. That nativity was short-lived.

I remember the first time I was told that my advocacy work for birth trauma was "fearmongering." I had just opened the direct messages on my Instagram page and was met with these words: "You fear-mongering bitch. Who do you think you are that you would try and turn a beautiful thing like birth into this. You should be ashamed of yourself." I remember the pounding of my heart, the sweating of my hands, and the tightness in my chest as I held back the tears, so confused as to what I was reading. This could not possibly be for me; this must be a mistake. I had to sit back and assess how someone could perceive my wanting to assist others on their birth trauma journey as negative. At that moment, I realized I was challenging the status quo by creating space to speak to the fact that birth is not always beautiful. I went from behaving myself—following the societal expectations and pressures that a woman expecting a child does as she embarks on that journey—to almost dying from birth trauma and breaking the silence around it. I went from celebrating my pregnancy and sharing the mandatory monthly bump photos to planning my perfect dream homebirth in the water and memorizing all the right affirmations (e.g., "Your body is made for this") to reporting my midwife for sexual assault, abuse, and neglect.

I remember responding to that first person on Instagram, as many good girls do, with an apology. I did not know at the time that I was engaging in fawning, a not easily spotted trauma response. But women are conditioned to engage in it from a young age. As I began to respond to that stranger through direct messaging, I started overexplaining myself, sharing why I started this page, and what my intentions were. I was so sorry I had upset them. And for a long time, I sat with it, for weeks asking myself if what I was doing was wrong. There are too many reasons to count as to why trolls on the internet get upset about my work in birth trauma. I get messages from people upset over this topic. People state, "Birth trauma is not cesarean sections, or is only cesarean sections." When I explore the intense pain experienced by birth trauma survivors who have lost a baby, I get messages asking, "Why are you talking about dead babies?" Other angles include "Not all providers are bad" or " Why are you talking about some providers being good when they are the cause of all birth trauma." I found myself going back and forth between fawning and wanting to please and appease people who were upset with my area of expertise and wanting to tell them to fuck off and face the fact that what I was speaking about was a reality for too many. Sometimes, it would feel like there was not much I could say right, yet these messages were not the norm. They were not filling my direct messages. But when they came, it was all I could focus on. Like most criticism, these messages wiped all the good from the path, like a tsunami. I rebuilt my confidence after messages like the ones above by connecting with other pages like mine that also received similar messages. These people told me not to give up, to keep going and to "build a thicker skin." I realized I had found my feral colony, people who were sharing the truth about childbirth.

My partner witnessed many tears those first few months of managing my Instagram. He would go back and forth between being supportive and telling me not to give up and that I was helping so many to asking if I should stop. Overall, his support was so meaningful as living on this side of the screen can feel lonely. But I do worry about the impact on my little one. What will my daughter think of this one day? Will she be in a domesticated state when she comes to find my vintage social media page and be disgusted and horrified that her mother would be so outrageous in her viewpoints of challenging childbirth conventions? Or will she think that she was to blame? Will she think it was something about her that led me astray to this wild and unnatural place of discussing how birth is not always beautiful. It is the only fear I have at this point in my work. It is the biggest thing that makes me question if my actions are correct because I never want her to feel unloved or unwanted. Neither one of those things is true. She is not the cause of my birth trauma but the very reason I fought hard to heal and why I want systems, policies, and procedures to change. There is this perception that we do not love or care for our child if we admit that we are struggling. I can attest to both judgment from others for discussing these difficulties and how inaccurate that judgment is. Fear of judgment silences women in talking about this.

I have never loved anything more in my life than my child. I do not think that I knew love until now. And it broke me in ways that, over two years later, I am still working hard to process. Birth trauma is this confusing place of dichotomy thinking, which makes it even more challenging to understand it by those who have never experienced it. This style of thinking is all or nothing, black or white, good or bad. It separates people into categories, propping one up on a pedestal and stepping over the other to get to it. In this type of thinking, domestication is the good and right way to be, and the feral side is the bad way that results in chaos. Bruno Bonfa-Araujo et al. explain dichotomous thinking as a binary and rigid way of processing information, influencing how people think, feel, and act (462). This type of thinking results in people not seeing the entire picture and feeling as if they must choose, not realizing that two things can be true at the same time. Because of how negative birth trauma appears to outsiders looking in, it is put into the category of wrong. This further isolates the survivors into thinking they should not disclose just how difficult things are. The danger in dichotomy thinking exists right here. Without a sense of connection and community, survivors' symptoms grow further, affecting their journey and identity as a parent and their bond with their baby, family unit, and so on. Explaining this style of thinking is one of the ways I support my followers and clients in understanding why that guilt and shame exist in the first place. Shedding light on guilt and shame in social media can upset people who dwell on the "good" end of this dichotomous thinking. Followers who do not understand birth trauma or do not have personal or professional experience with it often put up a fight about it.

My thousands of followers rarely saw this fight and the many others I have had over the last two years. I did not want them to know that by proxy, they were feral too by engaging with my content, agreeing, and sharing their stories of pain and anger. I did not want them to think that anything was wrong with them or for the intense fears and guilt they had already experienced to be further blown up by trolls on the internet. They did not know how many times I almost quit my page. For every hundred messages sharing the page's positive impact, there was one message that would break me. That one message would make me question if I was, in fact, wrong for talking about childbirth in a way that was not dripping in gratitude and joy. I do not think our domesticated parts die when we become feral again. They hibernate; they wait. Sometimes, they come out to survive a moment or out of habit, and other times because living in a wild state can be utterly exhausting. It requires tremendous energy, passion, determination, and relentless drive. It can be lonely, so the tame side arrives again to offer a false narrative: If one steps back and behaves themselves, their rewards are love and connection. Feral cats can either live on their own or within cat colonies, where they look after one another. As I reflect on this, I cannot help but see birth trauma survivors in the same way. They are either isolated or seek out those who just get it and will not use the infamous beginning of a sentence "At least..." (insert insensitive toxic positivity statement. I have felt the experience of both. I have felt alone and felt love and connection from the community. I think because of how my birth trauma unfolded, at the hands of a midwife, I felt deeply alone in my fight.

It is a surreal process to share that a provider, especially a midwife, has abused you. The messages I have received in my direct messages about this include "You are a liar," "Oh really, a midwife did that too, give me a break," and "There is no way a midwife did that; I am so shocked." I would watch random people tell my followers that if they just would have had a home birth, none of this would have happened for them. Those are painful moments as I watch my trauma be dismissed with a few taps on the keyboard. The deeper I get into the world of midwifery violence, the less alone I feel and the more I realize just how little it is discussed due to the ideals that society has about the role. Shining a light on midwifery violence upsets the natural idea that midwives are safer than doctors and, overall, challenges all providers in the system to start practising trauma-informed care. But birth trauma can happen anywhere, to anyone, and be committed by any provider. Society does not like this as we tend to feel safer if it is one specific group we can point to as the ones that harm. My role as an advocate has always existed throughout my career: I have helped survivors of domestic violence and sexual assault victims and served Indigenous communities. After years of being a therapist, I now understand that I was never able to fight my father in the way that I wished I could or save my mother in the way I always felt responsible for. So, I found ways to help people through my work with survivors. I had never felt such hate and anger towards my advocacy from strangers until I started to focus on birth trauma. Before my experience of birth trauma, I had been domesticated. I had followed the rules for me and those around me. I practised gratitude, did not complain, and was joyful and optimistic about childbirth. Stepping outside of that can be lonely. Jill Taylor discusses how when she began to teach women's studies at a university, she was often questioned about how she could teach that and how she was constantly challenged about why there were no "men's studies?" When women's experiences and pain are amplified, it tends to cause outrage.

Since becoming a birth trauma specialist and managing my Instagram page, I have been called a "cunt," "a liar," and an "attention whore" from everyday people because I was sharing stories and evidence-based research and asking for systems to change. I had never heard of tokophobia, a fear of pregnancy. The first time I was accused of causing this in other women, I turned to the research to educate me. Gerald Thomson et al. discuss secondary tokophobia, a fear of childbirth due to a previous traumatic birth, which affects the size of their family and the hopes and dreams they initially had tied to this. Here is the thing: Tokophobia is going to exist with or without pages like mine. I am sharing how I have watched so many people, my clients, my friends, and my followers, heal from their birth trauma and go on to have positive experiences. But this is not done by ignoring it, abolishing pages like mine, or slapping toxic positivity on it with a nice little bow. It is through facing it head-on, genuinely exploring what it all means, the pain and the grief alongside the dreams and the joy, that we find healing. Indeed, through connection and hearing other stories, we find a way to make sense of our own traumas and heal. Common humanity is this beautiful and challenging way of addressing what we have been through: It is the ability to notice our suffering while recognizing that others suffer, too. This creates a sense of community. I am told this daily when I receive messages of hope and survival. They often say, "Thank you so much for your page. Hearing other stories, knowing I am not alone, it saved me. I am doing a lot better these days." The reality is that tokophobia after birth trauma does exist. Researchers have shown that experiences of birth trauma affects the choice and ability to have more children (Dandan; Hendrix et al.; Reed et al.).

My wild side compels me to do something many may view as reckless: Take on systems and providers that physically create birth trauma. The statistic that drives my advocacy work and lights a fire in my belly is that 66 per cent of birth trauma survivors state that at the root of their birth trauma is provider mistreatment (Reed et al.). All birth trauma is preventable. Many in the medical field are uncomfortable, even angry, with my work and my belief that the treatment of birthing individuals needs to change. The flip side of this is that I have met and worked with many providers who embrace their feral side and wonder what it might be like to challenge the system, too. To make my situation that much more uncomfortable, I decided that a large part of my career and research would be dedicated to understanding how the "fawn" trauma response shows up in the childbirth experience. My hunch tells me that the mistreatment in so many birth trauma survivors' experiences activates that response in full force. The "fawn" trauma response is one of the lesser-known trauma responses. It is domestication. It is what we are conditioned, as women, to engage in from a young age. For many of us, it is an act of survival. Typically, people understand this to be the fight, flight, and freeze. Fawning is people pleasing, avoiding conflict, and walking on eggshells around abusive or intimidating people. It is being a so-called good girl despite feeling on the inside like you are screaming. In childbirth, the dynamics between the provider and the patient make a perfect fawn storm. Fawning focusses on the needs of the threat, not a person's personal needs. They act as if they were engaging with the threat instead of appearing scared or upset. Those who experience abuse from providers do all that they can to keep safe. Part of my rebellious side is asking what it might look like for us to no longer fawn and to use our voices when least allowed.

Becoming feral after birth trauma means speaking the truth, giving space to the uncomfortable, and challenging the ideals women who have given life have been forced to swallow silently for centuries. No one wants those values to be questioned because it threatens the sanctity of the family. But women, every day, are dying for those ideals to be upheld. The rates of maternal mortality are sky-high in the United States (US), as are the rates of birth trauma. According to the World Health Organization, an estimated 303,000 women died of maternal causes worldwide in 2015. Most are from low-income and middle-income countries, yet the US has one of the highest rates and is one of the wealthiest countries in the world. I had to make a choice running my Instagram page to either go back to domestication or embrace the feral side, which I think can help prevent birth trauma and heal from it.

It only feels right to end this chapter talking about my cat, Furiosa. I did not plan on this, but she walked across my lap as I sat at my kitchen table, finishing my thoughts. I stared down at this feisty calico cat and literally laughed out loud at how this moment was coming full circle for me. Although Furiosa was domesticated by being taken from her farm home as a feral kitten, she never cared to be tamed. The calico would not have it. That breed is known as being the "bitchiest" cats, and she can be at times. But I think she is content with who she is, which is admirable.

The name Furiosa comes from the 2015 movie *Mad Max*. Charlize Theron was cast as Furiosa. If you have yet to watch the film and want to, skip this last part, as it has some spoilers. I fell in love with this character when she arrived on the screen. She is a true badass, and with just one arm and barely any help, she saves an entire community of women who are being used and abused as sex slaves. She goes against everything she has ever known—every norm, rule, pressure, and expectation—and knows there is more beyond what her society has always convinced her of. She is a rebel well before her unruly acts of releasing the women by being a woman who cannot breed. She helps those women forced to use their bodies and never looks back. Those who think she betrayed their society and broke the rules set out to kill her, sending every well-known warrior to take her down. And none of them can. Furiosa wins against all odds, and she is the role model I want for my daughter. I realize I have become my own version of Furiosa—a feral, unkept, brave, courageous, and strong woman who broke from her domestication cage and embraced the wild. She did not ask for it; it was not an easy journey to get to this place, yet it felt precisely where she needed to be, like returning home again. As women, we do our absolute best work within these wild places.

Works Cited

Beck, Cheryl, and Sue Watson. "Subsequent Childbirth after a Previous Traumatic Birth." *Nursing Research*, vol. 59, no. 4, 2010, pp. 241–49.

Bonfa-Araujo, Bruno, et al. "Seeing Things in Black-and-White: A Scoping Review on Dichotomous Thinking Style." *Japanese Psychological Research*, vol. 64, no. 4, 2022, pp. 461–72.

Dandan, Ju, et al. "Childbirth Readiness Mediates the Effect of Social Support on Psychological Birth Trauma of Primiparous Women: A Nationwide Online Cross-Sectional Study in China." *Research Square*, vol. 1, no. 1, 2022, pp. 1–20.

Gurara, Mekdes, et al. "Traditional Birth Attendants' Roles and Homebirth Choices in Ethiopia: A Qualitative Study." *Women and Birth: Journal of the Australian College of Midwives*, vol. 33, no. 5, 2020, pp. e464–e472.

Hendrix, Y.M.G.A., et al. "Postpartum Early EMDR Therapy Intervention (PERCEIVE) Study for Women after a Traumatic Birth Experience: Study Protocol for a Randomized Controlled Trial." *Trials*, vol. 22, no. 599, 2021, pp. 1–11.

Reed, Rachel, et al. "Women's Descriptions of Childbirth Trauma Relating to Care Provider Actions and Interactions. *BMC Pregnancy Childbirth*, vol. 17, no. 21, 2017, https://bmcpregnancychildbirth. biomedcentral.com/articles/10.1186/s12884-016-1197-0. Accessed 7 Jan. 2025.

Roberts, James, and Meredith David. "The Social Media Party: Fear of Missing out (FoMo), Social Media Intensity, Connection, and Well-Being" *International Journal of Human-Computer Interaction*, vol. 36, no. 4, 2020, pp. 386–92.

Taylor, Jill. "What Took Me So Long? A Well-Behaved Woman Finds Women's Studies." In: Ginsberg, A.E. (eds), The Evolution of American Women's Studies. Edited by A.E. Ginsberg, Palgrave Macmillan.

Thomson, Gerald, et al. "COST after Birth Consortium. Policy, Service, and Training Provision for Women Following a Traumatic Birth: An International Knowledge Mapping Exercise." *B.M.C. Health Services Research*, vol. 21, no. 1206, 2021, pp. 1–10.

Ulrich Thatcher, Laurel. "Why Well-Behaved Women Seldom Make History." *B.Y.U. Studies Quarterly*, vol. 59, no. 3, 2020, pp. 197–203.

Wetherell, Silvia. "Investigating the Impact of Eye Movement Desensitization and Reprocessing (EMDR) in Reducing Birth Trauma symptoms." *Annals of Psychophysiology*, vol. 9, no. 2, 2022, pp. 67–75.

8

The Mess House: Wildness in the Domestic Realm

Batya Weinbaum

"What would a psychoanalyst say," my mother mused about my house on her last visit (even before the murals in the dining hall). She was implying that I was analyzable as aberrant from the norm. My daughter used to refer to our abode not so lovingly as the "mess house," and she was reluctant to ask even her homeschooler buddies to visit. She preferred her friend's house, where matching scented soaps adorned each bathroom of the stay-at-home mom, who made these high-end items, supported by a dashing up-and-coming director in the Cleveland advertising film industry.

But radical feminists such as myself? We have our own culture, and I am sure the differences in these excruciatingly painful instances were cultural. Now, years after my daughter left, and my mother died, no more homeschoolers or relatives create a trickling stream through my house. I clean and organize less and less, only sporadically. And I express myself more. For example, a Fuck Housework poster I bought on eBay for $108, a relic of the early period of the women's liberation movement, hangs on my refrigerator door, held there by magnets of Buddhas and the city of Santa Barbara where I used to live. At the time of the women's liberation movement, we loudly claimed the right to throw off all bonds of oppression, both outer and inner, and did so gallantly and defiantly.

The poster photographed below on my refrigerator is a drawing in blue on a cream background of a young woman breaking a broom in two. She is smiling and beaming. Commitment and determination are fiercely and proudly glowing all over her face. Shirley Boccacio explains how the poster was "born out of the anger and frustration of Women" and how she was "the artistic medium" (111). She "conceived it, designed and drew it and then had it printed as a poster" (111).

In "The Politics of Housework," Pat Mainardi further expounds upon the feelings of those early days of the second wave. As Pat Mainardi writes, the women's liberation movement addressed issues about housework. She discusses the difficulty of getting men to do chores around the house and explains all women suffer from something called "guilt over a messy house" thinking that housework is ultimately the woman's job (449). But what about the woman without a husband? Is there some path in this revolt against total identification with housework (as well as sexuality and physical helplessness) recommended by the second wave (Dunbar 478), which is too far to walk into messiness without falling into a tumultuous sea? Can we be too feral in our revolt against traditional concepts of femininity and motherhood represented in conventional markers and paradigms of domestication—the swept, mopped floor, the uncluttered shining feng shui of spaces, the organized linen cabinets, and the bare countertops in the spotless kitchens? Do we harm ourselves by reverting to wild domestic savages and taking the position that we will not clean our homes and instead use them to express our wild selves the way fat liberationists eschew the benefits of weight loss and reclaim their fat? Are there parallels between how we view our bodies and our houses in terms of the notion of the unkempt, the unpoliced, the wildly expressive, and the unclean? This chapter hopes to provoke thought and insight about what might or might not be such liberationist practices today.

Susan Griffin writes in her treatise *Woman and Nature*:

> Her womb from her body. Separation. Her clitoris from her vulva. Cleaving. Desire from her body. We were told that bodies rising to heaven lose their vulvas, their ovaries, wombs, that her body in resurrection becomes a male body.

> The Divine Image from woman, severing, immortality from the garden, exile, the golden calf split, birth, sorrow, suffering. We were told that the blood of a woman after childbirth conveys uncleanness. That if a woman's uterus is detached and falls to the ground, that she is unclean. Her body from the sacred. Spirit from flesh. We were told that if a woman has an issue and that issue in her flesh be blood, she shall be impure for seven days. The impure from the pure. The defiled from the holy. And whoever touches her, we heard, was also impure. Spirit from matter. And we were told that if our garments are stained, we are unclean back to the time we can remember seeing our garments unstained, that we must rub seven substances over these stains, and immerse our soiled garments.

> Separation. The clean from the unclean. The decaying, the putrid, the polluted, the fetid, the eroded, waste, defecation, from the unchanging. The changing from the sacred. We heard it spoken that if a grave is plowed up in a field so that the bones of the dead are lost in the soil of the field, this soil conveys uncleanness. That if a member is severed from a corpse, this too conveys uncleanness, even an olive pit's bulk of flesh. That if marrow is left in a bone there is uncleanness. And of the place where we gathered to weep near the graveyard, we heard that planting and sowing were

forbidden since our grieving may have tempted unclean flesh to the soil. And we learned that the dead body must be separated from the city.

Death from the city. Wilderness from the city. Wildness from the city. The Cemetery. The Garden. The Zoological Garden. We were told that a wolf circled the walls of the city. That he ate little children. That he ate women. That he lured us away from the city with his tricks. That he was a seducer, and he feasted on the flesh of the foolish, and the blood of the errant and sinful stained the snow under his jaws.

The errant from the city. The ghetto. The ghetto of Jews. The ghetto of Moors. The quarter of prostitutes. The ghetto of blacks. The neighborhood of lesbians. The prison. The witch houses. The underworld. The underground. The sewer. Space Divided. The inch. The foot. The mile. The boundary. The border. The nation. The promised land. The chosen ones.

Thus, there is much behind the noticeable symptom that Flo Kennedy notes in her essay on women's institutionalized oppression that women "are dirt searchers," and their greatest is eradicating "rings on collars and tables" (442). In doing so, and maintaining organization, they keep wildness at bay.

Furthermore, those born into female bodies get the most pressure from society to meet unrealistic expectations of physical beauty; this is why they have the hardest time going to a nudist community, where they might have the opportunity to live in a free, wild space (*Women and Naturism*). These unrealistic expectations of their bodies are parallel to the unrealistic expectations women are encouraged to have about their domestic space.

And what if we created free, wild spaces in our homes? As the following photos show, what if we bring the wildness of nature into our dining halls, painted on the walls (Figures. 1, 15, and 16)? What if we untamed our environments? What if we practiced reading tarot cards from our beds (Figure. 13), eradicating boundaries of workspace and private space? What if we used our walls and windowsills for storage (Figure. 12)? Painted dancing goddesses in our bedrooms (Figure. 2)?

Mounted our own wild, abstract, and impressionistic goddess paintings (Figures. 3 and 4)? Hung portraits where we vigorously celebrated our large unruly naked bodies (Figure. 5)? Decoupaged our kitchen cabinets and stools, mosaiced our floors, and brought in lucky rocks we painted with affirmations for the staircase (Figure. 6)? Made an ever-changing art gallery replete with protest signs on the front porch (Figure. 7)? Brightly tiled the bathroom basement floor (Figure. 8)? Left our beds unmade (Figure. 9), our bedclothes and laundry hanging (Figure. 17), and our bedroom coffee nooks untidy on unfinished tile tables (Figure. 10)? Carelessly left our glasses where we slept when we work out of our beds in the wee hours of the morning, crossing boundaries of time and space (Figure. 11)? Did our daily centering rituals amid chaos (Figs. 14 and 18)? Allowed animals on the furniture (Figures. 19 and 21)? And creatively painted and adorned our furniture (Figure. 20)?

Do all or any of these acts constitute the resistance to traditional concepts of femininity and notions of patriarchal domesticity as we know it? Do they bring ferality into our homes? As feral women, how does the mess of artmaking in and of our homes challenge cultural definitions of womanhood? Are we deemed mad, eccentric, bad mothers, and deviant instead of wise, creative, and crone? Are we merely perpetually punished by being devalued by assessments in real estate, or are we rewarded aesthetically for having the courage to claim the right to be expressive within the borders of our own homes?

Figure 1. Dining room mural.

Figure 2. Bedroom goddess of the Red Sea.

Figure 3. Annapurna Hindu goddess of food (my painting by my bed).

Figure 4. Celebration (my painting in front of my fireplace,
inspired by a vase from the Indus Valley Harapan civilization).

Figure 5. Self-Portrait (in front of my fireplace).

Figure 6. Decoupaged, mosaiced kitchen.

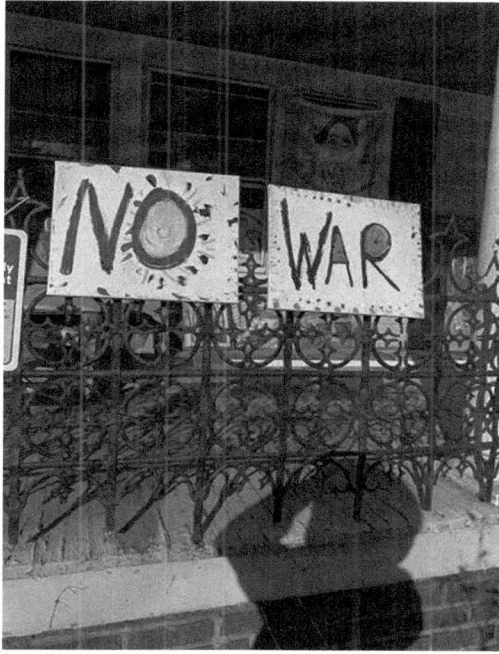

Figure 7. Art gallery on the front porch.

Figure 8. Tile project in basement bathroom floor.

Figure 9. Unmade bed.

Figure 10. Coffee nook in the bedroom, mural behind.

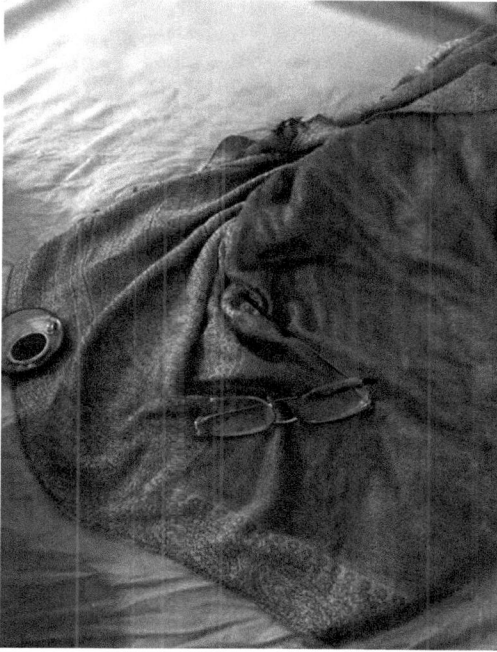

Figure 11. Glasses on the bed, where I frequently lose them, and a pendulum to use on calls as a phone psychic.

Figure 12. Unorthodox storage: jewelry on the wall, painkillers by the bed.

Figure 13. Making a living from my bed.

Figure 14. Bureau of transformation by a journalling chair.

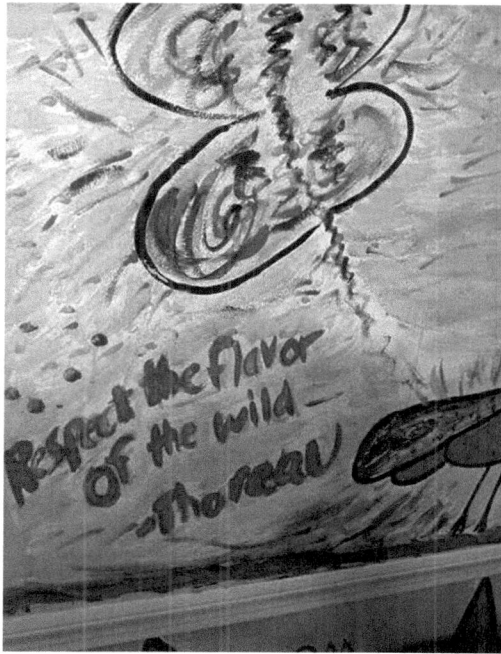

Figure 15. Wildness mural two.

Figure 16. Wildness mural.

Figure 17. Bed clothes and laundry hanging.

Figure 18. Centring amid chaos in the bedroom.

Figure 19. Animal on the furniture.

Figure 20. Adorning furniture.

Figure 21. Animal on the furniture two.

Works Cited

Boccacio, Shirley. "The Housework Poster Rip-Off." *Female Liberation: History and Current Politics.* Edited by Roberta Salper. Knopf, 1972, p. 111.

Dunbar, Roxanne. "Female Liberation as the Basis for Social Revolution." *Sisterhood Is Powerful: An Anthology of Writings from the Women's Liberation Movement.* Edited by Robin Morgan. Vintage, 1970, pp. 477–92.

Griffin, Susan. *Woman and Nature: The Roaring Inside Her.* Harper Colophon, 1984.

Kennedy, Flo. "Institutionalized Oppression of the Female" *Sisterhood Is Powerful: An Anthology of Writings from the Women's Liberation Movement.* Edited by Robin Morgan. Vintage, 1970, pp. 438–46.

Mainardi, Pat. "The Politics of Housework." Kennedy, Flo. "Institution-alized Oppression of the Female." *Sisterhood Is Powerful: An Anthology of Writings from the Women's Liberation Movement.* Edited by Robin Morgan. Vintage, 1970, pp. 447–54.

Morgan, Robin, editor. *Sisterhood is Powerful: An Anthology of Writings from the Women's Liberation Movement.* Vintage, 1970.

Deshane, Stefan, host. "Women and Naturism." *The Naturist Living Show,* episode 16, 17 May 2010, www.naturistlivingshow.com/podcast. Accessed 25 Jan. 2025.

II

Representations

9.

The Mother Shell
Selected Artwork

Alexandra Carter

A lexandra Carter's paintings explore the sensations of the female body through themes of fertility, maternity, and transformation, with a focus on the concept of the "monstrous feminine."

Using acrylic inks on translucent drafting film (mylar), she creates fluid, figurative forms that highlight the resilience and power of the maternal body.

Inspired by folklore, mythology, and her personal experiences of motherhood, Carter weaves imagery from her upbringing on a cranberry farm into her work, linking agricultural fertility to the physicality of the human body.

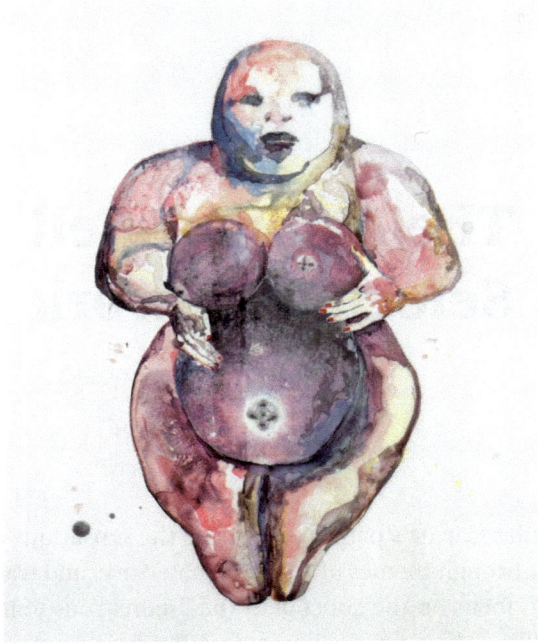

Bona Dea, 2020.

Mammalia, 2021.

Materna Sinistra, 2021.

Stigmama, 2021.

Gorgon, 2022.

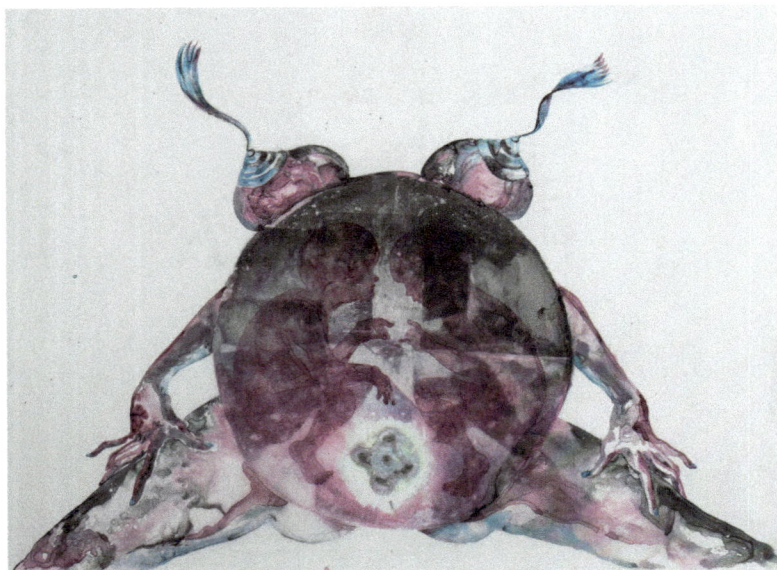

BurlyQ Berry, 2022.

Badass Mother Birther, 2022.

Amazons' Embryo, 2023.

Strike a Pose

Catherine Moeller

Artist Statement

This drawing is based on ancient stories of women lifting their skirts and baring their vulvas before their husbands and soldiers, in order to shame them. This wild skateboarding woman, is displaying her defiance and power in a refusal of conventional feminine behavior and imposed morality forced upon woman. It is a response to the aggressive patriarchy, created for personal support, confidence and self-love. This piece shows the ability to express anger is empowering to the self.

11.

From Bold, Going Feral: Xiao Lu's Feminist Art and Ferality

Li Yang

Xiao Lu, an established Chinese contemporary artist and a founder of China's self-proclaimed first feminist art collective, Bald Girls, made a provocative feminist splash in 1989. She fired a pistol twice at her own installation work *Dialogue* during the China/Avant-Garde exhibition opening at Beijing's China National Art Gallery (now National Art Museum of China). Xiao left the scene after the shots while police mistakenly arrested Tang Song, a male onlooker, in the panic-stricken crowds. A series of coincidences contributed to the distortion of the event, but the most significant catalyst was the subsequent propaganda spread by male-dominated art critics and curators, who monopolized the right of interpretation. The dominant male voices in the Chinese art world, assisted by the media, extensively dramatized, politicized, and canonized the shots yet ironically sidestepped the existence of Xiao and her authorship. Tang, who later became Xiao's partner, took the credit and was portrayed as a heroic forerunner daring to pull the trigger against the political backdrop. To escape the unstable political environment, Xiao migrated to Australia in 1989 to seek asylum and spent years in seclusion there with Tang, who smuggled himself into Australia in 1991. Fifteen years later, Xiao admitted being the exclusive author of the installation and shooting the guns, but the male-dominated art critics vehemently questioned her motives and prevented her from reclaiming authorship. They believed that Xiao's admission could never undo the grand narratives embodied by the shots. In recent decades, Xiao has made a comeback, performing more and making installation works in an untamed manner. She has revealed a "going feral" feminist focus, straying from her normative femininity after years of silence.

How does artistic untamed femininity disrupt patriarchal fantasies about women and women artists? Are there clear boundaries between domestication and ferality? How do women artists like Xiao negotiate the dynamics of going feral and moving between the normative and unruly, private and public, and personal and political realms? This chapter does detail Xiao's biography, but through the theory of feral feminism, it discusses how Xiao's art practice unveiled how heterosexuality, motherhood, and nonconformist femininity intertwine. The chapter first revisits Xiao's two early artworks related to gunshots to explore her boldness in a tamed context and her budding ferality in art as a means of breaking free from the hierarchy of reason over emotion. The section highlights how feral women are empowered by feminist separation while enduring punishment brought by ferality. I then approach Xiao's going feral through her work *Sperm*, introduce the concept of "untamed motherhood," and discuss ferality under the theme of motherhood. Subsequently, Xiao's more recent works and art practice with Bald Girls will be discussed while focusing on going feral in public and going feral as a collective empowering strategy for women artists.

Through an in-depth case study of Xiao Lu and her art, I argue that going feral, critically associated with feminist withdrawal and separation, entails inherent vulnerability. This is because the boundary between the tamed and the untamed is porous, dynamic, and often blurred and is shaped by intricate femininity, womanhood, and motherhood. By connecting feral theory with the concept of feminist mothering, I contend that untamed motherhood suggests an in-between space where feral beings exist and move between set definitions of identity, interruption, redefinition, and empowerment. Consequently, while celebrating their emancipation from gender norms and patriarchal oppression, feral women also endure punishment for their departure. Nonetheless, women artists, such as Xiao Lu, break through tamed spaces to enter a public unruly terrain, where they can juxtapose ferality in their art and lives, radically engaging with societal politics. Living with vulnerability, ambivalence, and diversity, feral women move between simultaneously blurring boundaries, striving to unshackle themselves from patriarchy.

Dialogue: Boldness within Taming

Born in 1962 into an influential and orthodox art family, Xiao Lu attended Beijing's Central Academy of Fine Arts High School and later graduated from the Zhejiang Academy of Fine Arts (now China Academy of Fine Arts) in 1988. In her fictional memoir *Dialogue* published in 2010, Xiao Lu recounts how she gave up dancing due to an injury and began art training under the guidance of her family. Despite a passive start, Xiao was not a feral outsider of the Chinese avant-garde art world as she received a standard and academic art education. During puberty, she was deeply bound to normative femininity, which permeated her family and society at large. Women were tamed under a patriarchal social order deeply ingrained in Confucianism, where little feminist practice had yet to take shape in China.

However, an undercover boldness began to bud when Xiao conceived the installation *Dialogue* in her final year as an undergraduate student in the oil painting department. Xiao submitted an installation work for her graduation exhibition but had no precedent to follow; thus, she had to overcome some administrative challenges. For this installation, Xiao modified two ready-made telephone booths, on which two life-sized photographs of a woman and a man were affixed inside respectively. The booths are connected by a mirror glass, before which a red phone sits on a central pedestal. Two figures appear to talk into a telephone while the hand receiver dangles off the hook. The scene contradicts the title of the work, just as the possibility of dialogue is harshly questioned in her memoir: "Have a dialogue with whom? ... Dialogue. A couple, man and woman, making a phone call. Were they really able to establish a dialogue?" (77). This installation was inspired by the sexual abuse Xiao suffered at the hands of a senior male artist, whom her parents trusted as a guardian. In an interview between Jonathan Goodman and Xiao, she stated the work dealt with "certain vexation and perplexities I had to deal with in puberty." All those feminine struggles and confusion triggered the shots in 1989 after the same work was launched at the China/Avant-Garde exhibition.

In the opening, Xiao fired two bullets in rapid succession into her own reflected image in the mirror (see Figure 1). The sudden event led to the temporary closure of the exhibition. In the chaos, Tang Song, a male art student, was mistakenly arrested because the police assumed the shooter had to be male. Xiao left the scene by chance after the shooting;

she later turned herself in to the police and was held in detention with Tang for three days. After the two were released, the curator and critic Li Xianting approached them to discuss how to explain the incident to the public. However, Li and Tang, the two men, spoke in Xiao's absence, marking the beginning of her deprivation of authorship. Although Xiao garnered attention and received credit from some Western press,[1] amid China's domestic uproar, Tang was initially and coincidentally attributed, and further deliberately aligned himself with other critics and curators to interpret the shots, thus being involved as the main author of the shots in the name of performance art. Although the intention behind Xiao's shooting was her individual catharsis, she found it hard to vocalize her personal affairs and experiences of sexual abuse behind the scenes. History written by the male-dominated art world identified the shots as the artistic herald of the Tiananmen Square protests. This social-political narrative is nothing but a product of hindsight. Nevertheless, the public opinion and political situation compelled her to remain silent. Another factor that played a part in Xiao's lasting repression was her relationship with Tang. Despite Xiao's shooting having no association with Tang, the subsequent events bonded them, leading to a romantic relationship lasting over ten years. It is conventional heterosexuality and romantic love that tame women to subordinate themselves to men, as was the case with Xiao. Her artistic career was disrupted, and Tang spoke in front of the public and shared authorship of the shooting incident.

Pulling the trigger in public in a country like China with rigid firearms regulations was undoubtedly bold behaviour. However, Xiao's boldness was immediately oppressed by more sophisticated factors after the incident: prudish convention mores in China; the gender stereotype that only men can fire a gun; the predominant role of male players in the art world; the narratives privileged by male critics, art historians, curators, and art bureaucracies; and the Matilda effect, which refers to the ubiquitous elimination of the achievements and contributions of women. Almost fifteen years after the incident, Xiao returned to her career and reclaimed the unique authorship of the bold shooting in 1989 by creating a new work in 2003. The performance titled *15 Shots... From 1989 to 2003* comprised fifteen shots respectively at fifteen black-and-white images of the artist pointing her pistol towards the viewer (see Figure 2). To commemorate the gunshots of 1989, Xiao fired through glass frames, leaving holes in her forehead in the images. These fifteen images, though similar in size and monochrome tone, gradually faded in sequence.

Xiao's *Dialogue* and fifteen shots have prompted multiple readings by researchers and curators. Adele Tan, for example, argues that Xiao's initial outburst and later return breached the inner circle of the Chinese art fraternity, repositioning feminine desires and emotions that have long been marginalized and ostracized in art history. Similarly, Laia Manonelles Moner discusses how Xiao Lu blurred the boundaries between the individual and the public through her art practice, which is strongly related to personal experience. Moner emphasizes that Xiao's resolute determination to reclaim her sole authorship helped resist and transform the institutional violence of patriarchy, as it aligns with the concept of "the personal is political," a slogan from the Western feminist movement of the 1960s.

Feral theories advance these insights. The subordination of emotion to reason, demanded by patriarchal ideology, is nearly universal in human societies. In Xiao's case, art and acts that derive from her innermost emotions were neglected and falsified because the social narrative denied what is personal and emotional, derogating women's emotions and personal space. From an animal liberation perspective, Brian Luke proposes an alternative metaethics, emphasizing going feral as a means of breaking free from the hierarchy of reason over emotion, hence the institutional objectification and exploitation imposed on females and animals. Moreover, some scholars working in the overlapping field of feminist theory and critical animal studies have foregrounded the interconnection of feminist separatism and feminist ferality (Montford and Taylor). When Xiao Lu withdrew from a patriarchal heterosexual relationship and refused to relinquish her authorship, she exhibited an aspect of feminist separation because she assumed power "by controlling access and simultaneously by undertaking definition" (Frye 105). Xiao's ferality, though not fully developed, facilitated the formation of new roles and new boundaries. In short, the sequence of her shooting fifteen times implied the passage of time and signified that Xiao had bid farewell to her past self. The separating and departing nature embedded in the concept of feminist ferality empowered her. She was ready to fight to recapture her accomplishment, cross the boundary that blocks and mutes the voice of women artists, and release herself from a subordinate role in a heterosexual relationship.

The dispute over authorship surrounding the *Dialogue* continues. The battle has allowed Xiao to assert her to rewrite "herstory" that challenges the singular masculine force. If the two shots in 1989 were only understood as bold under domestication instead of a truly untamed and unleashed statement, then the fifteen shots in 2003 and her decisive separation from Tang represented Xiao's critical transition towards going feral.

Sperm: Untamed Motherhood

In May 2006, while writing her fictional memoir, Xiao Lu was invited to a three-day workshop at the Kangda Hotel in Yan'an, where over forty artists and researchers gathered to develop an exhibition project. During this workshop, her installation and performance titled *Sperm* took place at a nearby lounge (see Figure 3). The installation featured a tall rack holding twelve empty jars for depositing sperm, along with a coordinate-measuring temperature-controlled machine. During the performance, Xiao set up the equipment and invited male participants from the workshop, as well as male visitors, to volunteer their sperm and deposit it in the temperature-controlled refrigerator. Xiao explained that she would use the collected sperm for artificial insemination in an attempt to get pregnant. However, at the end of the three-day collection period, no volunteers participated in the project. Again, Xiao's work was regarded as provocative, ludicrous, embarrassing, and transgressive because the potential male participants were treated as anonymous and subsidiary and were marginalized. Additionally, presenting insemination in art is taboo, just like showing pregnancy, maternal bodies, breastfeeding, and giving birth. The failure of Xiao's attempt and the response from male spectators, however, were what made the performance complete. Xiao showed ferality in this art project because she not only attempted to subvert the power dynamics within heterosexual reproduction but also incorporated this taboo and spurned subject into her art practice. The refusal and ignorance from male spectators also evidenced that this ferality occurred outside of their comfort zone, namely the domesticated realm where women should not hold dominance in reproduction.

The work was an artistic reproduction of the scientific method of sperm collection and depositing, which requires a freezing process to maintain the sperm's biological activity. However, in China, at the time, unmarried women were not allowed to undergo in vitro fertilization and become single mothers.[2] Accordingly, viewed through a feminist lens, critics generally believe this was a biting sarcastic work aimed at the policy; it questioned the traditional notions of motherhood. Julia Hartmann argues that Xiao raised awareness about state laws that restrain and control the reproduction autonomy of single women. Goodman stresses that although she is motivated by personal experiences and producing art in an often ironic way, Xiao cares acutely about the boundaries limiting women artists in China and the oppression women face in general. Tan argues that Xiao's experimental art engenders patriarchal anxiety because men's natural process of engaging in reproduction is robbed and replaced by autonomous and artificial techniques. More importantly, women's submission is reversed through an active refusal of heterosexual sex (Tan).

To further discuss the theme of motherhood that *Sperm* suggests, it is important to mention two contextual things. The first one is that Xiao had always wanted to be a mother during her reclusive life in Australia with Tang Song. Her eagerness and struggles with having children with Tang are depicted in her memoir. She became pregnant several times, but Tang always urged her to have an abortion, leading her to question herself: "That was in 1993, I was only thirty-one... Would I really be waiting and hoping forever with him?" (*Dialogue* 169). Tang's promise to eventually have children with Xiao turned out to be empty.

Second, Xiao had relocated to Beijing and separated from Tang before she produced *Sperm*. Her recuperation of authorship enraged leading male art critics based in Beijing. Xiao was, thus, excluded from the community and expelled from her residency and studio space in the 798 Art Zone.[3] Her marginalization and exclusion were punishment for her standing out as a feral woman who dared to confront canonized male narratives and reclaim authorship from men's hands. Driven by her failure to become a mother and the oppression against her career, Xiao doggedly embraced ferality as her explicit way of resistance. Although her male peers called her insane, she channelled her indignation into *Sperm*, openly presenting her ferality through art.

Xiao ultimately did not become a mother. However, this does not mean that the concepts of mother, motherhood, and mothering do not apply to the discussion of her work and identity. Motherhood enters women's lives in many ways, and its discourses affect nonmothers, not-yet-mothers, single mothers, lesbian mothers, mothers who have lost their children, and more. Therefore, motherhood is not a circumscribed role; instead, it encompasses reflection, judgment, and emotion, which Sara Ruddick calls "maternal thinking." As Ruddick argues, "Maternal thought does ... exist for all women in a radically different way than for men. It is because we are daughters, nurtured and trained by women, that we early receive maternal love with special attention to its implications for our bodies, our passions, and our ambitions" (107). Xiao's *Sperm* undoubtedly foregrounds her maternal thought in a way Elena Marchevska would call "maternal art," which seeks to "explore, reflect and critique the dominant cultural notion of motherhood and the role of 'the mother' in contemporary art practice" (2). At the time, Xiao had not been exposed to the concept of feminist mothering; nevertheless, she had consciously directed her satire at the institution of motherhood, which imprisons women through compulsory heterosexuality and male control. She experimented with "the potential relationship of any woman to her powers of reproduction" (Rich 13). For Adrienne Rich and Andrea O'Reilly, feminist mothering is a subversive mode of mothering that seeks to break the myth of patriarchal motherhood and to empower mothers. The domestic environment is one of the most important realms where women are domesticated and tamed by patriarchal reproduction and motherhood. Being feral means breaking this institutional control over how to define motherhood and how to mother. It is a journey of shedding, unlearning, and redefining; it is an empowering journey. Xiao's art thus suggests an essential interconnection between feminist mothering and ferality.

I argue that Xiao's maternal art practice specifies feminist mothering as feminist untamed motherhood, which places special focus on the process of untaming women from the patriarchal institution of motherhood and withdrawing from dependent heterosexual relationships to become a mother. Barbara Katz Rothman argues that the ideology of patriarchal society means far more than men in charge but indicates an essential and irreplaceable position of sperm—a worldview that permeates our thinking, parenting, and living. Feminist untamed motherhood abolishes the centrality of sperm and heterosexuality and withdraws from the relations shaped by this ideology. For Rothman, this means that the sentence "'Daddy plants a seed in Mommy' won't work any more" (392). Untamed motherhood redresses the fundamental structure of power and seeks female control of reproduction from the beginning. It thus involves both the tamed past and untamed future, suggesting that the boundary between the tamed and untamed is never sharp and unchangeable. The border instead tends to be fluid, porous, and ambivalent. Untamed motherhood is inherently vulnerable, as it can entail various forms of poignant punishment, unstable subjectivity, social stigma as barren or inadequate, and hidden anxieties and grief related to identity shifts, for example, being "unintentionally childless" (Tonkin 184). Xiao's longing for a child, experiencing pregnancy and abortion during her time in Australia, struggling between losing and gaining her subjectivity, and ultimately being "unintentionally childless"—while untaming reproduction by reclaiming power in art creation—reveal a new perspective of mothering as well as nonmothering, presenting women as active agents instead of passive others.

In addition, feminist untamed motherhood can encompass broader feminist concerns, such as mother-daughter relationships. The aspect can be glimpsed in Xiao's fictional memoir. Throughout her growth and artistic career, there has been a thread of resistance and estrangement from her mother: "The path of the inner world of mother and daughter had become completely blocked.... We stared at each other like strangers. I couldn't face this woman, who had given birth to me and raised me and was, of all people, the closest to me" (72). However, she deeply acknowledged that her tenacious personality and rebellious spirit were inherited from her mother, providing a matrilineal aspect of untamed motherhood. This matrilineal thread also plays a role in reproduction and maternity within the mother-daughter dyad. According to Xiao's account, during the period when she was determined to fight for her authorship, she travelled to Datianzhu Temple in Hangzhou and prayed to Guanyin Bodhisattva. She continues: "My mother told me that she had become pregnant with me on the sacred Buddhist mountain Putuo Shan [Mount Putuo], and that she was confident that the Bodhisattva Guanshiyin [Guanyin] would watch over me" (203). Her entwined submission and rebellion, along with all the tensions between her and her mother, suggest a critical in-between space—a space where untamed motherhood and ferality take shape and interweave and where women's porous identities could exist both within and outside the boundary of being feral.

Bald Girls, *Purge*, and More: Going Feral in Public

Looking back at Xiao's artistic career and all her past works, a clear trajectory can be observed. Both works, *15 Shots... From 1989 to 2003* and *Sperm*, are significant in her undoing of domestication, and from 2012, the establishment of the feminist art collective Bald Girls caused her art to shift from personal experiences to a broader concern for social politics. This shift in artistic creation reflects her going feral in public, a ferality initiated by further separation from the past context and a move towards a wilder, vast terrain.

Bald Girls, established in 2012 by Xiao and two other artists, Li Xinmo and Lan Jiny, and the curator Xu Juan, held its debut exhibition under the same name at the Iberia Centre for Contemporary Art in Beijing. During the opening, the three artists, including Xiao, engaged in a collaborative performance by shaving their heads (see Figure 4) in response to a statement written by Xu for the exhibition: "to fight against sexism, to expose the essence of social gender, to advocate a rebellious spirit in 'the Bald,' and an unconquerable will in 'the Guerrilla Girls,' and to move into a new age of gender" ("Bald Girls Preface" 6). Hair is a sexualized representation of normative femininity, a symbol of domestication that embodies the socially structured qualities of obedience and submissiveness, which are often associated with women. In traditional Chinese conventions, apart from religious reasons, the act of shaving one's head was historically regarded as a form of ethical and legal punishment. Women who were condemned for being promiscuous or not adhering to social standards of femininity might face this kind of punishment. Therefore, the performance was not only bold but also revealed a transgressive femininity that intends to subvert the patriarchal imagination of womanhood. The three artists did not care about being accused of madness or deviance; they instead celebrated it as a moment in which they broke free from domestication and went feral in public in a collective form.

The art world in China finds it hard to escape from state-controlled censorship. Shortly before the exhibition's opening, local police rushed into the space and confiscated paintings that contained nudity or profanity because they were deemed too radical and personal. The process of going feral inevitably entails a shift in living space; for artists, it also involves transforming their creative space. For women who have been relegated and exploited in the domestic sphere, the boundary between domestication and ferality involves emancipating care labour and breaking sexual oppression. Feral beings thus burst through the personal domestic space and enter a public space where they find alignment with other ferals. For female artists, the shift in space means they blur the boundary between the private and public spheres, juxtaposing their personal experiences with those of their female peers and developing greater sensitivity and concern for feminist careers and societal politics. Despite the interruption, the exhibition *Bald Girls* has had at least four profound meanings for Xiao and the wider community of Chinese women artists. It catalyzed Xiao's further ferality in her later artistic practice. It radicalized her active engagement in politics and social agendas and opened up a new bastion for women and women artists, where they could be empowered to resist patriarchal narratives. Finally, it demonstrated that working as a collective is an effective and vital feminist strategy for a nonhierarchical mode of solidarity, radical care, and being feral.

Going feral in public means more than being concerned about sociopolitical issues; it is a radical departure from domesticated contexts, particularly censorship and oppression from religions, cultures, and conventions. In May 2013, Xiao's original performance plan was unexpectedly denied on the opening day without prior notice by the authority of Museo Diocesana di Venezia, one of the exhibition venues of The Grand Canal—The 55th Venice Biennale. She intended to smear a bucket of sediment, taken from the Beijing–Hangzhou Grand Canal in China, all over her body before leaping into the canals of Venice. She was denied permission because of the belief that female nudity, even when covered in mud, would amount to blasphemy against the Christian religion. The planned performance then turned out to be a fortuitous act, as Xiao unexpectedly stripped off her clothes during the opening ceremony, traversed through the museum, and plunged into the canals for a naked swim (see Figure 5). The museum promptly shut down the exhibition and conducted a thorough cleansing the following day. In Western art history, which has been influenced by patriarchy and canonized by art institutions mostly controlled by men, the female nude is either sexualized as an object of gaze or degraded as vulgar. Presenting mature nudity, challenges this taboo. In the Western context, this dichotomy of the female nude derives from the Christian religion and has been constantly perpetuated by social mores. Women's bodies thus have been long domesticated and objectified by religion, history, and society. Xiao's *Purge* railed against the organizer's censorship of art and the domesticated female body behind which patriarchal ideology stands. From a perspective of feminist separatism, Marilyn Frye emphasizes that women's separation is only perceived as dramatic and impermissible by the patriarchal view, but for women, it represents a radical stance. *Purge* is indeed a satire and resisted normative femininity. Moreover, it showcases her unruly decision to disobey male-dominated institutions and withdraw from misogynistic contexts.

Kelly Struthers Montford and Chloë Taylor argue that going feral also brings punishments, including social alienation and various forms of abuse, discrimination, and exclusion. Even though Xiao's artwork *Dialogue* is a prominent milestone in the history of Chinese contemporary art, and her many other works in public have disrupted the boundaries of normative femininity, when celebrating her feminist achievements, we should recognize the punishments she has faced due to her boldness and ferality. From seeking asylum in Australia to being excluded from the domestic contemporary art community, Xiao has suffered various punishments. More recently, following her performance of *Skew*[4] and the delivery of a politically related artist statement at 10 Chancery Lane Gallery in Hong Kong in 2019, Xiao discovered that her name written in Chinese characters had been subject to censorship and removal within Chinese media. She can now only receive a visa to return to China by promising officials that she would never engage in any art-related activities in the country, including participating in exhibitions. When talking about her years living in the diaspora, Xiao expressed her deep attachment to her identity as a Chinese woman. Living on the margins and in between identities, with no solid place to rest and thrive, is often the condition of being feral. It implies the possibility of perpetual homelessness, both socially and culturally. Xiao's going feral in public does not mean indifference towards women's situation in China and their feminist development, nor has she abandoned the socially domesticated space where feminists and activists strive to break through. It is a critical prism through which the boundary between tamed and untamed can always be explored and discussed.

Living with Ferality: Not a Conclusion

In January 2019, on the beach at Stanwell Park in Sydney, Xiao completed a performance of *Tides*, which is a retrospective of her life and artistic career spanning the past thirty years (see Figure 6). Confronted and surrounded by the incoming tides, Xiao planted thirty bamboo poles into the sand. Claire Roberts, the cocurator of Xiao's solo exhibition at 4A Centre for Contemporary Asian Art in Sydney, vividly recollects and depicts the scene: "Xiao Lu battles incoming waves that increase in intensity, destabilizing her footing and that of the poles. Head down, body bent, using both hands and feet, it takes all of her energy to wield the poles into position" (*Time and Tides* 70). All the organic and inorganic elements involved in this work serve as metaphors. The bamboo poles, firmly erected but easily washed away, appear to symbolize her thirty-year journey or trenchant yet vulnerable statements she has etched into patriarchal art history. The rising and falling tides might allude to the hardships she has faced and the undulating social and political contexts she has navigated—space in which she could withdraw and advance, resist and let go, ruminate and shout, define and break free. Shorelines are ambiguous, shifting, and liminal spaces. They are boundaries connecting oceans, the unruly wild, and lands, the human-dominated terrain.

Feminist art is a crucial realm where women artists can redefine their erased identities and diverse femininities and where those who have gone feral can deliberately distance themselves from patriarchal domestication. Xiao persists in taking back forbidden territories through her artistic practice and dismantling patriarchal barriers that have historically separated women's artistic creation from social-political life. For Chinese female artists like Xiao, going feral in her personal life and artistic practice is more a matter of navigating the intricacies and dynamics of femininity and living with them. It is a matter of moving between and blurring boundaries, as the existing art canon has yet to radically transform and gender equality remains elusive. Nevertheless, the realm is no longer uncharted by feminists and activists, and foremothers are passing the baton, just as Xiao reiterated in our conversation: "I place my hopes in the younger generations."

Figure 1. Xiao Lu. *Dialogue.* 1989. Chromogenic print, printed 2006, 81 x 119.7 cm. Collected by New York: MoMA. https://www.moma.org/collection/works/114901.

Figure 2. Xiao Lu. *15 Shots... From 1989 to 2003.* 2003. Photography by Li Songsong. https://xiaolu.com.au/index.php?c=show&id=28.

Figure 3. Xiao Lu. *Sperm*. Installation and performance documentation. 2006. Photography by Yuan Yang. https://xiaolu.com.au/index.php?c=show&id=37.

Figure 4. Xiao Lu et al. *Bald Girls*. Performance with Li Xinmo and Lan Jiny. 2012. Beijing. https://xiaolu.com.au/index.php?c=show&id=39.

Figure 5. Xiao Lu. *Purge.* 2013. Venice. https://xiaolu.com.au/index.php?c=show &id=32.

Figure 6. Xiao Lu. *Tides.* 2019. Sydney. Photography by Jacquie Manning. https://xiaolu.com.au/index.php?c=show&id=35.

Endnotes

1. See "Police Close Rare 'Avant-garde' Art Exhibit in China" in United Press International (5 Feb. 1989); "China's Dada Shock" in the *Washington Post* (13 Feb. 1989); "Condoms, Eggs and Gunshots" in *Time Magazine* (6 Mar. 1989).

2. Although China's Law on Population and Family Planning (formerly centred around the one-child policy) did not explicitly address the reproductive rights of unmarried women, the subtle discrimination against unmarried women and single mothers regarding reproductive rights was only alleviated with the implementation of the three-child policy in 2021.

3. The information is based on Xiao's account during a dialogue with the author in August 2023.

4. See Xiao's website: https://xiaolu.com.au/index.php?c=show&id=6, and the interview by Art Asia Pacific, https://www.youtube.com/watch?v=OzBbkaJhJtA&ab_channel=ArtAsiaPacific.

Works Cited

Art Asia Pacific. "Interview with Xiao Lu." *YouTube*, 8 May 2020, https://www.youtube.com/watch?v=OzBbkaJhJtA.

Frye, Marilyn. "Some Reflections on Separatism and Power." *The Politics of Reality: Essays in Feminist Theory.* The Crossing Press, 1983, pp. 95–109.

Gomez, Edward. "Condoms, Eggs and Gunshots." *Time*, 6 Mar. 1989, p. 44.

Goodman, Jonathan. "Xiao Lu: The Confluence of Life and Art." *Yishu: Journal of Contemporary Chinese Art*, vol. 8, no. 2, 2009, https://yishu-online.com/wp-content/uploads/mm-products/uploads/2009_v08_02_goodman_j_p025.pdf. Accessed 13 June 2023.

Hartmann, Julia. "Bold Characters: Motherhood and Censorship in Chinese Art and Curating." *Radicalizing Care: Feminist and Queer Activism in Curating.* Edited by Elke Krasny et al. Sternberg Press, 2021, pp. 230–41.

Luke, Brian. "Taming Ourselves or Going Feral? Toward a Nonpatriarchal Metaethic of Animal Liberation." *Animals and Women: Feminist*

Theoretical Explorations. Edited by Carol J. Adams and Josephine Donovan. Duke University Press, 1999, pp. 790–867.

Marchevska, Elena. "Maternal Art Practice: An Emerging Field of Artistic Enquiry into Motherhood, Care, and Time." *The Maternal in Creative Work.* Edited by Elena Marchevska and Valerie Walkerdine. Routledge, 2020, pp. 1–10.

Moner, Laia Manonelles. "Xiao Lu: Asserting Her Voice through Artistic Practice." *Revista Brasileira de Estudos da Presença*, vol. 13, no. 2, 2023, https://www.scielo.br/j/rbep/a/BTDFZWDgtn6WYpDHv6PKY mR/?lang=en. Accessed 13 June 2023.

Montford, Kelly Struthers, and Chloë Taylor. "Feral Theory: Editors' Introduction." *Feral Feminisms*, vol. 6, 2016, https://feralfeminisms. com/issue1/issue-6-feral-theory/. Accessed 3 June 2023.

O'Reilly, Andrea. "Feminist Mothering." *Maternal Theory: Essential Readings.* Edited by Andrea O'Reilly, Demeter Press. 2007, pp. 792–821.

Rich, Adrienne. *Of Woman Born: Motherhood as Experience and Institution.* W.W. Norton & Company, 1995.

Roberts, Claire. "Time and Tides: Xiao Lu's Recursive Art, 1989–2019." *Playground*, 12 (2023), pp. 67–79.

Rothman, Barbara Katz. "Beyond Mothers and Fathers: Ideology in a Patriarchal Society." *Maternal Theory: Essential Readings.* Edited by Andrea O'Reilly. Demeter Press, 2007, pp. 390–407.

Ruddick, Sarah. "Maternal Thinking." *Maternal Theory: Essential Readings.* Edited by Andrea O'Reilly. Demeter Press, 2007, pp. 96–113.

Southerland, Daniel. "China's Dada Shock." *The Washington Post*, 13 Feb., 1989, p. B2.

Tan, Adele. "Elusive Disclosures, Shooting Desire. Xiao Lu and the Missing Sex of Post-89 Performance Art in China." *Negotiating Difference: Contemporary Chinese Art in the Global Context.* Edited by Birgit Hopfener et al. Verlag und Datenbank für Geisteswissenschaften, 2012, pp. 127–40.

Tonkin, Lois. "Drawing as a Creative Exploration of 'Circumstantial Childlessness.'" *The Maternal in Creative Work.* Edited by Elena Marchevska and Valerie Walkerdine. Routledge, 2020, pp. 184–92.

UPI Archives. "Police Close Rare 'Avant-garde' Art Exhibit in China." *United Press International*, 5 Feb. 1989, https://www.upi.com/Archives/ 1989/02/05/Police-close-rare-avant-garde-art-exhibit-in-China/368 5602658000/. Accessed 26 Jan. 2025.

Xiao, Lu. *Dialogue*, translated by Archibald McKenzie. Hong Kong University Press, 2010.

Xiao, Lu. Personal interview. 3 Aug. 2023.

Xiao, Lu. "Skew (Performance/Installation)." XIAOLU, https://xiaolu. com.au/index.php?c=show&id=6. Accessed 26 Jan. 2025.

Xu, Juan. "Bald Girls Preface." *Bald Girls: Exhibition of Xiao Lu, Li Xinmo and Lan Jiny*. Edited by Xu Juan. Iberia Center for Contemporary Art, 2012, pp. 2–6.

12.

Selected Poetry

Victoria Smits

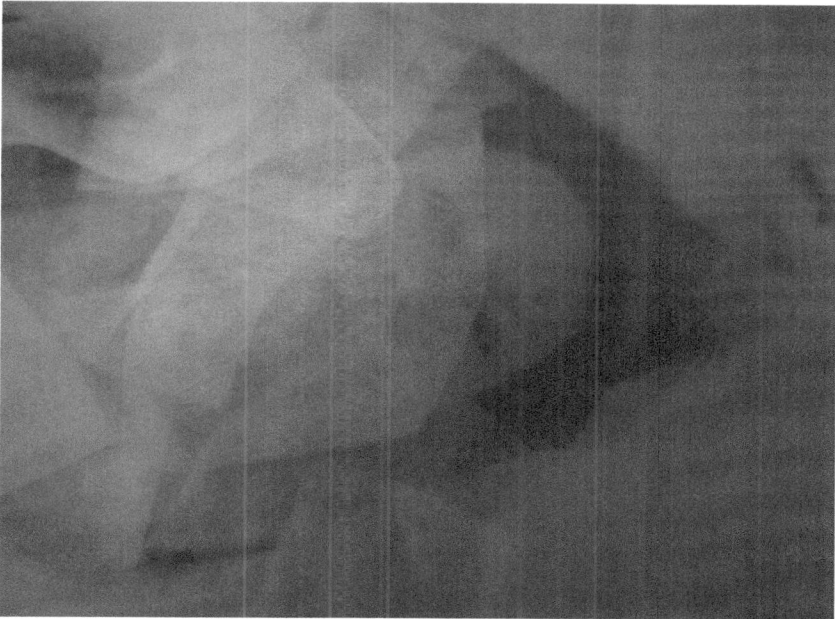

I Am (Not) Drowning, self-portrait
Archival pigment print on Hahnemühle paper, dryer sheet used as filter,
2021.

My Countess Truth

Was I born
to hold you up,
celebrate only you
          and your easy gaze?
Was I born
to be your plinth,
        soft and strong,
        a firm frame
        for each moment
        of your existence?
     Here you are!
     Here, I have you!
     Here, I will always
     be there!

I am a rock,
     a wooden structure
     designed to raise
     you up
     to be consecrated
     among the rest.
I am your servant,
     your maid,
     your willing
     domestic dog
     exalting your future
     accomplishments.
I am the lineage of women,
     offered as heralder of you,
     man, men, boys, men
     so that you may be
     extolled and honoured.

I am nothing but a bench
for you to stand on.

The Countess and Her Will

Lord, Thy Will Be Done
  to me.
Your will is done
  to me.
But are you the God of men
  or of women?

You are Not
  my god,
  my creator,
  my mother.
    This chaos of space and time,
    of screaming and nursing
    of succumbing to whims
  is born
  not of intellect
  or life
but of your limbs and loin
  your desires,
  not mine.

I thrive in my own
  aliveness
    and thoughts of an earth
  traversed
  by me,
  for me,
  with me,
and me alone.

I long for blood and vessels
  overflowing
    in rivers and streams
  with my joy,

my ideas,
my living
with myself,
and me alone.

Your will swallows me whole,
a Jonah joke forcing
your plan on me
inside the caverns of a whale,
the caverns of this home.

In dwindling courageous hope,
I find my will, spit myself out,
and leave,
like Ibsen's Nora did,
leave to find myself,
with me,
alone,
so beautifully alone.

The Countess and Her Bath

I am gentle
with me
as I bathe and baptize
myself,
caress my body,
my breasts.

Your longing
for this
is not yours
anymore.

It is mine.
I am mine.
I am the only one
>who will touch
>and know in the way
>knowing must be,
>should be,
>>should have always been.

Leave me be.
Leave this body
>alone.
>It is mine
>and mine only
and not yours to own.

The worn path
>away from domesticity,
>fringed with threads
>of oneness,
>patches of identity
>>are stitched
>>into wholeness.

I bless myself and my becoming.
I bless who I must be.

Ode to the Mundane

This dryer lint here
collects upon itself,
standing by, biding time,
until it looms whole,
a modest cloud
of undecipherable days:
maybe tears, or wails,
merriment, or joy.
Maybe, just maybe,
a sliver of repose.

Ethereal and light
but a stone cloak nonetheless,
spinning sheets scent my place,
always and ever discarded.
If I sew the edges into one,
neatly aligned in rows
and checks, will I become,
yes, become, whole again?

The selves of mother-labour
convene, sip wine,
and merrily collude
en masse. They erect
a goddess effigy,
celestial and astute
who hails these heritors
of daily life, with a gala
of feral ubiquity,
becoming Hera and Zeus as one.
She bears their load
devotedly, nourishing
each body, each life
as her own.

An Ode to Mahsa Amini

We are organs
and bodies, breath
and being,
oozing out
of other bodies
and back to earth:
children beaten
down to fleshy
heat, screaming and
swirling winds,
raw and infertile
dust, fires
unfreezing fossils
of what was.

In the midst
you emerged
alive, a torch,
a youthful
pledge to self
sovereignty,
to the sanguine.
Oh hallowed martyr,
monarch in death,
we hear your cries,
your invocation
to independence
while they bludgeoned
your broken body.
You bled
for us, the soldier
of all soldiers,
taken for righteousness,
for truth.

Homeland rally cries
call your spirit,
now wind and storm,
forcing freedom,
fists against the hijab,
manacle of death.
We must collect
ourselves, gather
ourselves and hold
fast to Eve
as she cuts her hair
to make us a nest.

13

Unfaithful Domestics: Ferality and Domestic Disorder in John McPherson's *Strays*

Casey O'Reilly-Conlin

The cat is a faithless domestic.... They are, naturally, inclined to theft, and the best education only converts them into servile and flattering robbers.... They readily conform to the habits of society but never quite its manners; for of attachment, they have only appearance, as may be seen by the obliquity of their motions and duplicity of their looks.... Very different from the faithful dog, whose sentiments are all directed to the person of his Master, the cat appears only to feel for himself, only to love conditionally, only to partake of society that he may abuse it.... It cannot be said that cats, though living in our houses, are entirely domestic. The most familiar are not under any subjection, but rather enjoy perfect freedom, as they do just what they please, and nothing is capable of returning them in a place which they are inclined to desert.

—George-Louis Leclerc de Buffon (qtd. in Vocelle, 210-212)

Paul Wells suggests that "dichotomies never work in opposition; they only work in oscillation and tension" (48). John McPherson's 1991 horror film *Strays* employs and reinforces a series of dichotomies while also creating the potential to probe, blur, or even resist their meanings: masculinity-femininity, ideal-deviant femininity, marital bliss-strife, human-animal, culture-nature, tame-wild, dog-cat. The most pertinent representation of dichotomies in oscillation is showcased through the concept of ferality and the figure of the feral cat. The feral is constructed as neither culturally domesticated nor naturally wild. It can neither return to the culture that abandoned or continues to reject it nor return to the wild—the nature that no longer exists or never fully existed for it. The feral cannot be defined in absolute terms as belonging to nature or culture; it exists in both yet belongs to neither. In representation and reality, the feral oscillates between the constructed categories of domesticity and wilderness, pet and vermin, and culture and nature. Feral is a definition that evades definition.

The film poster for *Strays* (see Figure. 1) effectively illuminates the oscillating nature of the feral cat and the film's central themes. The domestic, visualized through the house, is presented as ultimately vulnerable to outside threats. A horde of cats leaps from the darkness towards the house, symbolizing nature's impending encroachment on culture. A single cat, the leader of this feral colony, towers over the home, mouth open and teeth bared, threatening to swallow the supposed tranquillity of domesticity whole. *Strays,* like so many films within the horror genre, revolves around a white, middle-class family, the Jarrets, who move from the city to a rural area to escape the hustle and bustle of urban life only to have their newly acquired serenity disrupted by outside forces. Because of the complex and dualistic legacy of human-feline relationships across Western history, cats have become an ideal symbolic figure to enact the common trope of disordered domesticity within the horror genre.

Strays plays with a repertoire of ambivalent symbolisms and histories inherent to human-feline "naturecultures" (Haraway). Cats symbolize domesticity (e.g., kittens in baskets) and represent its destruction (e.g., invasive feral cats). Most of the film's action takes place in the typically domestic settings of the kitchen and bedroom. Feminine trinkets of domesticity, such as fluffy pillows and vases of flowers, are used as weapons against the invading cat colony. Bad women and bad cats, both threatening domestic order, become extensions of one another and must be punished, killed, or culled to restore the sanctity of the institutions they seek to destroy.

Figure 1: Film poster for *Strays.*

In this chapter, I use McPherson's *Strays* to probe ferality through its conjoined portrayal of women and cats and explore how this concept exposes man-made anxieties about the tenuousness of dichotomies, the porous boundaries between binaries, identities existing in flux, and the beings and beasts who defy and evade fixed definitions. I begin with a brief overview of naturecultures, a concept through which human-feline cohistories and relationalities may be interrogated. I then focus on two historical periods (the late Middle Ages/early modern period and the Victorian era), which hold particular significance to these relationalities. This is followed by a close analysis of McPherson's *Strays* and its portrayal of disobedient beings. The constant hostility towards and desire to punish such beings—those who dare stray from the rigid, predetermined path-ways of society proper—affirms the continued threat they pose to the illusion of impenetrable fortresses of fixed, binaristic categorization and is resultant of an underlying societal fear that some beings can never be fully brought under control and are always at risk of straying.

Naturecultures

> What distinguished man from animals was the human capacity for
> symbolic thought, the capacity which was inseparable from the
> development of language in which words were not mere signals, but
> signifiers of something other than themselves. Yet the first symbols
> were animals. What distinguished man from animals was born of
> their relationship with them.
>
> —John Berger, *About Looking* 9

Jody Berland argues that the cat, "as a liminal animal, an animal that crosses between worlds, an animal that threatens boundaries and taxonomies, [is] an animal onto which anything can be projected" ("Symbiotics" 155). Mysterious yet intimately familiar, homey but occult, cats are at once both "revered and reviled" (Vocelle 1). Although this chapter focusses on the representation of feral cats in *Strays*, this representation cannot be extricated from the complex and contradictory sociohistorical figure of the domestic cat, as both descriptors—domestic and feral—are intertwined with and dependent on the other. The symbolism, social status, and treatment of cats in Western history have shifted drastically from era to era, with each transition retaining remnants of prior associations that contribute to the cat's "ambiguous status" today (Berland, "Symbiotics" 155). If symbolism is the domain of human culture and essence is that of nature, then the two become inextricably entangled in what Donna Haraway has termed "naturecultures" ("Companion Species Manifesto"). In naturecultures, neither term— nature or culture—can be individuated or extricated from the other. Rather, they coevolve symbiotically. Nature and culture, material and semiotic, body and mind, or corporeality and cognition—neither opposing term makes sense without the other. These binary categories mutually influence each other and become intertwined in the implosive, relational, and contradictory dance of naturecultures.

Berland observes: "Cats have been known to humans for so many centuries that it is fair to say that the two species co-evolved in connection with one another. The histories of agriculture, gender, class, religion, and urbanization are punctuated with the presence of cats; each bears the marks of radical transformations in attitudes toward these animals" ("Symbiotics" 433–34). Cats have been symbols of domestic disorder and emblems of pacified and infantilized femininity; they are the companions of impoverished witches and bourgeois Victorian housewives. Embodying numerous symbolic definitions at once, cats never fully adhere to the rules of traditional domesticity and instead demonstrate an admirable propensity for fierce autonomy. This muddled embodiment results from the inconsistent and entangled histories, conjoined and ambivalent symbolisms, intimate encounters, and proximate geographies of human-feline naturecultures. For this chapter, I focus on two key periods that highlight the complexity and contradictory nature of feline-human relationships and cat symbolism in Western history: The late Middle Ages/early modern period and the Victorian era. I also examine the explicit (inter)connection between concepts of femininity and felinity during these periods.

Cohistories

> The phrase "domestic cat" is an oxymoron.
> —George Will ("Millions and Millions of Cats")

Late Middle Ages, Early Modern Era

The solidification of Christianity as the dominant religion throughout Europe in the Middle Ages began a period of intense vilification of the feline species (Vocelle). The proximate observability of feline behaviour rendered cats an available and renewable source of symbolic and moral projections. A cat unabashedly displaying her rear end, for example, was imbued with moral implications, which, in turn, were attributed to certain groups of people who thus became associated with cats. All this then redounded on the character and treatment of cats in an elaborate dance of naturecultures. On June 13, 1233, Pope Gregory IX issued a papal bull, the *Vox in Rama,* that declared the cat a "vessel for the devil" (Vocelle 108–09). Just over 250 years after the *Vox in Rama,* the domestic cat would appear again in a book that would cast a dark shadow over European history: *Malleus Maleficarum,* written by Dominican inquisitors Heinrich Kramer and Jacob Sprenger and published in 1487. A bestseller, second only to the Bible, for roughly two hundred years in Europe, the *Malleus* was an instruction manual of sorts, discussing heresy and witchcraft beliefs, women's inherent susceptibility to the temptations of the devil, and investigatory and legal proceedings for suspected witches.

Cats were common familiars of early modern witches. Superstition and occult associations surrounding cats are also prevalent in the annals of natural and medical history. Ambroise Paré and Joannes Jonstonus proclaimed that proximity to cats could cause tuberculosis or madness (Rogers), and in *The History of Four Footed Beasts,* Edward Topsell suggests that the "familiars of witches do most commonly appear in the shape of cats, which is an argument that this beast is dangerous to the soul and body" (qtd. in Vocelle 144). Cats were regularly killed in public spectacles alongside their human witchy counterparts (Berland, "Symbiotics" 155). They were ceremoniously tortured and killed in charivaris, such as the French Faire le chat and German Katzenmusik, their anguished shrieks providing music for the festivities (Darnton 83). In the United Kingdom, they were whipped for entertainment or placed in bags or baskets and used for target practice (Boehrer 27, 29). The Reformation certainly did not improve the social status of the domestic cat as it was reimagined as an enduring emblem of the Catholic Church and burned alive in anti-Catholic processions (Boehrer 40) while being made a recurring character in anti-Catholic propaganda and satire.

The early modern period did not quell the turbulence of the Middle Ages. A rapidly changing social, religious, economic, and political climate—including the privatization of land, home, and the female body—led to the reconfiguration of the family, gendered labour, domestic conduct, class divisions, and an intensified fear over the blurring of species boundaries and interspecies relationships between women and animals, particularly as they subverted social conventions of marriage and motherhood. Silvia Federici argues that the implementation of the enclosure system in early modern England and the subsequent reconfiguration of physical and social spatial boundaries directly contributed to the English witch hunts through the consequent privatization of land, home, family, and body as social and symbolic spaces. She writes:

> Not only did cooperation in agricultural labor die when land was privatized ... differences among the rural population deepened.... Social cohesion broke down; families disintegrated, the youth left the village to join the increasing number of vagabonds or itinerant workers—soon to become the social problem of the age—while the elderly were left behind to fend for themselves. Particularly disadvantaged were older women who, no longer supported by their children, fell onto the poor rolls or survived by borrowing,

petty theft, and delayed payments. The outcome was a peasantry divided not only by deepening economic inequalities, but by a web of hatred and resentments that is well-documented in the records of the witch-hunt, which shows that quarrels relating to requests for help, the trespassing of animals, or unpaid rents were in the background of many accusations. (72)

In short, the enclosure system unleashed a rampant criminalization and feminization of poverty. Federici observes that "following the loss of the commons and the reorganization of family life, which gave priority to child-raising at the expense of the care previously provided to the elderly" (200), elderly women and unmarried women, in particular, found themselves in increasingly precarious and vulnerable situations. Many were forced to beg for their livelihood "at the very time when the new Protestant ethic was beginning to finger alms-giving as a waste and encouragement to sloth" (Federici 200). The emergent Protestant valorization of work, imbued as it was with theological and social significance, rendered beggars as social pariahs. As beggars, women faced particular scrutiny as their status as (often) unmarried and their frequent movement throughout the community rendered them immediately suspicious. Not permanently fixed in the confines of the home, or under male supervision through the newly defined sacraments of marriage and motherhood, the bodies and behaviours of female beggars were less easily controlled.

The implementation of the enclosure system, produced a pervasive obsession with boundaries in early modern thought and practice. Diane Purkiss argues the following:

> The housewife's role involves maintaining boundaries, boundaries between nature and culture, between inside and outside, pollution and purity.... In early modern communities, one of the principal ways of representing the border of nature or culture was the boundary of the house ... [and] the boundaries of the house were invested with ideological significance for the woman's own identity as chaste. (97)

However, she concedes that these boundaries "were always being crossed" (98). The structuring of the early modern household was dependent upon the transcendence of boundaries: the enmeshment of natural and civilized worlds, the passage of bodies, both human and nonhuman, through the threshold of the house, and the transferal of fluids like semen or breastmilk between bodies. Such permeable boundaries meant that the household was always at the mercy of unfamiliar, even unsavoury, influences, and women, as preservers of these boundaries, faced particular scrutiny. Domestic conduct books, popularized in the early modern period, stressed a woman's responsibility to "keep house," linking "household containment [to] the enclosed chaste body of the virtuous woman" and thus associating women who were not "virtuously enclosed" with "sexual availability, economic profligacy and political disorder" (Purkiss 97). Towards the end of the sixteenth century, a social archetype emerged onto which early modern citizens could project their fears and insecurities and blame for all natural phenomena threatening the stability of early modern life—the witch.

The witch existed in stark contrast to that of the virtuous woman. She was constructed as lazy, scolding, unproductive, and barren; her actions were intentionally antagonistic to the productivity and industriousness of proper femininity. In fact, as Purkiss notes, accusations of witchcraft usually revolved around "housewifery gone awry" (94). Accused witches, Merry Wiesner-Hanks argues, were:

> often charged with actions that were the inversion of the nurturing expected of a good wife and mother—poisoning children with food instead of sustaining them, talking back to men instead of obeying them, souring cream rather than turning it into butter ... [and arose] in situations which were largely confined to women— food preparation and preservation, pregnancy and childbirth, [and] the care of young children. (90)

Nowhere is this more evident than in the bizarre and taboo narratives of interspecies intimacy and deformed maternities of the witch-familiar pairing.

One of the key elements of this witch lore, which Anne Llewellyn Barstow describes as a "uniquely English contribution," was the "belief in the imp or familiar, a demon who took the shape of a cat, dog, or toad, assisting the witch with her *maleficarum* [witchcraft], and being allowed to suck from her special teat in return" (76). The domestic cat has inarguably endured as the most prominent familiar representation and, like the broom and cauldron, has remained an emblem of subversive domesticity and femininity in modern depictions of witchcraft. Ironically, cats served an important utilitarian function as pest control in both rural and urban early modern settings, but their innate refusal to respond to human commands symbolically aligned felinity with the "social problem" (Federici) of the age. While their aptitude for catching and killing vermin could have situated cats alongside the virtuous housewife as protectors and preservers of the household, their disobedience, opportunism, love of rest, propensity to wander, and proclivity for sneaking unattended food symbolically rendered them an ideal companion for the scolding, idle, and disobedient witch.

In a time when spatial boundaries had acquired new significance, the familiars' ability to transcend these boundaries gained symbolic importance. The magical, liminal abilities of familiars allowed them to cross spatial boundaries at the witch's behest. They were easily able to enter the private space of the home when the witch herself was denied entry. The solidified bond between witch and familiar, through the blending of exteriors and interiors, allowed the witch to violate the most private and intimate spaces of her neighbouring villagers through her familiar— entering neighbouring farms to kill livestock, sneaking into homes to suffocate babies, and creeping into kitchens and bedrooms to spoil dairy and cause infertility and impotence. Lash Keith Vance argues that contracts with familiars often represent a "devotion to a corrupted domestic" (119). For example, the relationships between the St Osyth witches (1582) and their familiars, Vance observes, were regularly represented as tender and motherly. Witchcraft pamphlets often emphasized the "domestic nature of caring for these strange animals and that ... witches ... changed their house space into a foul perversion of motherhood" (Vance 130). The witch and her familiar companion served as figures through which early modern women could measure themselves against, demonstrating "the proper way a woman should run her house by showing the way monstrous mothers run their houses" (135). Vance continues: "Familiars become devilish versions of long lost children that are sweetly cared for by these witches. They are given milk, a place to sleep, and blood directly from the witch. This perverts any type of social or moral order to create a hybrid discourse of normality that shocks the reader far more than if the deponents simply contracted with the devil" (135). Purkiss also notes that the relationship "between witch and familiar was often represented in the witch's own confession as an elaborate maternal or quasi-maternal interchange" and "the popular notion of a blood pact between a familiar and a witch could be reshaped into a model of deformed maternity" (135).

Louise Jackson, in contrast to Purkiss, describes the relationship between witch and familiar as sexual. Familiars, she notes, were often described as hiding in the "sexual parts" of women, and their witches' teats, often represented as excess flaps of skin, were commonly located on their genitals.

Even if not explicitly related to witchcraft, early modern women's relationships with animals were regularly viewed as deviant or dangerous, often represented as a conflation of maternity and sexuality in perverse interspecies exchanges. As Erica Fudge demonstrates:

> In sixteenth and seventeenth-century thought a pet was sometimes understood to upset the boundary between human and animal. For Edward Topsell, writing in 1607, the lap-dog, that epitome of the ladylike pet, represented women's inferiority. He wrote that "these dogs are little, pretty, proper and fine, and sought for to satisfy the delicateness of dainty dames and wanton women's wills.... [They are] instruments of folly for them to play and dally withal, to trifle away the treasure of time, to withdraw their minds from more commendable exercises, and to content their corrupted concupiscences with vain disport." The relationship between the woman and her lap-dog was regarded as dangerously maternal, and even, perhaps, dangerously erotic. (28)

Like the relationship between a witch and her familiar, women who lavished care and attention on animals and invested time in such relationships with no apparent productive outcome were rendered frivolous, suspicious, and dangerous. A pet or familiar, imagined as a surrogate husband or child and a usurper of nurturant or romantic affections, had the potential to distract women from more noble domestic and marital pursuits. While the category of "pet" was a relatively new concept in early modern English thought and usually reserved for upper-class circles, as the Topsell quote reflects, attitudes towards economically marginalized women and their familiars reveal the same anxieties about upper-class women and their lapdogs. In both instances, a woman's relationship with a nonhuman companion represents a form of self-indulgence and an impediment to modesty. In the context of the early modern household, the expenditure of nurturance on beings and relationships outside of the care of offspring or spouses or for nonutilitarian purposes represented a direct threat to the harmonious operation of the household and, by proxy, the state. For upper-class women, the attention and luxury bestowed upon a pet rather than a husband or child were imagined to reflect the woman's vanity and profligacy. In the witch-familiar relationship, the familiar reciprocated the witch's nurturance by doing her bidding. Acting as an extension of the witch herself, the affection lavished upon her familiar can be understood as a form of radical self-love in staunch opposition to obligatory self-effacement idealized in the figure of the virtuous housewife.

Victorian Era

By the latter half of the early modern period, the status of some animals had drastically shifted, and cats were reclassified from "utilitarian domestic assistants to pets" (Rogers 9), at least in upper-class circles. As Berland explains: "With the growth of industrialism in England and across Europe.... Human and animal bodies and their meanings were reorganized together by the discursive regime of industrial capitalism. Once nature seemed comfortably under control, pets were safe for middle- and upper-class households to love and to embrace" ("Iconographics" 439–40). Cats were increasingly featured in domestic portraiture, often accompanied by children or perched on the laps of girls and young women in frilled dresses. In the nineteenth century, the domestic cat was reimagined and reimaged as an emblem of cleanliness, innocence, femininity, and bourgeois domesticity. In Victorian society, it became "fashionable to pamper cats" (Rogers 82). As Katherine Rogers observes, the domestic cat "became an embodiment of domestic virtue—a high calling at a time when the pure and harmonious home was idealized as never before" (97–98).

Defiant and demonic feline imagery was pacified to illustrate that the animal spirits of women and cats have the potential to be tamed by domestic institutions. The prowling scavenger cats of early modern paintings were replaced with fluffy white kittens in scenes of domestic tranquillity. As Rogers demonstrates, these kittens are pictured as "engaged in the mildest form of mischief: they never break or steal ... rather, they tiptoe around a formally set table, investigating the place settings without disarranging anything" (98). As the domestic cat was granted new heights of acceptance, certain aspects of its representation were pacified to comply with the standards of Victorian domesticity.

"Popular artists," Rogers writes, "constantly included cats in their wholesome domestic scenes to reinforce family values" (98), accomplished by "the tendency to sentimentalize away their aloofness and potential for fierceness" (97). St. George Jackson Minvart, in 1881, commented: "The cat is ... favoured by that half of the human race which is the more concerned with domestic care; for it is the home-loving animal and one exceptionally clean and orderly in its habits, and thus naturally commends itself to the good will of the thrifty housewife" (1). The cat became an emblem of ideal femininity. Women pictured with cats, cats and children (particularly girls), and "families of playful kittens, generally supervised by a benevolent mother" (Rogers 99) became stock images of the Victorian era. Little girls were given kittens to teach them about devoted and nurturing motherhood (Vocelle 261). Furthermore, cats were regularly anthropomorphized and infantilized as "living dolls" and eternal children (Vocelle 264) in both "narrative and imagery through a refeminized ideology of natural innocence" (Berland, "Symbiotics" 157). The idle cat was reimagined as the passive cat. Despite the representational loss of their species animality, their claws, fangs, and predation, cats "were so thoroughly rescued by Victorian culture that by the beginning of the twentieth century their depictions involved a sweeter, more decorous femininity allowing cats the safety of domestic life" (Berland, "Symbiotics" 157). This period, however, also birthed a new cultural archetype that effectively inverted the Victorian association of cats with domestic tranquillity.

The increased popularity of pet ownership in Victorian culture contributed to the partial reinvention of cats from the demonic accomplices of witches to the very emblem of domestic tranquillity. However, just as the witch figure was antagonistic to that of the virtuous housewife, the Victorian era too birthed a cultural archetype in opposition to traditional domesticity: the Crazy Cat Lady. Although reclaimed and celebrated by many feline-loving women, the Crazy Cat Lady is a pejorative archetype, utilized as a cautionary tale of what becomes of women who stray from their predetermined roles as wives and mothers. At best, she is a comical figure to be ridiculed and laughed at or an image of tragedy to be pitied. At worst, she is a creature of revulsion.

Newspaper articles about such women from the Victorian era highlighted their commitment to domestic disorder (Vocelle); cat ladies forsook homely aesthetics and desirable domestic conduct by surrendering their homes to the creature comforts and messy animality of their feline companions. As the earlier Minvart quote reflects, a woman's concern "with domestic care" was a reflection of her character or "good will." Thus, the animal messiness of the homes of cat ladies was understood as evidence of their abject animality. Ann Lloyd, a cat lady who lived with her two "spinster sisters" and an unknown number of cats, was charged with being a public nuisance. When asked by the court if her home had an "offensive smell," a testifying officer replied, "There was, your worships, but I don't know what it came from. I have thought perhaps it was from the ladies' bodies" (qtd. in Vocelle 250). The women, the cats, and the home are conjoined in abject animality that ruptures contained and ordered Victorian femininity and domestic interiors. While represented as bizarre, repulsive, and even terrifying, these women expressed a sincere compassion for creatures similarly misunderstood and disregarded by conventional society.

A common trope of contemporary pop cultural representations of woman and cat pairings—prevalent in modern depictions of the Crazy Cat Lady archetype—is that the woman must die. Her death acts as comic relief, putting an end to her tragic narrative. Like the condemned witch who meets her fate at the gallows, the lonely death of the Crazy Cat Lady is evoked as a cautionary reminder to women not to stray from the conventions of traditional domesticity. A newspaper article highlighting the curious case of Countess de la Torre, who in 1887 was criminally charged with having too many cats, describes her home as having a "poverty-stricken air, being altogether given up to the animals" (qtd. in Vocelle 255) and details the harassment and taunting the Countess received from her neighbours in an accompanying interview: "'Hoh ! hoh ! mother of dogs and cats ! Though shoudst be burned, thou wicked one ! Harbourer of unclean animals, thou shoudst be drowned as a witch'" (qtd. in Vocelle, 253). The newspaper article concludes with reference to the commonplace unhappy ending of the Crazy Cat Lady: "Someday [the cats] may devour the Countess. There may be no gratitude from man or beast. It would be a sublime ending" (qtd. in Vocelle, 258). The author insinuates that despite the Countess' compassion, her cats have no real allegiance to her. The image of an old woman dying alone only to be discovered days later half eaten by her cats is symbolic affirmation that the company of cats will never compensate for matrimonial and maternal fulfillment or the quiet security of domestic life. Like the witch's inversion of traditional domesticity and femininity, the Crazy Cat Lady either fails to live up to, or worse, intentionally deviates from feminine conventionality. Reduced to a joke, the pitifulness ascribed to the Crazy Cat Lady masks the terror she arouses as a deeply subversive figure.

Strays

> The Jarrets have finally found their dream house.
> Now it's about to become their worst nightmare.
>
> —*Strays* trailer

In *Strays,* before we are introduced to the Jarret family, we are introduced to the former occupant of their newly acquired dream house. The perspective of *Strays*'s opening scene is that of an unknown creature who in the dead of night leaps from the darkness towards the home before entering it through an unlocked cat door. Once inside, the creature encounters an elderly woman asleep on the couch, surrounded by her many cat companions, cradling a bottle of liquor as a grandmother might cradle her grandchild. This is reminiscent of the portrayal of another Crazy Cat Lady, Eleanor Abernathy, a recurring character in *The Simpsons,* who forsaking marriage and motherhood to pursue an education and career conciliates her loneliness with the company of cats until she succumbs to alcoholism and eventual madness. The elderly woman of *Strays* awakens to a chorus of demanding meows. She lovingly coos "my babies" at her many cats before venturing outside, leaving the door open behind her, to retrieve a store of cat food from her cellar. She stops momentarily to greet and lavish affection on the swarm of feral cats that have congregated on her doorstep. The boundaries of this cat lady's home are already established as porous; the cat door is unlocked so that cats— domestic and feral alike—may pass through at their leisure, and she leaves her front door open and vulnerable to outside forces. "So many guests tonight," she coos; she is not surprised by or fearful of the invading colony and instead greets them as welcomed guests. As she opens the cellar door to retrieve the cat food, she hears a menacing growl. She looks out into the wilderness bordering her property. From this angle, the wilderness stares back, the camera acting as an extension of the feral cat, representing his point of view. The camera-cat hybrid leaps towards her as she lets out a harrowing scream.

Following the implied death of the elderly woman, the setting changes, and we are introduced to the film's central human characters, the Jarrets: Paul, husband, father and lawyer; Lindsay, wife and mother; and Tessa, their picturesque infant daughter. They are driving towards their prospective new home recommended by Lindsay's real estate agent sister, Claire. Paul is immediately emasculated as the family patriarch (as he frequently is throughout the film) as Lindsay is shown driving the car and, evidently, calling the shots. Lindsay insists that Claire thinks the house would be perfect for them to which Paul replies that Claire "isn't exactly an expert on domestic bliss." It is established that Claire is in the middle of a bitter divorce and that Paul is her attorney. Like the Crazy Cat Lady, Claire does not adhere to traditional domestic femininity. She does not have children and is getting divorced. When she later admits her infidelity to Paul, Claire protests that her former husband was neglectful and defiantly posits, "What was I supposed to do, sit around the house baking cookies?" further disengaging her character from feminine domesticity. Throughout the film, Claire embodies the trope of the homewrecker and like the feral cats threatens to destroy the family's domestic bliss. She makes several sexual advances towards Paul that he naively and unintentionally reciprocates causing tension in his and Lindsay's marriage.

Both Claire and the Crazy Cat Lady represent what Berland has termed "questionable women" (159) and are ultimately animalized, again borrowing from Berland's work, as "lusty" (171) in the case of Claire, who was unfaithful in her marriage and a threat to her sister's, and "mentally ill" (171) in the case of the Crazy Cat Lady. Both women are themselves strays: The Crazy Cat Lady strays entirely from the social conventions of marriage and motherhood, whereas Claire strays from her own marriage bed and attempts to crawl into that of her sister. Even the trailer for *Strays* sets the two sisters apart as antagonists in this domestic showdown: Domestic Lindsay is shown retrieving items from the fridge, and immediately after, Claire, adulteress and unabashed temptress, is shown seductively applying lipstick while gazing at her reflection in a *vanity* mirror.

In *Passional Zoology* (1852), Alphonse Toussenel describes the cat as: "An animal so keen on maintaining her appearance ... so eager for caresses, so ardent and responsive, so graceful and supple ... an animal that makes the night her day. and who shocks decent people with the noise of her orgies can have only one single analogy in this world, and that analogy is of the feminine kind" (qtd. in Vocelle 247). Cats, already condemned in gendered terms as cunning, disloyal, hypersexual, and promiscuous, when firmly cemented under the category of pet in the Victorian era, earned an equally gendered reputation as vain, frivolous, and spoiled. Like Claire, who condemns her husband as neglectful, but also forsakes her own domestic responsibilities through infidelity and her refusal to bake cookies, cats are imagined as enjoying the comforts and spoils of domestic life without ever fully adhering to its mandates. Toussenel continues: "Lazy and frivolous and spending entire days in contemplation and sleep, while pretending to be hunting mice … incapable of the least effort when it comes to anything repugnant, but indefatigable when it is a matter of pleasure, of play, of sex, love of the night. Of whom are we writing, of the (female) cat or the other?" (qtd. in Vocelle, 247). Charles Dickens continued this trend in his 1860–61 collection *The Uncommercial Traveler*, wherein he writes: "There [is] a moral and politico-economical haggardness to [cats].… In appearance, they are very like the women among whom they live. They seem to turn out of their unwholesome beds into the street.… They leave their young families to stagger about the gutters" (qtd. in Vocelle 277).

Feline-feminine correlations have a recurrent theme: straying, often accompanied by the conjoined themes of animal amorality, selfishness, vanity, and the abandonment of predetermined responsibilities. L.A. Vocelle notes "Chaucer highlighted the belief that it was a woman's nature to stray just like a cat" (123). Bartholomew Angilcus, author of the compendium *De Proprietatibus Rerum* (thirteenth century), argues that a cat that "normally parades around the neighborhood proud of its appearance can be kept at home by singeing its fur" (qtd. in Rogers 35–36). Nicholas Bozon (1320) similarly comments: "Just as a cat can be made to stay at home by shortening her tail, cutting her ears and singeing her fur, women can be kept there by shortening the trains of their dresses, disarranging their headdresses and staining their clothes" (qtd. in Vocelle 123). Medieval preachers also applied feline character-istics to vain women (Rogers 36), and this association has persisted into the modern age and is prevalent in *Strays* through the character of Claire.

The Jarrets settle into their new home. The camera frequently switches perspectives, and the audience's viewpoint blends with that of the cat. We later learn that the owner of this shared gaze—between cat, camera, and audience—is a large, feral tom-cat (from here on referred to as "Tom") who stalks the family from the periphery of their property while secretly living in their cellar among a colony of feral cats. Tom is not fully visualized to the audience until about halfway into the film, although he is ever-present through the camera's frequent switching of perspectives and Paul's frequent sneezing, as he is allergic to cats. However, we do catch a glimpse of the film's antagonist when, while driving, the family hits something causing them to veer off the road and into a ditch. Paul asks "what was that?" and Lindsay, catching a brief glimpse of a cat trotting away from the scene unfazed, replies "bad luck," evoking a commonplace negative feline stereotype and the implication of cats having nine lives.

We first fully view Tom when a repair man enters the cellar to fix the phone line and is viciously killed by the invading colony of cats at Tom's behest. At the same time, while in the attic, Lindsay discovers a mother cat and kitten living there. She lovingly places them in a wicker basket and introduces them to picturesque and doll-like Tessa. The imagery evokes the "refeminized ideology of natural innocence" (Berland, "Symbiotics" 157) ascribed to cats in Victorian culture and is vividly reminiscent of a Victorian greeting card (see Figure 2). Lindsay surprises Paul at his office, with their daughter and the kitten in tow, and finds him and Claire in an inappropriate embrace. In an act of defiance driven by revenge, Lindsay insists that they are keeping the mother cat and kitten despite Paul's allergies and distaste for cats. Later, the couple continues to argue as the camera focusses on a vent in their bedroom, where Tom watches on, seemingly revelling in this domestic disturbance. The couple angrily go to bed, and in the morning, Paul awakens to find his pillow soaked in cat urine and a dead rat at the foot of his side of the bed. He blames the mother cat and kitten, and when Lindsay protests his accusations and suggests they call a vet, Paul proclaims, "I don't need a vet to teach me how cats behave. I know how they behave. That's why I have a dog!" At that moment, he realizes that Benny, the family dog, is missing. Unlike the Crazy Cat Lady, the Jarrets had kept the cat door (or in their case, the dog door) locked until Paul, distracted by his argument with Lindsay the night before, had unlocked the door to let Benny out and forgotten about him. With this action, opposing worlds have now been bridged; the boundary has broken, the fortress is now penetrable, and the domestic is rendered acutely vulnerable.

Figure 2: Left: still from *Strays*; right: Victorian greeting card.

Paul eventually finds Benny, injured and yelping, under the porch stairs. They call a vet to their home, and as he tends to Benny, they inquire about the scene in their bedroom. Upon inspecting the scene, the vet suggests that a dominant male cat could be responsible "especially if he's feral." When asked by Lindsay to explain the term, the vet responds "Gone wild." Taken aback, Lindsay questions if they have a wild cat living in their backyard to which, in a quote that encapsulates the oscillating nature of ferality, the vet clarifies: "No. A wild cat, a real wild cat like an ocelot, if they saw you, they'd run. But a feral, well, they've been around people all their lives, so they're not afraid at all. Makes them much more dangerous than any wild cat." It is its very proximity to and familiarity with human and domestic realms that renders the feral dangerous.

Later, while Paul is at work, Lindsay checks on Tessa only to discover that her crib is filled with cats (see Figure 3). The image recalls the Crazy Cat Lady referring to her cats as "my babies" and echoes the deformed maternity of the witch-familiar pairing and early modern fears of familiars sneaking into cribs to suffocate babies. Lindsay, expecting her child may be injured or suffocating under the weight of the cats, frantically throws them from the crib before noticing Tessa, terrified, and weeping the corner. When she rushes to comfort her daughter, she is confronted by Tom who, aided by his feral colony, goes on the attack. The film then erupts into chaos as the human characters are launched into a frantic showdown with the invading cats. During the struggle, the home literally and symbolically collapses all around them. Lindsay fends off Tom's violent advances with fluffy pillows and a flower vase (symbols of feminine domesticity) before retreating with Tessa and hiding in her playhouse (a microcosm of the domestic). Claire arrives at the house and, surprised by Tom, falls over a banister to her death. Soon after, Paul arrives and he and Tom become locked in an epic battle of multi-species masculinity. Tom scratches and bites at Paul's neck as he unsuccessfully attempts to fling the cat from his body. Eventually, Paul notices a flickering electric wire. He tentatively holds the wire up and goads Tom towards him. Tom leaps onto Paul who plunges the wire into Tom's open mouth, electrocuting and killing him. Paul stares at the dead cat before, in a moment of apparent comic relief, he sneezes into his face and tosses his corpse to the floor. Culture triumphs over nature, domesticity prevails, and Paul's masculinity is effectively restored.

Figure 3: Still from *Strays.*

Conclusions

> Those who'll play with cats must expect to be scratched.
> —Miguel de Cervantes (*Don Quixote de la Mancha* 222)

Anat Pick argues that "cinema [can act as] an apparatus for the disciplining of [nonhuman] bodies, but it is also a space in which these disciplinary practices are publicly negotiated and so potentially resisted"

(315). Although by the end of *Strays* the patriarch Paul eventually triumphs over the colony leader Tom—his feline shrieks as he's electrocuted echoing those of felines past tortured during festivities like the Faire le Chat and Katzenmusik (Darnton)—and the harmony of the family unit is restored (in part through the death of Claire), the film ends with a cliff hanger. The family is forced to give up their dream home and while the remaining cats are seized by animal services (to a likely fate of euthanasia), the film ends with a new couple coming to view the property. We hear an innocent, yet menacing, squeak of the surviving kitten, and the perspective again shifts to the camera-cat hybrid. We are left to assume that the surviving colony member will pick up where his father left off, seizing ownership of the household, wreaking havoc on its new occupants, and pissing all over their newly acquired domestic bliss.

Carl Jung, highlighting the connection between women and cats, infers that cats "resembled women...'because cats are the least domesticated of the domesticated animals'" (qtd. in Rogers 139). United by common tropes, shared stereotypes, and entangled histories, women and cats arouse anxieties that their primal animality always has the potential to rear its fanged head no matter how domesticated they become. In naturecultures, as Rogers observes the following:

> Cats conveniently represent what men have long and bitterly complained of in women: they do not obey.... Men who cannot control women as they would like to, associate them with animals that cannot be controlled.... [This] association was used to censure wives for incorrigible insubordination or to reduce them to unobtrusive little homebodies. Cats enhanced the sexual allure of women, but also supplied images of passive softness or lasciviousness or cold unresponsiveness or treachery. The qualities that are simply natural in a cat are immoral in a woman, and their immorality in the human context redounds upon the cat's character. (140)

The anxiety and terror aroused by women-cat pairings must be pacified through complacent imagery, belittled through jokes, or punished with violence. This is evidence of their enduring subversive power. The cat evokes a serpent-in-the-garden anxiety about the dual nature of womanhood—that Mary-Eve and virgin-whore dichotomies can collapse within a woman when she is permitted to stray too far from domestic confines and into the abject realm of her animal nature. The cat is used as a more intimately familiar incarnation and convenient surrogate of the serpent—a reminder that we are not safe from its temptation even in our own homes. The serpent may be in the garden, but the cat is in the cradle. The rebellious cohistories of women and cats are subtly evoked as reminders and warnings that the rebellion is never entirely quelled and that if not contained or controlled, the animal spirits of these two domesticated creatures may very well rear fanged heads and clawed paws. And no marriage bed or singed fur, no chastity belt or tail amputation, can keep them from straying.

Works Cited

"A Midsummer Nice Dream." *The Simpsons,* Season 22, episode 16, Gracie Films and 20th Century Fox Television, 13 Mar. 2011.

Barstow, Anne Llewellyn. *Witchcraze: A New History of the European Witch Hunts.* Pandora Publishing, 1994.

Berger, John. *About Looking.* University of Massachusetts Press, 1980.

Berland, Jody. "Cat and Mouse: Iconographics of Nature and Desire." *Cultural Studies,* vol. 22, no. 4, Routledge, 2008, pp. 431–54.

Berland, Jody. "Cat and Mouse: Symbiotics of Social Media." *Virtual Menageries: Animals as Mediators in Network Cultures.* MIT Press, 2019, pp. 149–74.

Boehrer, Bruce. "Gamer Gurton's Cat of Sorrows" *English Literary Renaissance,* vol. 39, no. 2, 2009, pp. 267–89.

Cervantes, Miguel de. *Don Quixote de la Mancha.* Francisco de Robles, 1605.

Darnton, Robert. *The Great Cat Massacre and Other Episodes in French Cultural History.* Basic Books, 1984.

Federici, Silvia. *Caliban and the Witch: Women, the Body, and Primitive Accumulation.* Autonomedia, 2004.

Fudge, Erica. *Animal.* Reaktion Books, 2002.

Haraway, Donna J. *Manifestly Haraway.* University of Minnesota Press, 2016.

Jackson, Louise. "Witches, Wives, and Mothers: Witchcraft Persecution and Women's Confessions in Seventeenth-Century England." *Women's History Review,* vol. 4, no. 1, 1995, pp. 63–84.

Kramer, Heinrich, and Jacob Sprenger. *The Hammer of the Witches: A Complete Translation of the Malleus Maleficarum*. Translated by Christopher S. Mackay. Cambridge University Press, 2009.

Mivart, St. George. *The Cat: An Introduction to the History of Backboned Animals Especially Mammals*. J Murray, 1881.

Pick, Anat. "Executing Species: Animal Attractions in Thomas Edison and Douglas Gordon." *The Palgrave Handbook of Posthumanism in Film and Television*. Hauskeller, M., T.D. Philbeck, C.D Carbonell, eds. Palgrave Macmillan, 2015.

Purkiss, Diane. *The Witch in History, Early Modern and Twentieth Century Representations*. Routledge, 1996.

Rogers, Katherine M. *Cat*. Reaktion Books, 2006.

Strays. Directed by John McPherson, performances by Kathleen Quinlan, Timothy Busfield, and Claudia Christian. Niki Marvin Productions and MCA Television Entertainment, 1991.

"*Strays* (1991)–Official Trailor." *YouTube*, uploaded by ScreamFactoryTV, 6 Mar. 2024. https://www.youtube.com/watch?v=QagMqrxsMMo. Accessed 17 Jan. 2025.

Vance, Lash Keith, Jr. *Theorizing Space in the Early Modern Period*. University of California, Riverside, ProQuest Dissertations Publishings, 2000.

Vocelle, L.A. *Revered and Reviled: A Complete History of the Domestic Cat*. Great Cat Publications, 2016.

Wells, Paul. *The Animated Bestiary: Animals, Cartoons, and Culture*. Rutgers University Press, 2009.

Wiesner-Hanks, Merry. *Christianity and Sexuality in the Early Modern World: Regulating Desire, Reforming Practice*. Routledge, 2000.

Will, George F. "Millions and Millions of Cats." *The Washington Post*, 13 July 1997, https://www.washingtonpost.com/archive/opinions/1997/07/13/millions-and-millions-of-cats/895adbal-aef2-4cf0-bb0b-9cdd0d8683a2/. Accessed 17 Jan. 2025.

14.

Releasing the (M)other within: Jeanette Winterson's Feral Journey from *Oranges Are Not the Only Fruit* to *Why Be Happy When You Could Be Normal?* [1]

Else Werring

The relation to the mother is a mad desire, because it is the dark continent par excellence. It remains in the shadow of our culture, it is night and hell ... our society and our culture operate on the basis of an original matricide

—Irigaray, "Body" 10–11

As Freud so elegantly theorized, this involves asking how the animal infans becomes human, or how the potential for animal life becomes subjectified.

—Griselda Pollock, Introduction 15

This chapter posits Jeanette Winterson as a feral feminist and Deleuzian "becoming-animal" through a reading of her daughterly journey from her debut novel *Oranges Are Not the Only Fruit* (1982, from here on referred to as *Oranges*) to her midlife memoir *Why Be Happy When You Could Be Normal* (2011, from here on referred to as

Happy). Winterson's ferality is closely tied to the motif of the mother. Both *Oranges* and *Happy* are matricidal texts—that is, texts in which a daughter reworks her internalized mother in an ongoing process of self-overcoming.[2] In *Oranges*, Winterson created herself as a linguistic turn feminist, weaving her fictional self into a colourful fabric of mythical and literary language. Thirty years and a "bout of madness"[3] later, the same story is retold in *Happy*. Linking feral theory to Deleuzian feminism, I argue that Winterson, through cyclically repeating her daughterly process, resists the patriarchal injunction to separate mothers from daughters. While the maternal body has long been contested in feminist theory, and motherhood has often been deemed unworthy of academic interest (O'Reilly), Winterson opens "lines of flight"[4] for reexperiencing daughterhood as a return to a long-lost interrelated self and acknowledging a maternal role in this process. Through ambivalently mourning the lost mother, Winterson enables a feral release of the animal within, thus challenging the binaries human-animal, nature-culture, and body-mind.

How the mother has been linked to the animal, not only in patriarchal thought but also by feminists like Simone de Beauvoir and Julia Kristeva,[5] makes the maternal an interesting category to think alongside the feral. The patriarchal motherhood institution (Rich) has been used through history to subjugate and domesticate the human female, and a feminist liberation from oppressive and essentialist maternal constructions has been necessary. But it is also arguable that much feminist theory, for fears of essentialism, has gone too far in its disavowal of the maternal body and that this has created a "domesticated feminist"—thus, necessitating a second feral undoing, working through a return to maternity, all the while being careful, of course, not to return to the mother as a patriarchal and reified construct. [6] Winterson's work provides an excellent opportunity for doing this. Her quest, in both *Oranges* and *Happy*, is one of reclaiming her body from the grips of heteropatriarchy through engaging with the mother-daughter relationship and a spiralling, repetitive narrative style. Even though it is her own body Winterson is out to reclaim, and not the maternal body per se, the two seem, for Winterson, inextricably linked—in Irigarayan terms, "the one doesn't stir without the other" (Irigaray, *And the One* 56).

Oranges and *Happy* both, in separate ways, linger with the mother-daughter body, neither as an essence nor entirely as a social construct but rather "a play of forces" and "spatio-temporal variables" (Braidotti

20–21). The difference between the two books lies in what sort of body Winterson is trying to reclaim. While *Oranges* displays the narrating I's active role in constructing herself linguistically and symbolically as a demonic, queer, and ludically postmodern agent, what seems to occur in *Happy*, by contrast, is a *dissolution* of agency through an encounter with passivity, narrative gaps, and non-knowledge. *Happy*'s return to the mother sketches a tentative link between the mother-daughter body and animality, affect, and the extra-linguistic, differentiating it from the intertextual play of *Oranges*,[7] Significantly, *Happy* adds Winterson's birth mother to the picture (who gave her up for adoption at six weeks old).

In what follows, I begin with some introductory remarks on *Oranges* and *Happy* and the role of the mother in Winterson's work. I then connect the concept of "the feral" to sexual difference theory and explore the link between maternity and animality. Next, I briefly outline Deleuzian feminism and the significance of Rosi Braidotti's version to my reading of Winterson. I then show how the "Winnet Stonejar" myth at the end of *Oranges* is linked to an important aspect of Winterson's repetition in *Happy*; namely, Winnet's insistence on remaining in an open and liminal position vis-à-vis her daughterly selves and different versions of her internalized mother. The last part of my chapter presents *Happy*'s repetition-with-a-difference of the *Oranges* plot and argues that this repetition unleashes a Deleuzian writing-as-becoming-animal in the second half of *Happy*.

Winterson and the Mother-Daughter Plot

Oranges is a semiautobiographical Kunstlerroman and Bildungsroman, as well as a lesbian coming out novel, where the young protagonist must separate from her humorously rendered, gothic-monstrous, and Christian-fundamentalist adoptive mother to become herself. The novel won the Whitbread prize for best first fiction, was made into a BBC TV series, became part of British school syllabi, and has, since its publication, received much critical attention, most of which points in either of two directions: one on Winterson as a lesbian writer and the other on postmodern aspects of her work (Mekinen 2). While the mother-daughter relationship is a concern in many of these studies, it tends to be secondary to other themes, such as the novel's intertextual elements, its subversion of the Bildung tradition, Winterson's treatment of love, time, and space, or her work's relation to lesbian and queer theory. Laurel Bollinger is an exception. She foregrounds the mother-daughter relationship in her analysis of Winterson's intertwining of her tale with the biblical Book of Ruth.[8] This chapter continues on the path staked out by Bollinger by emphasizing the mother-daughter theme as my primary concern. My main focus, however, is not on *Oranges'* narrative but on Winterson's repetition of it in *Happy*. Through highlighting the connections between maternity, animality, and ferality, repetition and materiality, and "matter" and "mater," I argue that *Happy* epitomizes a Deleuzo-Guattarian "becoming-animal."

In *Happy*, written almost thirty years after *Oranges*, Winterson claims that all her work, in some way or other, builds upon the underlying theme of her mother: "I have written love narratives and loss narratives—stories of longing and belonging. It all seems so obvious now—the Wintersonic obsessions of love, loss and longing. It is my mother. It is my mother. It is my mother" (160). Even though all of Winterson's fiction draws on her life experience, *Happy* is her first memoir. Its first two-thirds engage with *Oranges'* plot but warns its readers that the truth coming out this time is harsher: "And I suppose the saddest thing for me, thinking about the cover version that is *Oranges*, is that I wrote a story I could live with. The other one was too painful" (6). The last third of *Happy* covers new ground. It describes how *Oranges'* wound has been reopened for Winterson in midlife due to her recent break up from girlfriend Deborah Warner, which triggers her attachment trauma. Her "lost loss" (*Happy*, 161) resurfaced around the same time as Winterson found her adoption papers and began a search for her birth mother. This process eventually led to a nervous breakdown, culminating in a suicide attempt, from which, thankfully, Winterson survived to tell the tale. (*Happy*, 155–230; Werring, 12–13).

The story of child abuse related in *Happy* is chilling, even to readers familiar with the *Oranges* plot. Jeanette was "beaten as a child and learned early never to cry" (2). Mrs. Winterson was subject to labyrinthine, unpredictable dark moods (119), and Jeanette was often locked out of the house overnight—or inside the coal hole (21). Despite these harrowing incidents, however, Mrs. Winterson's extraordinary persona, often found in a deckchair, reading sensationalist literature about hell (104), defies easy categorization:

> She was a flamboyant depressive; a woman who kept a revolver in the duster drawer, and the bullets in a tin of Pledge. A woman who stayed up all night baking cakes to avoid sleeping in the same bed as my father. A woman with a prolapse, a thyroid condition, an enlarged heart, an ulcerated leg that never healed, and two sets of false teeth- matt for everyday, and a pearlized set for "best." (*Happy* 1)

Mrs. Winterson unquestionably had a dark side, but her monstrous side blended into a larger mosaic beyond good and evil—one that we, as readers, feel some degree of warmth for amid our horror and sadness on behalf of little Jeanette. If anything, she elicits mixed feelings, invoking Melanie Klein's theory of maturation as the ability to embrace and incorporate ambivalence. Upon finding her birth mother, Ann, Winterson notes that she does not feel a biological connection and that she cannot be the daughter Ann wants, any more than she could be Louie Winterson's daughter. She hates it when Ann criticizes her adoptive mother: "She was a monster, but she was my monster" (229).

Winterson acknowledges her artistic and writerly debt to her mother's incessant biblical teachings: "My mother taught me to read from the book of Deuteronomy because it was full of animals (mostly unclean)" (26). Mrs. Winterson was a gifted storyteller "in charge of language" (27), and Jeanette was "fed words and shod with them," which became the key to her eventual escape. Sadly, she had to break with her mother in the process, and Winterson's pervasive melancholia over—and compulsion to repeat—this break reverberates through her work.[9]

Winterson's adoptive mother has kept recurring in various guises[10] through much of her fiction since *Oranges* and has, according to one critic, become "one of the great horror mothers of English language literature" (Garner).[11] Julie Ellam points out how "the constant *fort/da*[12] return to the story of the adopted child in Winterson's fiction appears to have been used unconsciously as a place to master her own feeling of loss" (222). Since 2000, moreover, Winterson's work juggles two mothers: Her birth mother, who gave her up for adoption at six weeks old, makes fictive appearances in *Lighthousekeeping* (2004) and *The Stone Gods* (2007) and is rendered autobiographically in *Happy*. It is arguable that a shadow of the birth mother also flows as a watery undercurrent through much of Winterson's fiction.[13]

I read Winterson's continued occupation with mother- and daughter-hood as subversive because it maps onto a social field where the maternal body still flutters as an eerie shadow, haunting not only patriarchy (Irigaray, "Body"), but also strands of feminism (Braidotti; Cavarero; Jacobs; Kawash; O'Reilly; Wieland).

Feral Theory

The term "feral" refers to "wild strains of an otherwise domesticated species or to an organism that has reverted to a wild condition following escape from captivity" (Allaby). Ferality signals liminality and has often been perceived as an incommodious condition between the more accepted wild and domesticated states. The feral also has "positive associations with powerful spaces ... such as borderlands, margins, thresholds, hybrids, becomings, standpoints, situated knowing, nomadism, etcetera" (Milne 1). According to Anne Milne, the feral can be a useful lens through which to read "feminine spaces where meaning is not resolved" (2). Insofar as the maternal body constitutes an unresolved space for feminism (Kawash; O'Reilly), Winterson's continued tarrying with the maternal connects her work to the feral. For Nick Garside, the feral citizen is a "perpetual wanderer," free from commitment to any particular theory—but one who "inevitably disturbs and incites communities s/he visits" (7). The "wanderer" is a significant trope in all of Winterson's work, which may be aligned with Braidotti's "nomadic subject" (Meyer) and sustains the paradoxical, open, and unresolved as a central pillar (Bijon).[14]

Giorgio Agamben argues that the "anthropological machine" works to define the human by asserting what it is not i.e., "animal" or "savage" (37). This leads to a negative definition of man without which he is "faceless" (7, 30–31). But if we remove ourselves from the animal, in ourselves and in the world, we will remain in the dark, according to Agamben (Restuccia 415). To render the "anthropological machine" inoperative, he argues, we need to expose the emptiness at the core of "man"—the "hiatus between man and animal" (Agamben 92) and to risk ourselves in this emptiness and "non-knowledge" (91), which is connected to a special sort of inactivity. Agamben theorizes feral man (a human figure without language) as a messenger of man's inhumanity, a displayer of his fragile identity and a lack of a face of his own (30).

This points to how a significant way in which "man" has distinguished

himself from "the animal" is through specific understandings of "rationality" and "language." In *The Animal That Therefore I Am,* Jacques Derrida
argues that sexual difference and animal difference "trouble the same
horizon," since "they both infringe upon the fiction of the subject that
calls itself man" (qtd. in Turner 121). Just as women have been historically
marginalized through language, animals are often linguistically reduced
to objects. Derrida further troubles the distinction between speaking
and non-speaking or a strict separation between human and animal
communication. Such distinctions fail to take the unconscious into
account, as well as to consider the materiality of speech and the corporeality of language (*The Animal,* 125). This connects Derridean thought
to feminist theories on the silencing of women's voices and the desire to
speak otherwise. In *Philosophy and the Maternal Body,* Michelle Boulos
Walker claims that "the maternal body operates as the site of women's
radical silence" (1). But she, like Derrida and Agamben, troubles the
distinction between language and silence and questions the assumption
that silence must necessarily mean the absence of language. Building on
Luce Irigaray, Boulos Walker argues that Plato's philosophy represents
a male fantasy to self-engender through an erasure of the fleshy maternal body. Instead of staying with the trouble of maternal flesh, Plato's
philosophy (and a long tradition continuing to this day) reappropriates
it as the mute matter-passive ground from which active mind projects
itself forward. Both Deleuze and Irigaray aim to subvert the Platonic
version of the body-mind distinction through their different yet similar
theories of speaking/writing otherwise. As we shall see, Jeanette Winterson's "Winnet Stonejar" myth, at the end of *Oranges,* may be read as
taking issue with Plato as well—an aspect of *Oranges* that is repeated
with a difference in *Happy.* In both *Oranges* and *Happy,* Winterson's
in-betweenness regarding the terms "body" and "mind" and "mother"
and "daughter" are linked to a certain understanding of madness—not
as mental illness but rather as acts of feminist subversion.

In Kristeva's theory of abjection (*Powers*), there is a pervasive connection between the animal and the maternal. Such a connection also
shows up frequently in de Beauvoir's *The Second Sex,* combined with an
urging women to leave behind the animal realm of "immanence" in
order to "transcend" as humans (73, 165, 194, 524). The animal-feminine
link must be approached with caution, lest it reaffirms damaging constructions of both the maternal and the animal (Johnson). But in light of

the new materialist critique of liberal humanism, returning to the mother trope—like the animal trope—harbours subversive potential. The maternal shares with the animal that they are perceived as mysterious, unknown objects whose existence threatens the clean, unified body (Johnson). What is to gain through a return to the mother-animal matrix is a richer theory of subjectivity, embracing self-conceptions that acknowledge "embodiment, animality, physicality, dependence and vulnerability" (Russell 4). It is this self-conception, as contrasted with the autonomous subject of liberal humanism, that is at stake both for Winterson and in Deleuzian feminism.

Repetition, Becoming and the Matter-Mater link

Feminists building on the work of Gilles Deleuze and Félix Guattari tend to begin from the premise that the liberal humanist view of subjectivity needs scrutiny (Buchanan; Stark 7). Like other poststructuralists, they underline how liberal humanists view the human as universal man—a rational animal with language. This definition has worked to the exclusion of women, children, animals, queer and disabled people, as well as people of colour, who have all been forced to carry the burden of the irrational body. Deleuze's philosophy builds on Spinoza's monism, which rejects the philosophical and historically gendered privileging of the mind over the body (Stark 5). In *Difference and Repetition,* Deleuze argues that we need to think differently about difference; not defined negatively as the other of identity, but as a deeper form of untamed difference that is positive and generative and does not need an outside to define itself. This concept of difference resembles what Luce Irigaray, Elizabeth Grosz, and Braidotti describe as sexual difference.

The aim of Deleuzo-Guattarian "Schizoanalysis" is to break up "molar" (as in solid and unified) units and become a "molecular" self, speaking with multifarious voices. In *Difference and Repetition,* Deleuze argues that "the repetition of return" exposes us to a "demonic power" which might make us ill but also heals us (qtd. in Ansell Pearson 73). The repetition is one allowing for difference, like different performances of the same piece of music. Arguably, Winterson's constant repetitions of her adoptive mother (and also her birth mother) are Deleuzian in this sense.

Rather than blank slates onto which society writes its script, Deleuzian bodies are always already alive, affective, and forceful. This means that there is no strict nature-culture distinction because bodies and cultures interact from the beginning. To Deleuze and Guattari, the self is a "map": "open and connectable in all of its dimensions; it is detachable, reversible, susceptible to constant modification" (*Plateaus* 12).The aim of becoming is to connect oneself to the world and to other people but also to plants, animals, objects, technology, and ideas—to "construct one's own little machine, ready when needed to be plugged into other collective machines" (187). This theorizing of the body as "a machine" should not make us confuse it with a predetermined entity. What matters in terms of connection are not pure ideas but embodied affects—the ability to affect and be affected (*Plateaus* xv). It is bodies that affect and are affected, but the term "body" should not be taken to exclude the mind.

"Becoming" is connected to repetition and nonlinear time through which matter is released. Becoming-animal does not mean playing or imitating an animal; it involves "unbecoming-human" (Cimatti) in the sense that the rigid boundaries of liberal humanist subjectivity are diffused into a more enmeshed and interrelated mode of existence. Braidotti thinks we are at a moment in history where "the body strikes back" (16) and that the female feminist subject should "start with the revaluation of the bodily roots of subjectivity, rejecting any universal, neutral and consequently gender-free understanding of human embodiment" (22).[15]

For Braidotti, it is crucial to remember how the root of the term materialism is "mater." The material is at the root of the subject and at the same time "expresses the specificity of the female subject" (23). This fact has been denied in patriarchal history, with the effect that women have borne "materially and symbolically the costs of masculine privilege of autonomous self-definition" (23). For Braidotti, Irigaray's thought helps us on this quest through delving into the maternal imaginary: "[But] there is no sentimentality in this reappraisal of the maternal/material feminine. Irigaray acknowledges that motherhood is also the site of women's capture into the specular logic of the same" (24). Nevertheless, what we may gain is a source for women (and men) to investigate physical modes of perception, empathy, and interconnectedness that transcend androcentric thought: "Even the most traditional image, that of mother and child, can be repossessed by strategic repetitions and revisitations, for Irigaray, and by becoming de-stratified and de-territorrialized, for Deleuze" (24).

Winnet Stonejar

The ending of Winterson's *Oranges* illustrates how young Jeanette inhabited body and mind separately but felt homeless in both worlds. Winterson's matricidal writing is geared towards tearing down the wall between the two worlds to create a nomadic home from which to speak, live, and write freely. Winnet Stonejar is an anagram for Jeanette Winterson and casts young Jeanette as a sorcerer's apprentice. Mrs. Winterson plays the part of the sorcerer—father of this fable. Winnet is tricked by the sorcerer into his territory, where she learns his language, one that can travel in time and create reality. When Winnet looks about her in the wizard's room, she cannot see the couch the wizard talks of. "What couch?" she asks. "Why, that one, said the sorcerer, surprised. She looked again, and there it was" (*Oranges* 186). The sorcerer, a Platonic dualist, inhabits the realm of pure mind and mistrusts all things embodied.[16] He expects complete obedience from Winnet in return for teaching her about music and mathematics. When Winnet falls in love, the sorcerer throws her out, since her embodied version of love differs from his abstract ideal.[17] Luckily, however, it turns out the magician-father cannot take his magic—the creative power of language—back, even as he rejects his daughter. Winnet has to leave, lest her heart be turned to stone. But her father has fastened an invisible thread around her button to pull when he pleases (189).

Having realized the life of pure mind is not for her, Winnet is now cast into a woman's world of pure body, where she must conceal a part of herself to survive. She learns the words but not the language (195). But the world of the body is just as alienating to Winnet as that of the mind.[18] Winnet hears of a distant city where people do not "sow or toil" but contemplate the world (196). She longs to go there and eventually succeeds after an arduous descent through the underworld of her own body: she dreams of entering a spiral staircase running down into her gut. Winnet "must pass through the blood and bones that swill round the bottom step, in the huge space under her skin" (203).

The myth reflects and sums up Jeanette's story related in *Oranges* about finding an embodied release reading fiction in secret and how her illicit reading culminated in a dream of going to Oxford to study literature. But Winnet's academic journey turned out a disappointment.

Even so, the journey to the distant city of learning brings on a significant turning point in the Winnet fable: The narrating voice now switches from the third person/Winnet to the first person/I (206). The city is full of towers, which the city dwellers seem obsessed with climbing. But the view from the top is chilling: "At the top there is a keen wind and everything is so far away it's impossible to say what is what. There is no one to discuss it with" (206). Winnet ends up dreaming of firm ground and concludes that "If the demons lie within they travel with you" (206).

The fable ends with a return home by way of the last train. Jeanette sits in her carriage clutching a copy of *Middlemarch*, observing a sighing man, as the train halts in a snowstorm. A strange bundle enters, chanting "Bloody hell, bloody hell, bloody hell" (207). The bundle, a fat woman with a bad heart, gets stuck in the door but eventually squiggles her way in, as the sighing man starts muttering and eventually singing about love and the lack of it.

The train carriage, we infer, is Jeanette's nomadic self, undertaking a journey of rebirth. She had almost succeeded in separating from her mother before Mrs. Winterson persistently squeezes her way back into her psyche. Her new self, clutching *Middlemarch*, alludes to her dream of becoming a writer and the man muttering/singing about love foreshadows what she will be writing about, namely love and the lack of it. Jeanette concludes: "It is not one thing nor the other that leads to madness, but the space in between them" (207). Being stuck in a liminal position in between mind and body—and in between mother and daughter—may lead to madness. Jeanette nevertheless chooses this mad path.

The train journey symbolizes Jeanette's search for the lost body. But the lost body is entangled with the mother-daughter relation (Irigaray, *And the One*). Patriarchy is invested in separating daughters from mothers (Rich), meaning that a battle against patriarchy must include restoring this relationship, however difficult. Blaming a mother for her patriarchal parenting fails to acknowledge how that mother herself has been a victim. *Oranges*' ending remains open: Jeanette has left her mother yet also returned, as she will continue to do repeatedly through her artistic career. She will continue to sing her "song of love and the lack of it" (224). Jeanette's mother has tied a string around her button, to tug when she pleases

Oranges' Irigarayan "cat's-cradle" (DeLong) of literary, mythical, and plain prose points to young Jeanette taking the "linguistic" turn: By mastering language, she can, in effect "create" reality. But this does not mean that she can just get up and leave her past and her mother behind.

The power of the mother to pull her back suggests a certain material excess—a stickiness that shadows the critique levelled against the "linguistic turn" by the new materialist and posthumanist feminists. In the words of Susan Hekman: "We have learned much from the linguistic turn. Language does construct our reality. What we are discovering now, however, is that this is not the end of the story" (92).

Winterson echoes this insight at the end of *Oranges* before leaving her ending open. The open question of material stickiness and maternal excess is what Winterson dusts off in in midlife, through the writing of *Happy*.[19]

Winterson's "Matricidal" Journey from *Oranges* to *Happy*

Happy swivels back, almost thirty years later, to the same mother-daughter plot as *Oranges*. The first two thirds of *Happy* repeats but does so with a difference (Deleuze, *Difference*). What remains the same is how the mother-daughter plot is framed as a battle against the body-mind distinction. Louie Winterson (i.e., Winterson's mother) "didn't want her body resurrected because she had never, ever loved it" (*Happy*, 66). She esteemed a life of disembodiment, which meant death for herself and a chaste missionary's life for her daughter. The problem was not just that of her own or her daughter's bodies but all bodies in general:

> [Her] own, my dad's, their bodies together, and mine. She had muffled her own body flesh in clothes, suppressed its appetites with a fearful mix of nicotine and Jesus, dosed it with purgatives that made her vomit, submitted it to doctors, who administered enemas and pelvic rings, subdued its desires for ordinary touch and comfort, and suddenly, not out of her own body, and with no preparation, she had a thing that was all body. (21)

The "thing that was all body" was baby Janet, renamed Jeanette after adoption. Winterson imagines what it must have been like for herself as a baby to be subjected to the rule of someone who hated bodies: "I had lost my warm safe place, however chaotic, of the first person I loved. I had lost my name and my identity. Adopted children are dislodged. My mother felt that the whole of life was a dislodgement. We both wanted to go home" (23).

Mother and daughter shared a longing for home. But while Mrs. Winterson thought of home as an escape from the body, Jeanette thought of it as a place where she could fully embrace embodiment. Louie Winterson projected onto Jeanette the parts of herself that she found unacceptable—in much the same way as Irigaray describes patriarchal thought's historical projection onto women of all things embodied so that universal man and his concepts could be free of them (Irigaray, *Speculum*). Mrs. Winterson decided early on that her daughter was "the Wrong Crib" (*Happy* 53) and constantly watched her for signs of possession. By elevating herself to the status of pure mind and pious suffering, Mrs. Winterson transferred her body hatred onto her daughter, as well as to Jeanette's birth mother, Ann: "She invented many bad mothers for me, fallen women, drug addicts, drinkers, men-chasers. The other mother had a lot to carry but I carried it for her, wanting to defend her and feeling ashamed of her all at the same time" (220).[20]

Happy's last third describes Winterson's search, and eventually finding of, her birth mother, who displays an "ease in her body" that Jeanette feels she has inherited from her (216). Even if the finding of the birth mother presents a significant turning point in the story, it is not as simple as presenting a return to the essentialized maternal body. As Braidotti underlines, the Deleuzian body is "not an essence, let alone a biological substance, but rather a play of forces" (20–21).

To return home, yet again, in *Happy*, Winterson needs to revisit her past traumas because they contain the sources of embodied rejection that she still, in middle age, struggles with, even if they take a different form at this later time. The ending of *Oranges*, as we have seen, remains open because the world leaves Jeanette no space in which she can be both mind and body. She felt compelled to choose and ended up on the verge of madness in between. This Wintersonesque madness, however, should not be confused with mental illness. Rather, it seems connected to feminist interventions into discourses on sanity, rationality, and health—an implicit nod to theories articulated by Sandra M. Gilbert and Susan Gubar (*Madwoman*) and Elaine Showalter (*The Female*)—which constitutes a critique of the hystericizing of women "and the reclaiming of hysteria as a form of feminist resistance" (Gruen and Probyn-Rapsey, 2).

In the case of Winnet, and Winterson's work more generally, the madness in question may be linked to the daughter's desire for the mother which to Irigaray represents a "mad desire" and our culture's "dark continent" ("Body" 10). Gilbert and Gubar, for their part, connect the woman writer's madness to imaginative returns to Plato's cave, which in Plato's philosophy represents shadows, illusions, and irrationality. In their feminist reworking, "the womb-shaped cave is also the place of female power, the *umbilicus mundi,* one of the great ante-chambers of the mysteries of transformation" (*Madwoman* 95). Winnet refuses to settle her identity as a bounded agent, split off from her internalized mother (the loud, cursing tramp, as well as the Platonist master of language and reality), even as she does renegotiate her view of herself as an artist and prophet (the man singing about love) and a woman writer, indebted to a tradition of powerful women writers before her (herself clutching a copy of *Middlemarch*). She acknowledges her debt to her matrilineal heritage and follows Virginia Woolf's injunction to "think back through our mothers" (*Room* 76).

Winterson's fight against the body-mind distinction is a prominent feature of all her work. But since this fight contains so many different aspects, not least in terms of feminist interventions into the sex-gender-distinction, the way in which Winterson takes up the battle in *Happy* is different from the way in which she conducted it in *Oranges.* The enemy might be the same (patriarchal thought in all its forms), but different contexts demand different weapons. Jeanette's insistence on remaining in a liminal position points to seeds of a feral undoing already having started in *Oranges.*[21] The main gist of *Oranges,* however, points towards a linguistic turn undoing from the strictures of heteropatriarchal sex-gender systems. The new materialist turn happens later in *Happy.*[22] In order to show why, I shall compare two scenes from *Oranges* to the repeated narration of those same memories in *Happy.*[23] Through this, I want to explore the differences between these two texts as concerns Jeanette's relation to the body. The first episode concerns a hospital scene when Mrs. Winterson leaves her terrified daughter alone in the hospital. The second concerns the exorcism to which her mother subjected Jeanette to rid her of lesbianism.

Happy's Repetition with a Difference

Happy repeats an episode that was earlier depicted in *Oranges,* namely an incident where Jeanette experiences momentary deafness. Her mother assumes her deafness to have some religious import and does not take her to the hospital. In *Oranges*, Mrs. Winterson's religious interpretation of Jeanette's deafness is that she is in a state of rapture (31)—the story told in *Happy* is that Jeanette is believed to be possessed by the devil due to masturbation (53). Either way, Jeanette eventually has to have her adenoids removed. She is terrified of being left alone at the hospital by her mother, but Mrs. Winterson shows no mercy and refuses to sit by her daughter's bedside. This scene is linked to the title of the novel. Louie Winterson leaves Jeanette alone in hospital with only a letter and a bag of oranges—the only fruit—to symbolize her embodied presence (37). To Jeanette, this symbolic presence, devoid of the actual body, felt like a horrifying abyss. Winterson's quest in *Oranges* is partly about getting rid of the Platonic and Christian clean cut between body and thought and language—the injunction that in the beginning was the word because such a belief entails a rejection of our prelinguistic, corporeal beginning (Kristeva, *Revolution*). If oranges represent an absent body to Jeanette, her insistence that oranges are not the only fruit reinstalls herself as embodied presence (Werring 69).

Winterson's process in *Oranges* is one of mirroring her own experience using myths and fairy tales, an act that may be construed as Winnicottian, since for Donald Winnicott, mirroring is one of two central maternal functions (Werring 41–42, 70). In *Oranges*, the fictive character of "testifying Elsie" acts as facilitator for this maternal mirror through introducing Jeanette to the world of literature and the imagination (40). Fiction and the imagination are, for Winterson, connected to the body and were as such vehemently objected to by Mrs. Winterson, who "knew that Lawrence was a satanist and a pornographer" and set her daughter's books on fire (41). Elsie, in contrast, joyfully proclaims the link between fiction, body, and affect by gushing over Rossetti, Swinburne, and Yeats while boisterously ingesting Mrs. Winterson's oranges with Jeanette: "Elsie had no teeth, so she sucked and champed. I dropped my pieces like oysters, far back into the throat. People used to watch us, but we didn't mind" (40).

With Elsie at the hospital, orange juice is like breastmilk, although this life-sustaining liquid is consumed by mother and daughter together. Elsie is referred to in *Happy* as a fiction. Winterson frequently problematizes the fact-fiction binary in *Happy* and her other work, emphasizing how important it is for her to write herself as both so that her writing remains true to herself (Winterson, *Art*). She subverts her adoptive mother's oranges (symbolizing the absence of the maternal body) by inventing Elsie through whom oranges reintroduce maternal flesh. This flesh is not essentialized, however: It is not real breastmilk but alludes to the physical and symbolic attachment represented by it.

Oranges's fictive characters illustrate processes inside Jeanette, artfully blended with the bible, *Jane Eyre*, myths, and fables.[24] These fantastic and fictive elements are no longer there in *Happy*, which is written in a plainness of prose that, for one critic, makes it "unwintersonesque" (Sayers); another critic calls it "harrowing and candid" (Myerson). *Happy*'s plainness of prose seems designed to release affects from an extralinguistic, material excess.

The hospital scene in *Happy* is rewritten without testifying Elsie and is much shorter than its *Oranges* equivalent. The one evocative scene we are given this time is the image—lodged in Winterson's memory—of her mother's abandoning her in a high-sided children's bed. Jeanette scrambles over the bed's edge and runs after her, her mother's "tall, massy, solitary back in a Crimplene coat" (53) and the slippery feeling of polished linoleum under Jeanette's feet as she scrambles after her mother. The scene is initially rendered in the past tense, but then abruptly switches to the present in the following sentence: "Panic. I can feel it now" (53). Then follows an instant flash memory of child Jeanette's making up a story about a rabbit with no fur: "His mother gave him a jewelled coat to wear but a weasel stole it and it was winter..." (53–54). The flash is followed by another reflection in the present: "I suppose I should finish that story one day" (54). Winterson's narrating "I" takes over the Winnicottian function performed by Elsie in *Oranges*—namely, the function of mirroring and making sense of Jeanette's experiences. Memories from the past are pegged onto affects in the present. This mediating between past and present selves also seems to have a productive intent—constructing another sort of self for the future, one that has integrated traumatic memories while acknowledging the insufficiency of language to incorporate them. The frequent tense switches invoke the feral or animal aspect of herself: An animal lives in their present even if affected by memories. The tense switches invoke ferality as a liminal state between the wild (living in the present) and domestic (more time for boredom, daydreaming, and imaginative play with memories).

We may think of Winterson's tense switches in terms of what Brian Massumi calls "intensity," which "vaguely but insistently connects what is normally indexed as separate" (85). Intensity, states Massumi, is nonlinear "resonation and feedback giving rise to static-temporal and narrative noise," which creates a "temporal sink, a hole in time," an opening between activity and passivity: "Not exactly passivity, because it is filled with motion, vibratory motion, resonation. And it is not yet activity, because the motion is not of a kind that can be directed... toward practical ends" (Massumi 86). There is a marked difference between *Oranges'* active narrative style continually engaged in intertextual creation and the aesthetically speaking passive narrative voice we encounter in *Happy*. This is not to say that *Happy*'s narrative voice is per definition passive. It is active in the sense of being a clear and personal voice, but the activity of this voice is aesthetically more passive than the narrative voice of *Oranges*. Unlike Winterson's other work, *Happy* falls into line with the millennial memoir boom and, as mentioned above, is written in an "unwintersonian" plainness of prose. What we are witnessing in *Happy* is the voice of a narrator who is dissolving her identity as an artist, letting her everyday persona seep through and switching between active repetitions of her memories and a passive resignation or letting go.

A gap follows the hospital and rabbit episode in the text, signalling that the process engaging Winterson at this point is one of "anamnesis."[25] She is remembering a traumatic event from a time in her life before she had any idea of what constituted trauma. By repeating the traumatic memory to her adult self—who does have knowledge of trauma—Winterson prefers to go through an embodied reenactment in the present rather than creating a literary and fictive container through which to handle the memory.[26] For Reina van der Wiel, this means that Winterson's work, with the exception of *Oranges*, to a large extent remains stuck in a compulsion to repeat trauma rather than work through it. This begs the question of what working through trauma means. Van der Wiel's illuminating study, where she compares texts by Virginia Woolf and Jeanette Winterson, offers a complex model of artistic and writerly working through based in several strands of psychoanalytic theory, such as those of Christopher Bollas and Donald Winnicott. It seems, however, that van der Wiel's models of working through are more in tune with the British object-relations model of psychoanalytic thought than the Lacanian tradition (which is the intellectual inheritance of Kristeva and Irigaray). The Lacanian model places a stronger emphasis on the death drive and a split, decentred subjectivity (Luepniz). On the object relations model, working through trauma might mean something like a return to one's authentic true self. Based on the Lacanian understanding by contrast, a self cannot truly be made whole again, since it was never whole to begin with. A self is by nature decentred. Healing, on this scheme, is less about aesthetic integration through symbol formation than about incorporating shadow selves, digging out glimmers of hope and insight in the cracks of inner contradiction and chaos. On such an understanding of working through, almost disintegrating into madness may be a constructive step on the road towards healing.

According to Winterson in *Happy*, she has obfuscated her past: "For a writer, what you leave out says as much as those things you include.... And perhaps we hope that the silences will be heard by someone else, and the story can continue, can be retold" (8). This time, Winterson wants her reader to hear her silences rather than be carried away by her fantastic tales. What does it mean to hear silence? And why does Winterson find it so pressing that her readers engage in this activity?[27]

Ginette Carpenter notes how Winterson often inserts aspects of her autobiography into her texts and how her work highlights reading as an activity in-between embodied and disembodied modes of existence (77). Winterson often appeals to her readers, hoping they will hear her. She thereby accentuates the visceral qualities of reading, displaying a desire for change and transformation. Significantly, this signals how change, for Winterson, happens in an interrelational sphere, requiring that she herself be in a porous state of openness. Even if she is sitting alone writing, imagining her readers seems to induce a transformation of the writerly self. If we link these musings about silence and listening to Boulos-Walker's theory in *Philosophy and the Maternal Body*, we may argue that Winterson, through remembering and reenacting her daughterly longing or mad desire for the mother, affirms Boulos-Walker's positioning of the maternal body as a significant site of radical silence. As we saw above, this feminist point about the maternal body positions the mother— like the animal—as something that has been othered in patriarchal culture. Approaching both the animal and the mother within ourselves becomes an act of subversion. Like Agamben and Derrida (regarding the animal), Winterson displays a longing to explore what takes place in the hiatus between our so-called linguistic and extralinguistic selves. *Oranges* was about allowing more of a body to seep into Jeanette's definition of mind, into her language—the sort of "body" in question was the one

Mrs. Winterson associated with literature and fiction. *Happy*'s return to the body is concerned, instead, with the extralinguistic body, the body without analytic support. Winterson needs to retell the hospital scene from *Oranges* because she feels, thirty years later, that her wound has begun to fester beneath the cotton wool of Rossetti, Yeats, and testifying Elsie. Underneath is a quivering flayed rabbit (Werring 71). The image of the rabbit invokes a vulnerable, animal aspect of her psyche. What we learn from the second half of *Happy* is how this reenactment of her past prepared Winterson for a Deleuzian becoming-animal. Before delving into this becoming, however, I will compare another of Winterson's memories, which she repeats in *Happy*.

The memory in question is that of the exorcism to which Jeanette was subjected to rid her of her lesbianism.[28] Upon catching her daughter in bed with another girl, Mrs. Winterson colluded with the church community in deciding that "Satan must be cast out" through violent exorcism. In *Oranges*' version of the story, Jeanette's factual experience of being subjected to exorcism is mingled with her hallucinations about the "Orange demon" (138–40), her dream of "the city of Lost Chances" (*Oranges*,141–44) and the fable of the "secret garden, cunningly walled" (145–46). Many of the facts are similar in the two books: Jeanette's mother and senior members of the church sit at her house from morning till night, laying hands on her and trying to convince her to renounce "Satan" (i.e. her lesbian desire). When that does not work, the senior priest tells Mrs Winterson to lock Jeanette in the parlour for thirty-six hours without food or drink (*Oranges* 136–37; *Happy* 81–82). This is where the *Oranges* narrative turns into dreams and fables, while *Happy* remains with the naked facts: Jeanette is subjected to attempted rape, sleep deprivation, and repeated beatings by a church elder during those thirty-six hours. Like with the hospital memory, *Happy*'s narrative is shorter and less intended to lift factual experience to a higher level of literary meaning through the use of myth than *Oranges*. These memories invoke a brute physical violence without any fictional world of escape.

While *Oranges*' plot may be conceived of as young Jeanette constructing herself as a poststructuralist feminist, *Happy*'s plot, by contrast, portrays a feral undoing within poststructuralist feminism—emphasizing the feminist stance as a constantly shifting rather than fixed position. *Happy* explores the interface between activity and passivity and between language and silence, as well as exposing what Agamben calls the emptiness at the core of man—the "hiatus between man and animal" (92). In *Happy*, Winterson risks herself in affective nonknowledge, connected to a special sort of inactivity.

Becoming-Creature

As my above discussion of *Oranges'* Winnet Stonejar tale shows, Winterson positions herself within the feminist tradition of reclaiming hysteria, epitomized by the work of Gilbert, Gubar, and Showalter. I also connected this madness to Luce Irigaray's claim that the daughter's desire for the mother is a mad desire, not because there is something wrong with it but rather because there is something amiss in patriarchal culture. Winterson's tale of becoming-creature in *Happy*, which I now turn to, is a repetition with a difference of this theme; only this time, the madness also connects to the animal within.

Animal studies activists aiming to deconstruct the human-animal binary, such as Lori Gruen and Fiona Probyn-Rapsey, build on the tradition of Gilbert, Gubar, and Showalter in coining their term "Animaladies": "'Animaladies' conjoins two words, 'animal' and 'maladies' or, looked at another way, 'animal' and 'ladies.' Whichever two words you see when you look at it, it is always three: 'animal,' 'malady,' and 'ladies,' a triangulation within Animal Studies that draws gender, animals, and maladies together" (1). While Winterson's becoming-creature is not concerned with her engaging with animals or imagining becoming one, it may be linked to Deleuze and Guattari's concept of "becoming-animal," which connotes an opening towards a pack or multitude in one's inner being—a stranger within that also connects rhizomatically to other selves, entities, or concepts.[29] This stranger is not one but several, and for Winterson (if not for Deleuze and Guattari), such a stranger may be linked to an infant's connection to the mother, with all the blurring of boundaries this entails.[30]

Like *Oranges*, *Happy* is structured around a metafictional chapter reflecting on the nature of time, alluding to Virginia Woolf's *To the Lighthouse*, another text of matricidal mourning. The metafictional chapter in *Oranges*, "Deuteronomy," is mirrored by the *Happy* chapter "Intermission." It marks the end of Winterson's dialogue with the *Oranges* plot, and ends with the proclamation that she is now going to skip twenty-five years. We learn in the subsequent chapter that *Oranges'* publication and success were what led to the ultimate break with her mother, and that Winterson cannot quench the awareness of "something written over.... The ghost in the machine that breaks through into the new recording" (*Happy*, 157). This realization sends Winterson "down an abyss"; at the bottom of which, she realizes: "It is my mother. It is my mother. It is my mother" (160).

While Winterson acknowledges that she has wilfully opened the door to the abyss, her depiction of this fall mirrors how, for Deleuze and Guattari, becomings both are and are not acts of conscious choice. Winterson reflects: "The psyche is much smarter than consciousness allows. We bury things so deep we no longer remember there was anything to bury. Our bodies remember.... But we don't" (162). For Rosi Braidotti, this complex interplay between "active" and "passive" wills is missing from linguistic turn feminism. Her critique centres on how our lives are influenced by unconscious drives and affects, how often we thwart our most well intended rational plans if we allow ourselves to drift "nomadically, the way of the flesh" (*Metamorphoses*, 42–43, 47). Deleuze would argue that even when we do decide to embark upon a molecular becoming, we have no way of knowing in advance the extent of what it is we are consenting to. Becoming is always a leap into the unknown. (*Plateaus* 292).

Winterson's descent had her waking up at night, finding herself on all fours and shouting for her mother (*Happy*, 162). This was followed by suicidal thoughts, from which she found the occasional relief reading poetry (163). Winterson was in a place before she had any language, yet poetry somehow evaded her definition of what constitutes language, echoing Kristeva's distinction between semiotic and symbolic language (Kristeva, *Revolution*). Winterson seems to identify her mother's, her church's, and education's language with what Irigaray and Kristeva, following Lacan, call "the symbolic order," while other types, like poetry, (which for Kristeva was more intimately linked to prelinguistic memories of the mother) were still available to her. She also discovered that she was able to write children's books (*Happy*, 163–64).

Troubled by her oncoming crisis, Winterson decides to go to Paris, where her friend Sylvia takes care of her (165). Allowing herself to be cared for, however, does not make Winterson better but worse: "I had a sense of myself as a haunted house. I never knew when the invisible thing would strike—and it was like a blow, a kind of winding in the chest or stomach" (166). Winterson simultaneously starts to "become-nature," going for long walks and taking in the scenery of streams, hills, and fields. She eventually finds peace with her suicidal plans: "It was because I knew all this would be there when I was not that I thought I could go. The world was beautiful. I was a speck in it" (166).

Winterson feels serene as her suicide plan solidifies. The narrative goes on to depict facts and figures about gas, alluding to how she has researched that particular way to die, while skilfully making this aspect of the suicidal mind a gap in her text. After facts and figures about gas in the United Kingdom (166–67) and some sentences about feeling that her time is up, the actual suicide attempt is curtly related. Winterson tries with gas in the car, but the cat saves her (168), and she survives, about which the narrative concludes: "It was.... the fierce and unseen return of the lost loss. The door in the dark room had swung open. The door at the bottom of the steps in our nightmares. The Bluebeard door with the bloodstained key.... The room had no floor. I had fallen and fallen. But I was alive (169). The next two pages switch to a present tense metacommentary: "I often hear voices.... We assume people who hear voices do terrible things; murderers and psychopaths hear voices, and so do religious fanatics and suicide bombers. But in the past, voices were respectable—desired. The visionary and the prophet, the shaman and the wise woman. And the poet, obviously" (170).

These musings about madness tie in with Jeanette's goal in *Oranges*, namely that of becoming a prophet and a poet. What is different this time around, however, is that her prophet-poet persona blends in with an everyday voice, readily sharing her plain musings about life: "Going mad is the beginning of a process. It is not supposed to be the end result.... Probably we are less tolerant of madness now than at any period in history. There is no place for it. Crucially, there is no time for it" (171).

While this might be read as plain memoir jargon, it also has a Deleuzo-Guattarian ring to it because Deleuze/Guattari, too, are critical of a cultural tendency to medicalize what we might simply call life.[31] Reflecting on her own madness, Winterson continues: "There was a person in me—a piece of me... so damaged that she was prepared to see me dead to find peace" (171). Winterson refers to her creature as the sinister figure recognizable from fairy tales—the one with whom the hero makes a pact to get themselves out of trouble (172). Readers familiar with *Oranges* will recognize the "orange demon" as an earlier version of this figure, which emphasizes the multitudes at the core of subjectivity (*Oranges* 139). For Deleuze and Guattari, a becoming-animal process is always preceded by a pact with a demon, who "functions as the borderline of an animal pack, into which the human being passes or in which his or her becoming takes place, by contagion" (*Plateaus* 288).

Winterson labels her "becoming" a "bomb disposal":

> It is like bomb disposal but you are the bomb. That's the problem – the awful thing is you. It may be split off and living malevolently at the bottom of the garden, but it is sharing your blood and eating your food…. the creature loves a suicide… I am talking like this because what became clear to me in my madness was that I had to start talking – to the creature. (172)

The bomb metaphor recalls an earlier reference to adoption as a "bomb in the womb" (*Happy* 5), and of Winterson's process of searching out her birth mother as constituting a sort of explosion of self—that is, a fracturing into pieces. Winterson realizes that she has to "start talking to the creature" (172), and a voice outside her head—"not in it"—(172) tells her to get up and write. She writes a children's book because the "demented creature in me was a lost child. She was willing to be told a story. The grown-up me had to tell it to her" (173). The story Winterson makes up is about a "Creature Sawn in Two," one half male, the other female (173–74). It is a story about a split self, mirroring Deleuze and Guattari's aim with schizoanalysis—not to solidify a person into a well-integrated whole but to enable that person to handle inner contradiction and paradox. As Winterson starts talking to her creature, now described as part Mrs. Winterson, part Caliban, the creature starts talking back. When grown-up Winterson wants to talk about the coal hole, the creature replies reproachfully: "You'd sleep with anybody, wouldn't you?" (175). Winterson implements a daily dose of writing and placates the creature by reserving bouts of craziness for afternoons: "The afternoon madness session contained the oozing lunacy that had been everywhere. I noticed that I was no longer side-swiped and haunted. I was no longer being attacked by sweeping terrors and unnamed fears" (175).

About psychotherapy, Winterson states that she tried, but the creature refused to come to the sessions. The creature was "sometimes a baby. Sometimes she was seven, sometimes eleven, sometimes fifteen" (175). One day, however, Winterson notices while talking to the creature that she is using the word "us" rather than "you" to the creature. Some sort of deal has been struck. They both sit down and cry, agreeing that one day they "will learn how to love" (177).

The becoming-animal process begins when Winterson commits a semiconscious choice to open the door "at the bottom of the steps in our nightmares" (169). But once the door has been opened, there is no agent in charge of the process, at least not at first. Eventually, however, a "corporeal logic"[32] takes over and imposes some order in her chaos. Instead of talking to a therapist, Winterson begins writing and gardening and going for long walks outside. This is not the same as letting chaos take over by succumbing to drugs, self-harm, or extreme experiences, which Deleuze and Guattari guard against (*Plateaus*, 186–87). Winterson knows on some level that she does not want to see a doctor. She is also aware, however, of needing to safeguard herself and goes to see her friend Sylvia in Paris. The fact that she attempts suicide may be a sign that she does for a while "destratify too wildly" (Deleuzo-Guattarian jargon for not being careful enough), but another interpretation is also possible.

What if the fact that the cat saves her indicates that Winterson enters into some sort of molecular dialogue with her cat? If so, we might infer that Winterson knows, on some level, that the cat is there in the garage when she switches on her engine. Perhaps she suspects, somehow, that she may survive? Deleuze states that "a becoming-animal always involves a pack, a band, a population... in short, a multiplicity" (*Plateaus* 279). The fact that Winterson starts hearing voices suggests that she already feels like a multiplicity prior to her suicide attempt: The part of herself she wants to kill may be her molar self. There are, however, other parts of herself that she wants to survive. These are in league with nature, her voices, and her cat. Not all of her is a speck in nature, even if her molar personality feels that way. As Winterson suffers through her traumatic memories, she returns to a place of her split self. As Winterson finally befriends her creature, it is turned from an "it" or "she" to a "we" (177).[33]

The split self that Winterson finally embraces may be linked to Irgaray's idea of the "placental economy," a place of multiplicity and connection. For Irigaray, the placenta is a third term mediating between two: It works as a metaphor for intersubjective relations, where we can coexist (and cobecome) in a liminal state between separation and fusion. While this is a metaphor both for ideal forms of thought and action, there is also an element of material stickiness to the placenta, which recalls the roots of subjectivity in intrauterine life: a space forgotten or glossed over by the philosophers (Irigaray, "On the Maternal").[34]

This Wintersonian tale of madness is both a break and a continuation with Winnet Stonejar's mad desire for the mother (Irigaray, "Body"). It is one that turns madness into sanity. A similar subversion of madness may be linked to the deconstruction of the human-animal divide (Gruen and Probyn-Rapsey), as well as mad feminist ferality—in the sense of the in between nomadic subjectivity emphasized in feral theory (Garrard; Garside; Milne). This constitutes an embrace of the animal within, or in Agambean terms an acceptance of the hiatus between man and animal inside our human selves, discovered through inactivity and nonknowledge.

While Winterson emphasizes her daughterly madness vis-à-vis her adoptive mother already in *Oranges*, the feral aspects of this madness seem to be painted with broader strokes in *Happy*'s repetition and subsequent becoming-creature. While *Oranges*' "madness" performed a magnificent linguistic turn, *Happy* describes a material return, incorporating child selves partly like human-animal hybrid Caliban (175), partly like larger-than-life Mrs. Winterson, and partly like differentially aged child creatures who refuse to partake in grown-up discourses. These creatures do not accept being told what to do, but they do accept being told stories. This fact links madness again to the mother, since being told stories was an important part of Winterson's childhood.

Winterson's narrative is highly personal, and Deleuzians may object to my applications of his theory to her story, since Deleuze and Guattari are not interested in familial dramas. But Winterson's personal journey maps mother-daughter madness onto a larger social field. Her arduous search for birth mother Ann demonstrates how there is structural violence in language (labelled "masculine legalese" by Winterson) against which she relates feeling powerless to the point of surrender, simply emitting a cry and wetting herself in the judge's office (*Happy*, 189). Only through her powerful friends and education, we learn, is Winterson able to get through this process. As her readers, we imagine how this would have been entirely impossible for someone without Winterson's means: "The law is grandiose and designed to intimidate, even when there is no reason for it to do so" (190). That this is the sort of quest that might interest Deleuze and Guattari is evident from their book *Kafka – Toward a Minor Literature* (1986),[35] where Kafka goes through what we might call a familial quest for his father. Kafka's quest contains oedipal elements, but Deleuze and Guattari applaud it for bringing to life "the Russian bureaucracy," the "machinery of fascism," "judges, commissioners, and bureaucrats" (Deleuze and Guattari *Kafka*; Lorraine 176). Becoming-animal, they argue, tends to express the experiences of "minoritarian groups that are oppressed" (*Plateaus* 288).

Conclusion

Jeanette Winterson has repetitively, almost obsessively, continued to bring her adoptive mother to life in various guises through much of her fiction. More recently, she has also presented her readers with versions of her birth mother, who gave her up for adoption at six weeks old.

If we understand feminist ferality as a release from domestication, it is arguable that Winterson undergoes feral undoings in *Oranges* and *Happy*, which are both intimately linked to the protagonist's oscillation between separation and return to the mother. Underlying this oscillation is Winterson's battle with the body-mind distinction and how this distinction, since Plato, has treated matter-mater as the passive ground from which an active mind projects itself forwards (Boulos-Walker). By refusing to partake in heteropatriarchal linearity and a tidy mother-daughter separation and by, in Gilbert and Gubar's terms, returning to Plato's cave instead of escaping it on a "rational" search for truth, (Gilbert and Gubar, 93–107), Winterson chooses the alternative path of continuously tarrying with the past and with motherhood. This links Winterson's work to the feminist philosophy of birth tradition, representing a challenge to the historical prioritization of linear transcendence and philosophy toward death. What is gained through this perspective is a rethinking of feminist subjectivity as porous, enmeshed, and interrelated (Cavarero; Stone).

As Zoe Williams writes in her review for British newspaper *The Guardian*, *Happy* seems the most turbulent and least controlled of Winterson's books: "In Lilliputian fashion, what appears to be a straight narrative of her early life, is actually tying the reader down with a thousand imperceptible guy ropes, so that when she unleashes a terrible sorrow, there is no escaping it and no looking away." *Happy* insists that a return to motherhood—both individually and collectively—may harbour revolutionary potential, although anyone willing to try may have to risk a bout of madness.

Endnotes

1. An earlier version of this chapter can be found in chapter three of my master's thesis (Werring).

2. Melanie Klein, Julia Kristeva, and Luce Irigaray argue that Freud's theory is androcentric and that his view of female individuation, modelled on the Oedipus myth (in which the mother's voice is silent) is faulty and limited. They think Freud's theory of patricide glosses over an earlier matricide and theorizes matricide as a continuous process, recurring through life.

3. The Wintersonian definition of "madness" is not to be confused with mental illness but should rather be considered in light of feminist theory that theorizes a certain madness as subversion of what patriarchal thought considers rational or sane (Gilbert and Gubar; Showalter).

4. This is a term used by Deleuze and Guattari in *A Thousand Plateaus*, which refers to the movement away from established norms, structures, or boundaries. It represents the path that systems or selves take when they break free from established limitations and enter a state of becoming.

5. See also Johnson; Oliver.

6. Adrienne Rich distinguishes between motherhood as empowering experience versus patriarchal institution. Andrea O'Reilly, who argues that motherhood is the "unfinished business of feminism" thinks there has been an academic disavowal of motherhood because feminists have confused the two (i.e., they have theorized all aspects of motherhood as oppressive for women).

7. Although it is arguable that *Happy*, like Winterson's novel *Lighthousekeeping* (2004), alludes intertextually to Virginia Woolf's *To the Lighthouse*.

8. Bollinger foregrounds how Jeanette's return to the mother in *Oranges* constitutes a subversion of the masculine Bildung trajectory and how, unlike the classical fairy tale, with its passive heroine engaged in rivalry with the mother and stepmother, is subverted by Jeanette's return to the mother, intricately woven into the biblical story of Ruth

and Naomi as models of female loyalty, outside the bounds of heter-onormative marriage (Mekinen 33).

9. The last three paragraphs are adapted from Werring, 15–16.

10. *Boating for Beginners* (1985), *Sexing the Cherry* (1989), and *The Power Book* (2000) feature versions of the adoptive mother as well as versions of Winterson's coming-of-age narrative that we recognize from *Oranges*. *Lighthousekeeping* (2004) and *The Stone Gods* (2007) feature Winterson's birth mother. The theme of motherhood/adoption and the lost child is repeated in *The Gap of Time* (2015), while Winterson's own mother-daughter story is woven into the myth of Atlas in *Weight* (2008). *Frankissstein* (2018) plays with the topic of maternal, generative waters in various Irigarayan ways, as I shall argue in my Ph.D mono-graph (forthcoming).

11. Several critics have emphasized Winterson's play with horror/the gothic and its links to the mother trope as versions of Bakhtinian carnival and the grotesque (e.g. Haslett).

12. Freud theorizes children's play of "fort-da" ("gone-back")—the re-peated play of infants, where they drop or lose something and then "find it" again—as a reaction to the early trauma of the absent mother. He links this to his theory of repetition and the "death drive," which interplays with the "life drive" through life (*Beyond*).

13. *Boating for Beginners*, *Sexing the Cherry*, *Lighthousekeeping*, *The Stone Gods*, *The Passion* and *Frankissstein*.

14. Winterson's Woolfian affinities (*Art Objects*) are worth noting regard-ing the trope of the female wanderer because Woolf is one of Deleuze and Guattari's foremost examples of writing-as-becoming-animal (*Plateaus*).

15. Elizabeth Grosz's work aligns with Braidotti's in these respects, too. Although there are significant differences between these two thinkers, they both link the work of Deleuze and Irigaray in their feminist materialisms.

16. For Plato, all that existed before the imposed order of "Logos" was the boundless, watery "Chora," out of which the Demiurge created the forms (which represent, for Plato, what "ultimate reality" consists of). This view of reality is for Plato connected to truth and beauty and sharply split off from our empirical embodied existence, which is

linked to irrationality and illusion. This is the hierarchy of values that Irigaray and Deleuze try to subvert, and so does Winterson.

17. This connects the sorcerer's view of love to Plato's conception of it in the *Symposium*, and Winterson's implicit critique through her Winnet-story can be linked to feminist reactions to Plato on this theme (see Cavarero; Irigaray *Ethics*; Nussbaum).

18. This woman's world as all body may be linked to what Irigaray thinks of as a patriarchal construction of femininity as passive ground and silent matter, a difference that depends on its opposite "Man" rather than the sort of sexual difference that she wants to promote, which is an active force, as of yet unrealized.

19. This reading of the ending of *Oranges* is adapted from Werring 64–67.

20. The two previous paragraphs are adapted from Werring 67–68.

21. Jesse Bordwin alerts us to another seed of Winterson's neomaterialist feminism in *Oranges,* namely the very "thingness" of the novel's objects, which are, like the myths, woven into the protagonist's trajectory of becoming herself.

22. Emma McKenna also reads a "return of the body" into the *Happy* narrative, although for her, it is the classed body that is resurrected by Winterson and that she ambivalently works both to reject and by returning to her childhood and revisiting "the double" of Freud's *Uncanny.*

23. I compare three such memories in Werring, see the first note above.

24. Reina van der Wiel argues that *Oranges*, therefore, is the only example of Winterson's work that successfully works as a "maternal container," enabling her to work through trauma, while the rest of Winterson's work largely remains stuck in a compulsion to repeat.

25. I link Winterson's "anamnesis" to the thought of Jean Francois Lyotard in Werring 2020.

26. Van der Wiel argues that creating such literary containers can help victims work through trauma aesthetically and provides a compelling argument for how this is successfully undertaken by Virginia Woolf in *To the Lighthouse.* Van der Wiel argues that Winterson's work, with the exception of *Oranges,* fails in its attempt at working through trauma in this way, even if *Happy* might be partially successful.

27. The three previous paragraphs are adapted from Werring 69–71.

28. Winterson also repeats another memory in *Happy* (54–56) that was first related in *Oranges* (29–63), which may be similarly compared, namely the memory of when she started school.

29. Rhizomatic thought is a term used by Deleuze and Guattari to connote a nonhierarchical and interconnected way of thinking: Thought is compared to a root system allowing ideas to spread and connect without needing to be centred around a core. The point is to allow multiple entry and exit points and foster new thought.

30. Julia Kristeva's *Strangers to Ourselves* is another relevant connection to this material, which is connected to her theory of abjection and engages with Freud's uncanny. All these theories are relevant in terms of mother-daughter relations, but beyond the scope of this paper.

31. In *Anti-Oedipus*, Deleuze and Guattari relate their experiences with an alternative mental health institution called "La Borde." These reflections are critical of what is considered to be normal or sane versus mad. It is important to Deleuze and Guattari not to romanticize mental illness, but equally important to critique the medicalization of culture/life.

32. This is a term used by Tamsin Lorraine in her fusion of Deleuze and Irigaray's thought as an alternative to patriarchal or liberal humanist constructions of rationality.

33. The five previous pages are adapted from Werring 75–78.

34. See also Irigaray, *Ethics*.

35. This reading of Deleuze and Guattari's work on Kafka is influenced by Tamsin Lorraine (176). See also Werring 79.

Works Cited

Agamben, Giorgio. *The Open: Man and Animal*. Translated by Kevin Attell. Stanford University Press, 2004.

Alaimo, Stacy, and Susan Hekman, editors. *Material Feminisms*. Indiana University Press, 2008.

Allaby, Michael. "Feral." *A Dictionary of Zoology*, 2020, https://www-oxfordreference-com.ezproxy.uio.no/view/10.1093/acref/9780198845089.001.0001/acref-9780198845089-e-3251. Accessed 8 Jan. 2025.

Ansell Pearson, Keith. "Living the Eternal Return as the Event: Nietzsche with Deleuze." *Journal of Nietzsche Studies*, no. 14, 1997, pp. 64–94.

Bollinger, Laurel. "Models for Female Loyalty: The Biblical Ruth in Jeanette Winterson's *Oranges Are Not the Only Fruit.*" *Tulsa Studies in Women's Literature*, vol. 13, no. 2, 1994, pp. 363–80.

Bordwin, Jesse. "Queer Objects: Gendered Interests and Distant Things in Jeanette Winterson's *Oranges Are Not the Only Fruit.*" *Contemporary Literature*, vol. 60, no. 2, 2019, pp. 227–52.

Boulos-Walker, Michelle. *Philosophy and the Maternal Body: Reading Silence.* Routledge, 1998.

Braidotti, Rosi. *Metamorphoses: Towards a Materialist Theory of Becoming.* Polity Press, 2002.

Carpenter, Ginette. "Reading and the Reader." *Jeanette Winterson: A Contemporary Critical Guide.* Edited by Sonya Andemahr. Continuum, 2007, pp. 69–81.

Cavarero, Adriana. *In Spite of Plato: A Feminist Rewriting of Ancient Philosophy.* Translated by Serena Anderlini-D'Onofrio and Aine O'Healy. Polity Press, 1995.

Cimatti, Felice. *Unbecoming Human. Philosophy of Animality after Deleuze.* Edinburgh University Press, 2020.

Deleuze, Gilles. *Difference and Repetition.* 1968. Translated by Paul Patton, Columbia University Press, 1994.

Deleuze, Gilles, and Félix Guattari. *Anti-Oedipus: Capitalism and Schizophrenia.* Viking Press, 1977.

Deleuze, Gilles, and Félix Guattari. *Kafka. Toward a Minor Literature.* University of Minnesota Press, 2006.

Deleuze, Gilles, and Félix Guattari. *A Thousand Plateaus: Capitalism and Schizophrenia.* 1988. Bloomsbury Academic, 2020.

De Long, Anne. "The Cat's Cradle: Multiple Discursive Threads in Jeanette Winterson's *Oranges Are Not the Only Fruit.*" *Literature Interpretation Theory*, vol. 17, no. 3–4, 2006, pp. 263–75.

Derrida, Jacques. *The Animal That Therefore I Am.* Translated by David Wills. Fordham University Press, 2008.

Ellam, Julie. *Love in Jeanette Winterson's Novels.* Costerus New Series 181. Rodopi, 2010.

Freud, Sigmund. *Beyond the Pleasure Principle*. Translated by John Reddick. Penguin Modern Classics, 2003.

Garner, Dwight. "On a Path to Salvation, Jane Austen as a Guide." *New York Times*. 8 Mar., 2012, https://www.nytimes.com/2012/03/09/books/jeanette-wintersons-why-be-happy-when-you-could-be-normal.html. Accessed 25 Jan. 2025.

Garrard, Greg. "Ferality Tales." *The Oxford Handbook of Ecocriticism*. Edited by Greg Garrard. Oxford University Press, 2014, pp. 241–59.

Garside, Nick. *The Roving Life of a Feral Citizen. Democratic Ideals and the Politicization of Nature*. Palgrave Macmillan, 2013.

Gilbert, Sandra M., and Susan Gubar. *The Madwoman in the Attic: The Woman Writer and the Nineteenth-Century Literary Imagination*. Second Edition. Yale University Press, 2000.

Grosz, Elizabeth. *Volatile Bodies: Toward a Corporeal Feminism*. Indiana University Press, 1994.

Gruen, Lori, and Fiona Probyn-Rapsey, editors. *Animaladies: Gender, Animals and Madness*. Bloomsbury Academic, 2019.

Gustar, Jennifer. "Language and the Limits of Desire." *Jeanette Winterson: A Contemporary Critical Guide*. Edited by Sonya Andemahr. Continuum, 2007, pp. 55–68.

Haslett, Jane. "Winterson's Fabulous Bodies." *Jeanette Winterson: A Contemporary Critical Guide*. Edited by Sonya Andemahr. Continuum, 2007, pp. 41–54.

Hekman, Susan. "Constructing the Ballast: An Ontology for Feminism." *Material Feminisms*. Edited by Stacy Alaimo and Sudan Hekman. Indiana University Press, 2008, pp. 85–119.

Irigaray, Luce, and Wenzel, Hélène Vivienne. "And the One Doesn't Stir without the Other." *Signs: Journal of Women in Culture and Society*, vol 7, no. 1, 1981, pp. 60–67.

Irigaray, Luce. *An Ethics of Sexual Difference*. Translated by Carolyn Burke and Gillian C. Gill. Cornell University Press, 1993.

Irigaray, Luce. "Body against Body: In Relation to the Mother." *Sexes and Genealogies*. Translated by Gillian C. Gill. Columbia University Press, 1993, pp. 7–21.

Irigaray, Luce. "On the Maternal Order." *Je, Tu, Nous. Toward a Culture of Difference*. Translated by Alison Martin. Routledge Classics, 2007, pp. 31–38.

Irigaray, Luce. *Speculum of the Other Woman.* Translated by Gillian C. Gill. Cornell University Press, 1985.

Jacobs, Amber. *On Matricide: Myth, Psychoanalysis and the Law of the Mother.* Columbia University Press, 2007.

Johnson, Miranda. "'The Other Who Precedes and Possesses Me': Confronting the Maternal/Animal Divide Through the Art of Botched Taxidermy." *Feral Feminisms,* 2016, https://feralfeminisms.com/the-other-who-precedes-and-possesses-me/. Accessed 9 Jan. 2025.

Kawash, Samira. "New Directions in Motherhood Studies." *Signs,* vol. 36, no. 4, Summer 2011, pp. 969–1003.

Klein, Melanie. *Love and Gratitude and Other Works 1946–1963.* Virago, 1990.

Kristeva, Julia. *Powers of Horror: An Essay on Abjection.* Columbia University Press, 1982.

Kristeva, Julia. *Revolution in Poetic Language.* Translated by Margaret Waller. Columbia University Press, 1984.

Kristeva, Julia. *Strangers to Ourselves.* Translated by Leon S. Roudiez. Columbia University Press, 1991.

Lorraine, Tamsin. *Irigaray and Deleuze: Experiments in Visceral Philosophy.* Cornell University Press, 1999.

Massumi, Brian. "The Autonomy of Affect." *Cultural Critique,* no 31, 1995, pp. 83–109.

McKenna, Emma. "Double Melancholy: The (Class) Politics of Loss in Jeanette Winterson's *Why Be Happy When You Could Be Normal?" Women: A Cultural Review,* vol. 27, no. 3, 2016, pp. 296–316.

Mekinen, Merja. *The Novels of Jeanette Winterson. A Reader's Guide to Essential Criticism.* Palgrave, 2005.

Meyer, Kim Middleton. "Jeanette Winterson's Evolving Subject: Difficulty into Dream." *Contemporary British Fiction.* Edited by Richard J. Lane, et al., Polity, 2003, pp. 210–25.

Milne, Anne. "At the Precipice of Community: Feral Openness and the Work of Mary Robinson." *ABO: Interactive Journal for Women in the Arts,* vol. 2, no. 1, 2012, pp. 1–14.

Myerson, Julie. "Why Be Happy When You Could Be Normal? by

Jeanette Winterson–Review." *The Guardian*, 6 Nov. 2011, https://www.theguardian.com/books/2011/nov/06/why-happy-jeanette-winterson-review. Accessed 25 Jan. 2025.

Nussbaum, Martha. "The Speech of Alcibiades: A Reading of Plato's Symposium." *Philosophy and Literature*, vol. 3, no. 2, 1979, pp. 131–72.

Oliver, Kelly. *Animal Lessons: How They Teach Us to Be Human*. Columbia University Press.

O'Reilly, Andrea. *Matricentric Feminism: Theory, Activism, Practice*. Second edition. Demeter Press, 2021.

Pollock, Griselda. "Introduction. Femininity: Aporia or Sexual Difference?" In *The Matrixial Borderspace*, by Bracha Ettinger. Edited by Brian Massumi. University of Minnesota Press, 2006, pp. 1–37.

Restuccia, Frances L. "Agamben's Open: Coetzee's Dis-grace." *Comparative Literature*, vol. 69, no. 4, pp. 413–29.

Rich, Adrienne. *Of Woman Born: Motherhood as Experience and Institution*. Norton, 1986.

Russell, Kara M. "Lesbian Ferality: Bertha Harris's *Confessions of a Cherubino* as Disturbance Literature." *ISLE: Interdisciplinary Studies of Literature and Environment*, vol. 31, no. 4, 2024, pp. 838–59.

Sayers, Valerie. "Book World: 'Why Be Happy When You Could Be Normal?' by Jeanette Winterson." *Washington Post*, 2 Apr. 2012, https://www.washingtonpost.com/entertainment/books/2012/04/02/gIQAYlesrS_story.html. Accessed 25 Jan. 2025.

Showalter, Elaine. *The Female Malady: Women, Madness and English Culture 1830–1980*. Pantheon Books, 1985.

Stark, Hannah. *Feminist Theory After Deleuze*. Bloomsbury, 2017.

Stone, Alison. *Being Born: Birth and Philosophy*. Oxford University Press, 2019.

Turner, Lynn. "Animal and Sexual Difference: Kelly Oliver's Continental Bestiary." *Body & Society*, vol. 19, no. 4, 2013, pp. 120–33.

Werring, Else. *Electra or Persephone? Matricide in Rebecca Solnit and Jeanette Winterson*. 2020. University of Oslo, Master's thesis, https://www.duo.uio.no/bitstream/handle/10852/84352/Werring-MA-Thesis-FINAL.pdf?sequence=1&isAllowed=y. Accessed 9 Jan. 2025.

Wieland, Christina. *The Undead Mother: Psychoanalytic Explorations of Masculinity, Femininity and Matricide.* Karnac, 2000.

Williams, Zoe. "Why Be Happy When You Could Be Normal? By Jeanette Winterson – Review." *The Guardian*, 4 Nov. 2011, https://www.theguardian.com/books/2011/nov/04/why-be-happy-jeanette-winterson-review. Accessed 25 Jan. 2025.

Winnicott, Donald. *Playing and Reality.* Routledge Classics, 2005.

Winterson, Jeanette. *Art Objects: Essays on Ecstasy and Effrontery.* Vintage Books, 1996.

Winterson, Jeanette. *Oranges Are Not the Only Fruit.* Vintage Books, 1985.

Winterson, Jeanette. *Why Be Happy When You Could Be Normal?* Vintage Books, 2011.

Woolf, Virginia. *A Room of One's Own.* Penguin Classics, 2020.

15.

From Pig to Dog: Becoming Woman/Becoming Mother

Laura Bissell

I didn't dream about blood any more. I dreamed of ferns and damp
earth. My body kept me warm. I was just fine. When the sun came up
I felt the light run along my back and turn bright yellow in my head.
I got up on my trotters. I shook my head and stretched my hams.

—Marie Darrieussecq 69

We are at base animals, and to deny us either our animal nature or
our dignity as humans is a crime against existence. Womanhood and
motherhood are perhaps the most potent forces in human society,
which of course men have been hasty to quash, for they are right to
fear these forces.

—Rachel Yoder 237

Introduction

Written twenty-five years apart, Marie Darrieussecq's *Pig Tales*
(1996) and Rachel Yoder's *Nightbitch* (2021) offer subversive
critiques of societal expectations of women through narratives
of feral metamorphoses into a pig and dog, respectively. While these
creatures can connote both domesticity and ferality, I understand becoming
an animal (i.e., going feral) as an empowering act in this chapter.
Here, feral is "the process of returning to a wild state, escaping from
captivity or domestication" (Armstrong et al. xiii). This chapter explores

the institution of motherhood, becoming women/animals, women at work, conventions of womanhood, mothers and others, environment awareness, and kinship with animals. I argue that the social conventions governing womanhood and motherhood can be experienced as a form of captivity. The feral transformations within these novels provide an escape from gendered tropes and the opportunity for the creative potential of the protagonists to flourish.[1]

The Institution of Motherhood

Adrienne Rich writes the following about the "institution of motherhood" in *Of Woman Born* (1976): "In the most fundamental and bewildering of contradictions, it has alienated women from our bodies by incarcerating us in them" (13). As well as pregnancy being experienced by some as a bodily prison, the societal and cultural expectations of mothers can also be experienced as restrictive, inhibitive, and debilitating. By speaking about their experiences, mothers began to challenge the cages in which they found themselves: "The words are being spoken now, are being written down; the taboos are being broken, the masks of motherhood are cracking through" (Rich 24–25). This crack, or as Sara Ahmed describes it, the feminist "snap," marks the breaking point of women confined to the corset of their assigned role—"gender, a loop tightening" (Ahmed 25). This chapter explores womanhood and motherhood as a form of cultural domestication through *Pig Tales* and *Nightbitch* and argues that becoming feral is a feminist act in these novels.

In *Pig Tales*, narrated in first-person "piggy squiggles," a young woman employed at a cosmetics company and supposed beauty massage parlour (actually a brothel) notices changes in her body as she gains weight and develops a snout. As society in Paris crumbles around her and her wolf-lover, Yvan, this ironic fable exposes political and cultural hypocrisy around gender as the woman moves between sow and human forms. In *Nightbitch*, having found the expected performance of motherhood frustrating and deadening and mourning her previous life as an artist, the mother begins a performance art project exploring feral motherhood, through doggy games with her son and night-time hunts. She then transforms into the persona of Nightbitch as her art and life become one. Drawing on critical theory, this article argues that becoming-animal for the women in these novels provides a conduit for rage, violence, ferality, creativity, and animal kinship, as their animality erupts and disrupts normative expectations of them as women and mothers. Animals have been disempowered within Western culture, and the terms "pig" and "bitch" are often used as derisive. However, I argue that each protagonist's metamorphosis into animal forms is portrayed as joyful, empowering, fulfilling, and necessary to become their full creative selves. This feminist reclamation of these derogatory animal naming and shaming can also work to celebrate human-animal affinity and kinship (Haraway).

Pigs and dogs are culturally conceived as animals that can be both domesticated and feral; some studies acknowledge practices of human breastfeeding of these animals, which has partially led to their domestication (Simoons and Baldwin).[2] Dogs and pigs feature recurrently in culture and science as both companion animals and animals that stand in for humans. Carol J. Adams and Josephine Donovan argue that there is an intersection between sexism and speciesism and that domesticated animals are often feminized while wild animals are masculinized and therefore perceived to have higher status. The domesticated/feral species (pigs and dogs) have also historically been associated with female bodies, and the trajectory of cultural associations provides a useful context in understanding depictions of woman and mother as feral in these novels.

Becoming Woman/Animal

Jennifer Parker-Starbuck asks: "Is it time to look for more porous boundaries and examine how humanity might, as Deleuze and Guattari write, become-animal?" ("Becoming-Animate" 652). Gilles Deleuze and Félix Guattari suggest approaches to more-than-human affinities and challenges to perceived fixed boundaries. In these novels, the women do not arrive at either as a point of finality; instead, they oscillate between their human and animal states. As Anat Pick argues: "Darrieussecq is interested in how identities (human, pig, woman, whore) linger, travel, and seep into one another, flickering, as it were, in their own difference, their own becoming" (46). Similarly, in *Nightbitch*, the mother becomes a dog at times both opportune and not: eating lunch in public with her son, at the playpark, and alone at night. In one instance, her husband arrives home to find their child in a diaper on the floor next to a giant dog.

Parker-Starbuck examines how pigs are often abjected, ridiculed, consumed, and degraded in an article discussing the pig as a symbol of waste in our society ("Pig Bodies"). She notes that throughout history, the pig has been a metaphor for the human while symbolizing the grotesque. Pick argues that to recognize ourselves as pigs crosses the threshold of species and gender too and notes the Greek word "choiros" means both pig and "female genitalia" (49). Historically, it is the female body that is animalized for degrading or derogatory purposes. Both *Pig Tales* and *Nightbitch* include these threshold creatures—animals that we identify with, anthropomorphize, or have relationships with but also have the capacity to be repelled by or frightened of.

Nightbitch acquires her moniker after a particularly difficult night with her son. He lies between her and her husband screaming, and the woman waits, enraged that her husband sleeps on. She yowls, jumps up, breaks a lamp, and cuts her foot. In the morning, as the bloodied sheets spin in the washing machine, her husband says to her: "You were a real... *bitch* last night" (8). The word "bitch" originally referred to a female dog, but as early as the fifteenth century, it became a derogatory term applied to women who were deemed to be promiscuous (similar to the contemporary use of "slut" and "whore").[3] From the start of the twentieth century, the usage referred to annoying or difficult women, and this continued in the post-second-wave-feminism era. Attempts to reclaim the term since the 1990s have been deemed largely unsuccessful due to its misogynistic origin and the negative connotations that the word perpetuates. Cynthia Ngyuen argues:

> In many, if not all, instances, "bitch" creates an imbalanced power dynamic and enforces society's preference of what is deemed as "masculine." For example, by calling an inanimate object or intangible idea a "bitch," such as "That exam was a bitch" ... Most notably, "bitch" is often used to degrade men of their masculinity and to insult women who are seen as emasculating which again, enforces the patriarchy.

As Nightbitch says: "*Bitch* just had a ring to it, that condemning, inescapable ring, a ring that fucker or asshole could never fully conjure for a man. Bitch was flat and sharp and final" (30). In her chapter on *Nightbitch*, Andrea O'Reilly argues that it is the character's maternal rage that provokes her transformation and ultimately achieves maternal empowerment (220). I agree that rage is part of the alchemy of the metamorphosis but also contend that the mother's creative impetus plays a key part. Her return to artistic practice using her feral motherhood as a lens for her performance-making is an important empowering element.

Nightbitch is written in the third person, with a canny narrator offering ironic critique on the mother's situation. *Pig Tales*, in contrast, is written in the first person, the protagonist hoping the notebook she stole will be read by a publisher patient enough to read her handwriting (described as "piggy squiggles"). Donna Haraway recognises the potential for irony in her "Cyborg Manifesto": "Irony is about humour and serious play. It is also a rhetorical strategy and a political method" (149). Both novels are funny and have an underlying feminist politic that exposes the injustices that the women experience throughout their becomings.

While using humour, the novels also do not shy away from the realities of the women's experiences, including sex, birth, and encounters with death. In theories of the grotesque, the idea of a body exceeding its boundaries is understood literally. The body leaks, spills, and bleeds (all of which feature in both texts); however, I argue that the protagonists in these novels exceed their domesticated societal boundaries as well; they transgress their expected roles of good employee, woman, and mother to find creative outlets and fulfillment. In moving from the domestic to the feral, they inhabit their full creative selves beyond the cultural constraints of womanhood and motherhood.

Women at Work

Pig Tales, subtitled *A Novel of Lust and Transformation*, begins in Perfume Plus, a cosmetics company and beauty massage parlour, which acts as a façade for sexually corrupt clients to engage in "barnyard behaviour"; the characteristic smell of busy days is "massage oil and cold sperm" (65). Having become an employee of the company, with the director holding her "right breast in one hand, the job contract in the other" (2)—the nameless protagonist becomes hugely successful with the clients as she notices changes in her body: gaining weight, growing a snout, developing an aversion to ham, and becoming sexually aroused while at work. Her former lover, Honoré (ironically etymologically linked with "honour"), did not want her to work as he felt the work degraded women (7–8). Later, she claims: "Work had corrupted me: now I was moaning when we did it. Soon he wouldn't have anything to do with me, saying that I disgusted him" (30).

She begins to question her choices and the limited parameters of being a woman: "It would certainly have been simpler if I'd agreed to stay home, have a baby, and all that. I had regrets, and I was also ashamed of having failed ... I know it's hard to understand but I didn't feel at all like working any more" (59). The societal expectation of her to stay home and have a baby is framed as a simpler life, but the work she insists on continuing leaves her lacking, resulting in a sense of being torn and unsatisfied. In *Pig Tales*, the choice is between being a mother or being a worker, but neither option is satisfying to the protagonist, and this rupture seems to provoke her metamorphosis, a splitting between human and animal forms.

In *Nightbitch*, the mother has given up her "dream job" curating a gallery. She went back to work after her maternity leave, but the knowledge that her son was crying all day on a cold linoleum floor provided an impetus for her to leave:

> He used to cry a lot, one of them had told her months later, and it was as if with this offhand statement of ordinary fact, the day-care worker had sunk a finely sharpened blade into the mother's midsection, violently, for the mother felt severely—mortally, eternally—wounded, and at the same time murderous: why had the worker not picked up her son, most beloved? ... to tell the mother casually about her endlessly crying son, alone, on the linoleum floor, was a particular cruelty the mother would dwell on for weeks. After all, wasn't it actually, entirely, her fault to begin with that she had to leave her son in such a place? (It was. It was.) (11)

The visceral nature of the writing conveys the violence of this mother-love; matrescence is an embodied physical and emotional experience (as discussed in Lucy Jones's *Matrescence: On the Metamorphosis of Pregnancy, Childbirth and Motherhood*). In *Pig Tales*, the choice has been between motherhood and working; in *Nightbitch*, the mother is expected to do both but realizes that: "The whole fucking thing was a sham, the working and pumping and hurrying and not holding her baby" (15). The recognition that it "was all a trick, a trick to get them to do everything, a trick they could not escape" (15) leaves the mother bewildered and exhausted, so she gives up her ideal job to be "a privileged, overeducated lady in the middle of America, living the dream of holding her baby twenty-four hours a day" (16–17). But the reality of being on her own with her son constantly while her husband works away becomes deadening, and she fantasizes about her previous artistic life, and the possibility of staging the birth of her child as an artistic happening (23). The return to her previous job had exposed her lactating maternal body, while her guilt of leaving her child at daycare had felt like a violence. It is not the work so much as her return to artistic activity that allows her to transform. Through the feral transformation, the mother finds ways of escaping maternal gendered tropes. The merging of art and life within the mode of performance art allows her to be her full, rage-filled self. It allows her to be excessive and animal in her mothering.

Conventions of Womanhood

Both narratives explicitly comment on the sexualization of women's bodies, the expectation of women to be "hot", sexually attractive, young, and pleasing to men. Nightbitch realizes it is her expectations of herself that play a part in her misery: "Actually, if you thought about it, it really wasn't fair to call her a night *bitch*. Such a gendered slur didn't account for the fact she had made a boy with her own body, nurtured his multiplying cells for months and months to her own detriment, to her own fatness, to the decline of her youthful sex appeal, which wasn't supposed to matter" (29). She acknowledges that a real feminist would not care about such things as body shape or being thin or appealing to heteronormative cis men, but she admits that "she did care about being hot in her own eyes" (29). This notion that the expectation of being sexy (in her own eyes) and also being a mother-artist causes friction between her identities. Karina Quinn describes the "I-was battling quietly at the I-am" provoked by matrescence as the previous sense of self becomes destabilized by becoming a mother.

In both novels, the metamorphoses are not merely physical but are exemplified through emotional experiences and internal thoughts as animal imagery becomes fluid. Pick writes of the narrator of *Pig Tales*: "She oscillates between regarding her bodily transformations as hideous and as alluring, in full recognition of her incomplete humanity. In her very mindlessness, then, the heroine of *Pig Tales* arrives (perhaps more authentically and immediately than the theoretician or the philosopher) at the grotesque becoming of the human" (48). In *Pig Tales*, the protagonist says: "He looked at me and said 'No, not so hot.' That hurt. Then he hung up and turning to his men he added, 'The bosses never leave us anything but the pigs.' That hurt even more" (53). Again, the term "pig" is used as an insult, an indication that she is not attractive or desirable. Along with the protagonists' perceptions of themselves as sexually appealing (or not), both novels capture changing experiences of sexual activity. While working in the beauty parlour and undergoing her transformation, the woman in *Pig Tales* notices an increase in bestiality from her partner Honoré, her clients, and the manager who takes her on various "training" excursions, trips that would result in sexual activities. She says of the clients: "Their new inclinations turned the massage table into a sort of haystack out in a field. Some of the clients began to bray, others grunted like pigs, and little by little, most of them wound up on all fours" (17). The narrator begs any impressionable readers to skip the pages as she confesses "Bluntly put, I began really wanting sex" (26–27). Animal metaphors become fluid, as her boss tells her "There was no room in the firm for *bitches in heat*" (29). In becoming a pig, when sexualized, she is also perceived as a female dog in heat. Her desires animalize her further: "The director said it was a pity that even the best salesgirls went bad, and that you couldn't depend on anything these days. He said that I'd turned into—excuse me—a real bitch: those were his very words" (29).

A wealthy African Marabout rents her services "for an exorbitant price" (29), and she is expected to get down on all fours and make animal noises. She is chilled by what she sees in the mirror and does not disclose this to the reader, saying "You wouldn't believe me" (32). Later, she witnesses a "little corkscrew tail on [her] rear end" (69). Animal imagery resists straightforward readings about subjection and empowerment, playfully suggesting that the animal is nascent in all humans. Although the narrator and others see this as a source of shame, the language used by misogynistic characters (bitch, pig etc.) indicates it is patriarchal culture at fault in demonizing sexual urges. Arguably, women are supposed to present their sexuality within a tight parameter of behaviour; a large portion of pornography nods to the sexual abandon women are expected to perform ("women going wild"). But there are risks: If they engage too fully in the animality of their sexuality, their humanity is negated.

On a rare weekend of intimacy with her husband, Nightbitch describes their sexual encounter as being "only them there, together, animals alive in a house" (99). After a restorative lovemaking session, the mother returns to her preoccupations:

> And though the animalness of her being remained, she was also inside her full human-mother being, back to the usual worries and insecurities, the thoughts of career success, the burden of failure, the marital resentments, feminist rage and so on and so forth. All this was back but somehow transformed. She felt she could abide it as long as she still had Nightbitch. As long as she had that. (102)

This transformation is significant and powerful for the mother: "She was overwhelmed by her strength. She was awash in her own violence" (90). There is also a moment when she realizes that everything she had felt, experienced, and tried to articulate had been true, despite the dismissal of these things by her husband (who initially epitomizes societal and patriarchal expectations):

> The fact of the matter was that she had not been wrong about anything... Her feelings, in fact, about every single thing had been reasonable and precisely on point, not only about the dog stuff but even before, how she was so angry and tired, how she didn't feel it was right that she was now at home, out of the workforce, career on hold, art on hold, life on hold indefinitely, while her husband fulfilled himself. Not right that her work raising the child was devalued, women's work, housework, that once she became a housewife she began, ever so slowly, to disappear, until she only fully existed in the presence of her ward. When she considered how she spent each day, it was fair to wonder: without him did she even exist at all? (93–94)

These ideas are not new, appearing in feminist discourse since Betty Friedan's *The Feminine Mystique* (1963), but how this mother responds is significant. She rejects her internalized critique of herself as hysterical or unreasonable and trusts her experience of becoming an animal.

The physical transformation the women experience is extreme, but they are both in denial at the outset. The protagonist from *Pig Tales* says, "I rubbed every cream in the world on my third nipple but nothing helped, it wouldn't go away. When I noticed something like an actual breast swelling beneath it, I thought I was going to faint" (36). The woman notices the increasingly piggy appearance of her nose, and her altered physicality changes her mobility: "I tried to stand up and was surprised to find my body buckling beneath me. I wound up on all fours. It was frightening, because I couldn't move my hips—as though I were paralysed in the hindquarters, like an old dog" (43). Again, the animal comparison here is to a dog, as though she cannot quite come to terms with her pigginess. She reflects on her visit to the swimming pools at Aqualand:

> As for me, bending forward, I had what you might call an unparalleled view of my vulva, and I thought it was dangling rather strangely. I don't want to burden you with details, but the greater labia were hanging down a mite lower than normal, which is why I couldn't see them so well. In Woman's World, or My Beauty, My Health, I don't remember exactly, I'd read that the ancient Romans' favourite—and choiciest—dish was stuffed sow's vulva. (47)

This obscured recognition of her body as that of a pig and the connection she makes to an article that she has read in a women's magazine suggest she sees her own body as something to be consumed; her own internalized association between pigs and her female body is revealed.

In *Nightbitch*, the protagonist's transformation into a dog begins after her husband calls her a bitch, as though in naming her, he has made it so. The performative utterance is enacted: "In the days following this new naming, she found the patch of coarse black hair sprouting from the base of her neck and was, like, *What the fuck?*" (3). As she notices more hair on her arms, jaw, and on the top of her feet, she asks her husband if he thinks her incisors look sharper than usual. He responds: "Your tooth looks the same to me. You always think there's something wrong with you" (5). A dismissive and patronizing response to her lived experience is part of the genesis of her rage: "That single, white-hot light at the centre of the darkness of herself—that was the point of origin from which she births something new, from which all women do" (7). The new thing that is (re)birthed is her creative drive, as Lisa Baraitser argues, motherhood as generative of something new (7).

In the latter stages of the novella, the protagonist of *Pig Tales* shares that her lover, Yvan, said it was "fantastic to have two modes of being, two females for the price of one, in a way, and what a time we had" (109). She transitions between a sow and a woman, reflecting that "it's exhausting to wrestle with yourself like that" (132). News articles explicitly refer to her as a "*fat pig*" (110), although it is unclear if this is a comment on her as a human or sow. Nightbitch's metamorphosis offers freedom from her mother-life: "She likes the idea of being a dog because she can bark and snarl and not have to justify it. She can run free if she wants. She can be a body and instinct and urge. She can be hunger and rage, thirst and fear, nothing more. She can revert to a pure, throbbing state" (83–84). Ferality is freedom. And the realization that she could give in to what she felt she was being called to be—"an animal taking care of its young with no wishes or cares beyond that" (84)—is liberating, although the call of her artistic urges never fully recedes.

Mothers and Others

Nightbitch, written two and a half decades after *Pig Tales*, focusses on the experience of motherhood, and Darrieussecq's novel includes metaphoric references to a wide range of experiences of womanhood, such as puberty, pregnancy, pregnancy loss, menopause, and being mothered. In *Pig Tales*, the narrator explains that her mother has won Lotto and moved to the country but does not want her daughter to know: "because she didn't want me sponging off her" (37). In *Nightbitch*, it is revealed that her parents "never called and she never calls, so they knew nearly nothing about each other these days" (14–15). In both novels, the protagonists' mothers have become removed or are emotionally and geographically distant from their daughters. However, they both find affinities with older women. For the woman in *Pig Tales*, it is the older female client (referred to by the male customers as "the old hag") who takes joy in her radiance and is delighted at her supposed pregnancy.

Margaret Miles follows Mary Russo in claiming the female body is intrinsically grotesque due to its historical connection with the lower stratum, and its penetrability. At the same time, its bodily functions, such as pregnancy and birth, provide images of "natural grotesqueness" (Miles 93). Adrienne Rich suggests that becoming a mother evokes complex feelings about one's mother: "No one mentions the psychic crisis of bearing a first child, the excitation of long-buried feelings about one's own mother, the sense of confused power and powerlessness, of being taken over on one hand and of touching new physical and psychic potentialities on the other, a heightened sensibility which can be exhilarating, bewildering and exhausting" (36). In *Pig Tales*, the protagonist's mother appears on the TV show *Vanished Without a Trace*, weeping and appealing to her daughter to contact her. She argues with Yvan, as he thinks the mother is being bribed to "lure the wolf from the woods so to speak" (119). The program's host does, indeed, locate her and Ivan when she contacts the show. She reflects: "It killed me to see how frumpy I'd got, and it killed me to think my mother had recognised me in spite of that. Maternal instinct is a wonderful thing, a gut feeling, as they say" (120). Despite being estranged, the protagonist in *Pig Tales* still seeks her mother's approval.

In *Nightbitch*, an older woman, having witnessed the protagonist's appetite as she gobbles from a bowl of meat at an all-you-can-eat buffet, exclaims delightedly that she used to play doggies with her son: "And what a mother you are, she added. What a wonderful mother! To have such fun with your child. I remember the days.... We used to play doggies, too!" (80). Nightbitch feels a moment of recognition and affinity in her feral act: "She nearly wept with longing, to sit down across from the woman, take her old, soft, highly lotioned hands in hers, and ask questions, so many questions." Nightbitch also finds solace in the writings of Wanda White, an elusive academic studying the Bird Women of Peru whose *Field Guide to Magical Women* acts as a guide throughout her transformation. She reaches out to White by email but never receives a response, although she sees her at the edge of the dog park one day and chases her.

The "old hag" in *Pig Tales* and Wanda White in *Nightbitch* both stand in for the women's mothers in their passing down of knowledge and experience. These archetypes of cronelike figures and wise women are sought or found as othermothers when biological mothers have been absent or found lacking. In *The Queer Art of Failure*, Jack Halberstam calls for an "anti-social feminism, a form of feminism preoccupied with negativity and negation" (129), which traces broken mother-daughter relations: "This shadow feminism speaks in the language of self-destruction, masochism, an anti-social femininity and a refusal of the essential bond of mother and daughter that ensures that the daughter inhabits the legacy of the mother and in doing so reproduces her relationship to patriarchal forms of power" (124). There is an example of this in *Nightbitch*:

> She had once, while pregnant, attempted to talk to her [mother] about childbirth, what to expect, how she was scared of the pain, and how had her mother managed, to which her mother had only the offer of *It's called labor because it's hard work*—which she understood as a consolation. Sure, her mother was saying, it's bad, but since you are a woman, this is your lot in life, your work, to do what's hard, what's unspeakably painful, and then to keep this covenant of silence. (80–81)

The protagonist of *Pig Tales* has symptoms of pregnancy: "hunger, the nausea, the pudginess" (14). However, even though a gynecologist tells her she has experienced a miscarriage, she does not believe it, trusting her own body: "Personally, I'm certain I wasn't pregnant. I don't know what got into me all of a sudden to make me argue with the gynecologist about this. Anyway, he became furious and called me a little slut" (13). In between this false pregnancy (the symptoms she is experiencing perhaps due to her piggy metamorphosis) and an actual pregnancy, she encounters a human baby when she is in her sow form: "I could have easily eaten the baby, sunk my teeth into that really rosy flesh.... The baby smelled so good and seemed so roly-poly, like an inflatable doll" (72). Her animal urges almost turn her literally into a devouring mother and continue when she gets pregnant by a cleaner at the hotel. When a mobile crisis intervention unit arrives after the birth, the policeman with them declares that they should have called the Society for the Protection of Animals instead:

> On the ground next to me were six tiny wriggling things covered with blood. Given what they looked like I could tell they weren't long for this world. The policeman tried to come closer and I bared my teeth ... I struggled to my feet with this terrific pain in my belly. I took the six little things in my mouth, smashed in a manhole cover, and disappeared underground. I licked the poor mites as carefully as I could. When they grew cold, I felt as though I couldn't go on. I curled up in a ball and didn't think about anything anymore. (79)

She only overcomes her despair at her lost babies when piranhas attack her in the sewers, and she realizes that she still cares about life: "You could say it woke me up" (80). Despite rejecting the role of mother at the novel's outset, her moments of motherhood are significant to her. She threatens the policeman with violence and ultimately finds the loss of her babies devastating. The nameless protagonist does not become a mother in her human form, but when she is a sow, her motherhood is feral and occurs when she is freed of the conventions of womanhood. The term "mammal" comes from the Latin word "mamma" (breast), and this moment of feral motherhood serves to demonstrate the maternal experience shared by humans and other animals.

Kinship with Animals

Adams's and Donovan's *Animals and Women: Feminist Theoretical Explorations* calls for a feminism that includes humans and more-than-human life forms and encourages a departure from the submissive position of being oppressed, which has dominated women, animals, and the environment. They contend that both women and animals have historically been objectified as "other" in relation to the white, classical, and male (human) body. In both novels, the protagonists experience a heightened sense of the outdoors and feel the natural environment breaking down the boundaries between humans and animals. In *Pig Tales*, this includes eating flowers and apples and being surrounded by birds, the joy of the protagonist's life (12). The woman becomes frustrated when visiting the country house of a client as she can see fields, thickets, and trees outside the window and feels an intense urge to roll around in the grass and nibble it, but her hopes are dashed because the client keeps her "tied up the whole weekend" (13). The protagonist longs to frolic and roam free as a feral creature but is tied up due to her client's sexual proclivities.

Nightbitch also has an intense visceral experience of being outdoors, particularly on her night hunts where she chases rabbits and takes pleasure in defecating on her neighbours' grass. Her experiences of being in indoor environments, such as the supermarket and canteen, are also heightened by her canine senses. But it is in the outdoors that she feels a sense of affinity and freedom: "A wide-open field full of supple green grass through which we could run and run, and run, feeling the full power of our bodies, the blood careening through our muscles and fascia, a place where our lungs would open and we could take into us the entirety of the sky, a place where there were no humans but just the throb and thrust of life, life, life" (61). Part of this experience of the outside world is also a sense of kinship with other animals. In *Pig Tales*, Honoré brays about the woman's "menagerie" of pets (45), and she says the following: "At times I felt as though I understood everything the birds said. There were cats, too, and dogs; the dogs always barked when they saw me, while the cats gave me funny looks" (39). Affinities with animals (the little dog and the guinea pig she acquires which Honoré slaughters and puts in the pocket of her work uniform much to her dismay) further convey the feral kinships with other species she feels. Developing gut feelings and an aversion to eating meat develop in synchrony with the woman's metamorphosis.

The woman in *Pig Tales* develops an aversion to ham, offal, pork, "pate, sausages, and salami—all those handy luncheon meats" (40) and cannot stomach the idea of eating what are now her kin while indulging in raw unpeeled potatoes and the flowers she is given as gifts: "I had these cravings for bloodlettings. The clients themselves were getting fatter. My knees ached beneath their weight. I was seeing stars, I was seeing knives, cleavers" (17). She then later says, "As soon as I nodded off on my stool, images of blood and butchery flooded my mind. I saw Honoré looming over me, opening his mouth as if for a kiss, then biting me savagely in the bacon" (41).

The woman in *Pig Tales* fantasizes about being killed, and Nightbitch desires to kill. She murders small animals as she stalks the suburban gardens in the dark and finally slaughters their beloved pet cat in a harrowing scene of bloodlust. Nightbitch begins to suspect that the pack of dogs that visit her, led by a golden retriever, are Jen (one of the other mothers) and her friends: the long hair, the smell of strawberries, and the friend with a hangdog face. She wonders if all the moms are secretly turning into dogs and if this is a natural part of motherhood: matrescence as becoming feral. In addition to engaging in doggy games and behaviours, the mother is obsessed with raw meat. She feeds it to her son while they play doggies, causing her husband to ask if she intends to be a butcher. When she and her son are out for lunch, she is overtaken by an animal trance, of a "hunger that filled up every space inside her until she was nearly crazed" (78), and she loses herself eating meatloaf, stunning other customers. Although she has an affinity with other dogs, her tastes are true to her animal form. In *Pig Tales*, the woman who becomes a pig is a herbivore, while Nightbitch is a (murderous) carnivore. The protagonist of *Pig Tales* captures this ambivalence: "On the one hand, I was dreaming about blood night after night and had these vague impulses to hack up some plump flesh. On the other hand, flesh was precisely what repelled me the most. At the time I didn't understand these contradictions very well. Now I know that nature abounds in them, that opposites meet constantly in this world" (42). The oscillations in both novels between human and animal, domesticated and feral, contentment and rage, and the abundant contradictions and conflicts the protagonists in both novels experience convey the ambivalence many people experience during matrescence. In *Pig Tales*, after her lover Yvan is killed (to be later stuffed and displayed in the entrance hall of the Museum of Natural History), the woman is caught in a net, put in a van, and transferred to the zoo, where she is kept in a cage. Finally, the protagonist comes to, finding herself in a refrigerated truck on the way to the slaughterhouse. She is stark naked, in her human form, and escapes being turned into the offal to which she is so averse.

Towards the end of Darrieussecq's novella, the protagonist shifts between pig and human states; similarly, in *Nightbitch*, the mother oscillates between her human and dog form. Baraitser defines transformation as: "an induced or spontaneous change from one element or another. In common usage it describes what happens when something is changed utterly" (56). Baraitser draws on Luce Irigaray's concept of woman as that which overflows its idea, going beyond its conceptual frame for understanding itself (58), and she argues that the concept of transformation inherently blurs boundaries and challenges limits or edges (57). The transformations in these novels explore bodies in flux between a human and an animal state while also suggesting the human as an animal state.

Conclusion: From Pig to Dog

Both women learn to accept and enjoy their animal forms. In *Pig Tales*, the protagonist experiences a primal sense of life as she perceives her animal ancestors in her body:

> A craving for life sent shivers through me, engulfed me; it was like wild boars galloping in my brain, lightning streaking through my sinews, something that came from the depths of the wind, from the most ancient of bloodlines. I felt in the very fibres of my being the anguish of the dinosaurs, the tenacity of coelacanths, and knowing that these big fish were still alive impelled me to go on. (128)

Despite the acerbic wit of Darrieussecq's protagonist, she ends up being quite harmless. Her ferality is muted and she lives a contented life alone as a sow most of the time, although occasionally saddened "to think that now I would remain a poor dumb creature" (66). She only turns human at the full moon when she cranes her neck towards it "to show, once again, a human face" (134–35), mourn Yvan, and write her story in a notebook she found in the abandoned farm.

In *Nightbitch*, metamorphosis provides a more powerful and potent outcome. The mother is a successful performance artist with a lucrative career and sold-out shows for her strange public performance of *Nightbitch*. There is a sense that she has achieved an equilibrium between her woman-mother self, feral self, and creative self. The performance ends with her on stage with her son, to whom she delivers the limp body of a bunny that they have hunted for him to sniff and then caress. The final image is of "a feral woman and her offspring with the still-warm body of a rabbit in his hands" (238). This feral mother is celebrated, her animality part of her mothering.

In the twenty-five years between the novels, feminism has changed significantly. Intersectional feminism and matricentric feminism have influenced my reading of the ending of *Nightbitch*. *Pig Tales* offers transgression between human and animal boundaries, as the protagonist transforms from woman to pig, drawing attention to the sexism that the woman experiences. Within Western cultures, animals are abused and lack agency and there are moments within both novels where the women's transformation into an animal is confusing and disempowering.

However, ultimately, the transformation from woman to animal in *Pig Tales* and *Nightbitch* provides an alternative to the lie that women and mothers can have it all. This is the critique *Nightbitch* opens with, but the journey of the novel evokes a feral womanhood that arrives at a place of empowerment, creative energy, joy, alternative forms of mother love, and an expanded definition of what it is to be a good mother.

Endnotes

1. Andrea O'Reilly draws attention to the biological dimensions of women's lives: menstruation, pregnancy, childbirth, breastfeeding, and mothering in her article "Matricentric Feminism: A Feminism for Mothers" (2019):

   Mothers can no longer talk about their reproductive identities and experiences without being called essentialist. But maternal scholars do not reduce women's sense of self to motherhood, nor do they say that this is what makes her a woman or that motherhood is more important than other variables that constitute her self. They say only that motherhood matters and that it is central and integral to understanding the lives of women as mothers. Thus, mothers need a feminism, in both theory and practice, for and about their identities and experiences as mothers. (23)

   In this article I consider the protagonists of both novels as mothers although *Pig Tales* involves pregnancy loss and a breadth of experiences of being a woman.

2. One rationale for the connection between mothers as/of pigs and dogs is maternal practices, such as breastfeeding, that have been part of a cultural process of domestication.

3. The slur also was used to associate divine and powerful women (Artemis and Diana) with sexually depraved beasts, in which their followers were described by the phrase "son of a bitch" (Nguyen).

Works Cited

Adams, Carol J., and Josephine Donovan, editors. *Animals and Women: Feminist Theoretical Explorations*. Duke University Press, 1995.

Ahmed, Sara. *Living a Feminist Life*. Duke University Press, 2017.

Armstrong, Josh, et al. *Becoming Feral*. Objet-a Creative Studio, 2021.

Baraitser, Lisa. *Maternal Encounters: The Ethics of Interruption*. Routledge/ Taylor & Francis Group, 2009.

Braidotti, Rosi. *Nomadic Subjects*. Columbia University Press, 2011.

Darrieussecq, Marie. *Pig Tales: A Novel of Lust and Transformation*. Translated by Linda Coverdale. Faber and Faber, 1996.

Deleuze, Gilles, and Félix Guattari. *A Thousand Plateaus*. 1987. The Athlone Press, 2004.

Friedan, Betty. *The Feminine Mystique*. 1963. Dell/Laurel, 1984.

Haraway, Donna J. *Simians, Cyborgs, and Women*. Association Books, 1991.

Halberstam, Jack. *The Queer Art of Failure*. Duke University Press, 2011.

Miles, Margaret, "Carnal Abominations: The Female Body as Grotesque." *The Grotesque in Art and Literature: Theological Reflections*. Edited by James Luther et al. Wm. B. Eerdmans Publishing, 1997, pp. 83 –112.

Nguyen, Cecilia Posted. "The History of the Word 'Bitch' and Its Inherent Subordinating Nature." *The Revival Zine*, 27 Aug. 2020, https:// therevivalzine.wordpress.com/2020/08/27/the-history-of-the-word-bitch-and-its-inherent-subordinating-nature/. Accessed 5 Jan. 2025.

O'Reilly, Andrea. "The 'Wildness of Motherhood': Transforming Maternal Rage, Transgressing Patriarchal Motherhood to Realize Maternal Empowerment: A Reading of Rachel Yoder's *Nightbitch*." Edited by Andrea O'Reilly, Fiona Joy Green and Victoria Bailey. Demeter Press, 2023. pp. 215–36.

Parker-Starbuck, Jennifer. "Becoming-Animate: On the Performed Limits of 'Human.'" *Theatre Journal,* vol. 58, no. 4, 2006, pp. 649–68.

Parker-Starbuck, Jennifer. "Pig Bodies and Vegetative States: Diagnosing the Symptoms of a Culture of Excess." *Women & Performance: A Journal of Feminist Theory*, vol. 18, no. 2, 2008, pp. 133–47.

Pick, Anat. "Pigscripts: The Indignities of Species in Marie Darrieussecq's *Pig Tales*." *parallax*, vol. 12, no. 1, 2006, pp. 43–56.

Quinn, Karina. "The Body That Read the Laugh: Cixous, Kristeva, and Mothers Writing Mothers." *M/C Journal,* vol. 15, no. 4, 2012, https:// doi.org/10.5204/mcj.492. Accessed 25 Jan. 2025.

Rich, Adrienne. *Of Woman Born: Motherhood as Experience and Institution.* W.W. Norton and Company, 1976.

Russo, Mary. *The Female Grotesque: Risk, Excess and Modernity.* Routledge, 1994.

Simoons, Frederick J., and James A. Baldwin. "Breast-Feeding of Animals by Women: Its Socio-Cultural Context and Geographic Occurrence." *Anthropos*, vol. 77, no. 3–4, pp. 421–48.

Yoder, Rachel. *Nightbitch.* Penguin Random House, 2021.

16.

Gone Feral: Deviant Mothers, Defective Mothering, and the Undoing of Normative Motherhood in Katixa Agirre's *Mothers Don't* and Yewande B. Omotoso's *An Unusual Grief*

Andrea O'Reilly

This collection probes the concept of ferality concerning traditional, patriarchal concepts of womanhood and femininity and asks what becoming or being feral means for women. More specifically, the collection explores how untamed and undomesticated femininity may be positioned and understood as resistance to patriarchal culture. This chapter discusses these concepts and questions to explore how deviant mothers and their defective mothering may be read as enactments of ferality to destabilize and decentre normative motherhood in two recent novels: *Mothers Don't* (2022) by Basque writer Katixa Agirre and *An Unusual Grief* (2022) by Nigerian and South African author Yewande B. Omotoso. *Mothers Don't* examines the infanticide of twin infants, while *An Unusual Grief* explores the suicide of a twenty-four-year daughter who is estranged from her mother. In this chapter, I explore how the two novels in taking up two of the most tabooed maternal topics—infanticide and the suicide of a child—position mothers and their mothering as feral, deviant, and defective to unsettle and undo normative motherhood.

Compellingly, the titles of each novel signify this resistant stance on motherhood. The title *Mothers Don't* indicates that certain behaviours are not allowed for mothers, while the word "unusual" in the title of the second book implies that what the novel explores is peculiar if not aberrant. Indeed, the words "don't" and "unusual" when conveyed about motherhood signpost the good-bad mother dichotomy of patriarchal culture. In their introduction to *Bad Mothers: Regulations, Representations, and Resistance*, Michelle Hughes Miller, Tamar Hagar, and Rebecca Jaremko Bromwich argue that "the Bad Mother trope arises from the cultural inculcation of the Good Mother and its successful institutionalization" (6). Moreover, they continue, the "Good Mother shapes the Bad Mother through its mechanism of the accountability to the expectations that it holds" (6). The good and bad mother tropes are thus divergent yet symbiotic: The meaning of the one depends on that of the other. At the most rudimentary of its expectations, the good mother trope demands that mothers will not harm their children and will protect their children and keep them safe. In the introduction to *Mothers Who Kill*, Charlotte Beyer and Josephine Savarese argue that the association "of mothers and motherhood with care and nurturing is dramatically at odds with the figure of the mother who kills her child" (9). I suggest that the same could be said of a mother whose child commits suicide. As the mother Mojisola reflects in *An Unusual Grief*, "It is [her] fault that [her daughter] is dead" (90) and because of this, she is "a failed mother, the spectacle of a mother who lost a child" (18). Indeed, normative motherhood assumes and expects that good mothers will not harm their children and that the children of good mothers will not harm themselves.

Kelly Struthers Montford and Chloë Taylor argue that "one way in which women have been oppressed has been through their relegation to the domestic sphere and through the exploitation of their domestic labour" (6). Thus, going feral can be understood as a liberation from patriarchal culture, which has caged feminine spirits and neutered feminine authenticity. This chapter argues that the mothers of *Mother's Don't*—the narrator, her friend Lea, and Alice, the mother who commits infanticide—and Mojisola in *An Unusual Grief* go feral, and this ferality makes possible an undoing of normative motherhood.

Mother's Don't achieves this by positioning maternal ambivalence, rage, and even infanticide as understandable, relatable, and indeed commonplace to normalize maternal deviance and defectiveness and thus unsettle the normative assumption that motherlove is unconditional and that mothering is always experienced as fulfilling and gratifying. In an interview, Agirre explains that her intention in writing *Mothers Don't* was "to shock" and to "show how common infanticide is and how closely it is related to motherhood" (qtd. in Fraser). *An Unusual Grief* also presents a deviant mother and defective mothering in its descriptions of Mojisola's maternal reluctance, ambivalence, discontent, and estrangement from her daughter to unsettle the expectations of normative motherhood. The novel also activates ferality by connecting, as Omotoso explains, "death and desire" (qtd. in Hill) to show how the death of her child releases Mojisola's sexuality to renew and empower her as a woman and to forgive herself as a mother. The story is about, as the author explains, "Yinka [the daughter] dying and Mojisola [the mother] waking up" (qtd. in Hill) to position maternal loss, in Jeanne-Maire Jackson's words, as "the catalyst for all kinds of growth." In their descriptions of maternal reluctance, ambivalence, discontent, and estrangement—and in positioning infanticide as understandable and a child's suicide as transformative—the two novels enact maternal deviance and defectiveness to show how ferality can undo normative motherhood.

"It's Not Like Mothers Possess Some Magical Essence": Infanticide, Maternal Ambivalence, and Rage as Enactments of Ferality in *Mother's Don't*

The first chapter of *Mothers Don't*, titled "The Revelation," opens with an epigraph from the play *Medea* and describes how the nanny in *Mothers Don't* found the drowned twin infants as two little bundles on their parents' bed upon her return to the family's home. Beside the bed sat the mother, Alice Espanet, dressed in a nightgown with her left breast exposed. As Melanie, the nanny, touches the twins, who were "not moving" and had "purple lips and cold skin" (4), the mother Alice tells her "They're fine now" (4). The mother "spoke with perfect calm" and in a voice that struck Melanie "as terrible, unbearable" (4). Even worse though, Melanie thinks, is the mother's "placid, almost listless, indolent manner" (5). Alice's unnervingly calm behaviour as she sits beside her dead babies with her left breast exposed characterizes her as the disturbed Medea of the chapter's epigraph. Soon the police and ambulance arrive, and the children's father and Alice are taken to the hospital.

The narrative shifts to the first-person perspective of an unnamed narrator who mentions hearing the media furor over the alleged infanticide but consciously ignores it given that she will soon give birth to her first child. However, two weeks later as she is giving birth, the narrator experiences "in the most unexpected of ways, a revelation. A revelation that would determine, if not the rest of [her] life (out of deference for the child about to be born), then at least the next two to three years of it" (8). "The Revelation" the narrator refers to is the realization that she knew Alice, who then went by the name Jade, for several weeks eleven years ago when she was at university. It causes the narrator to break her focus as she is birthing her child and results in her asking for an epidural for pain relief. As the anesthesia takes effect, the narrator reflects: "I had to hang on to THE REVELATION at all costs" (10). After the birth, the narrator confides that "all she could think about was Alice Espanet" (11) and realizes that she knew [she] had no choice; [she] had to immerse [her]self in the inquietude. [She is] a writer, after all" (12). Moreover, the narrator further reflects: "Given my state at the time, it was easy to surrender to my obsession. I was at its mercy and that seemed just fine to me" (12). I argue that the opening chapter introduces us to two feral mothers: Alice who kills her twin infants and the narrator, an ambivalent mother who seems more preoccupied with a former friend who has murdered her children than with the child she is birthing.

The following chapter, opening with the epigraph "Mothers do not write, they are written," explores the unnamed narrator's early months of motherhood that "physically and psychologically sucked [her] dry" (17). When she learns that she has won a prestigious literary award for her first novel, the narrator realizes that "[her] identity as a mother had devoured all other identities and banished all [her] other selves into exile" (23). Moreover, as the narrator reflects further: "[The award] made it clear to [her] that she was no longer [herself] ... and that it was time to turn things around; somehow [she] had to start piecing back together [her] essential self" (22). For the narrator, the path to this reclaimed self was to write about Alice and the infanticide of her twins. The unnamed mother-writer becomes, as reviewer Fiona Graham notes, "obsessed with the infanticide and the crime feeds on her own ambivalent attitude to motherhood." The narrator takes a leave of absence from her job, not to care for her new baby as would be expected but to investigate and write about the infanticide committed by a woman she briefly knew while at university. With the money she receives from the literary award, the narrator places her six-month-old son in daycare and leaves the daycare as a free woman—"or as free a woman as a mother can be" (25). The narrator's newfound freedom from motherhood that concludes the chapter connects to Alice's determination to become a mother described in the following chapter.

After twenty-two visits to a fertility clinic, Alice became pregnant with twins. The narrator visits the clinic, but with no one willing to talk about Alice, she can only speculate on Alice's feelings on becoming a mother, wondering whether her inability to become pregnant was because she unconsciously did not want children, or, perhaps, she did want children and was willing to sacrifice everything to have her own baby. The narrator then contrasts Alice's planned pregnancy to the shock of her unexpected one (34). For the narrator, pregnancy "had been a latent menace, a skilled sharpshooter, ready to end [her] life as [she] liked it" (34). The narrator wonders if Alice saw it that way as well. Either way, in not conforming to the normative script of motherhood as desired, planned, and naturally occurring, Alice and the narrator are defective, if not deviant, in their maternal identities. Moreover, in disclosing her ambivalence, if not aversion, to motherhood, in wondering whether Alice felt the same, and in identifying with a woman who killed her children, the narrator reveals that mothers may not be as fulfilled and happy through motherhood as the institution of normative motherhood expects and requires them to be.

Indeed, the following chapters demonstrate and prove that maternal ambivalence and even the extreme of infanticide can be understood as understandable, relatable, and even commonplace. As noted above, Agirre's intent in writing the novel was "to shock" and "to show how common infanticide is and how closely it is related to motherhood" (qtd. in Fraser). Although patriarchal culture may insist that mothers do not harm children or dislike motherhood (as indicated in the novel's title of *Mothers Don't*), this narrative shows otherwise. The narrator shares the pre-Hispanic myth of La Llorona, a mother who throws her two children into a river and then, devastated by guilt, kills herself (44). This story is told in various iterations from Mexico to Chile. In Panama, the mother's negligence is understood to be the cause of the children's death, while in other cultures, the mother murders her children, as Medea does, to avenge the man who abandoned them. Later, the narrator mentions the author Muriel Spark, who abandoned her baby and left him in the care of his manic-depressive father in Rhodesia, and discusses Sylvia Plath's suicide when her children were two years and three months old. The narrator reflects that "[Plath's] all-encompassing love for her [children] made her suicide all the more unimaginable" (80) and questions "If only for their sakes, wasn't it worth it to go on a little bit longer? Wasn't the simple prospect of watching [them] grow up enough reason to stay alive?" (80). We later learn that Ted Hughes, Plath's husband, had another daughter with his lover and that his lover also "turned on the gas" and killed herself along with her young daughter (81). The chapter "Killing Children" provides a history of infanticide, which shows, in the narrator's words, that "historically speaking, killing your own children [was not] considered a crime" (89–90). And even when infanticide did become one, as the narrator explains, it did not stop but was only "performed in secret" (93). Indeed, as the narrator confirms: "Children have always been murdered.... We're just more now horrified by it" (95). Significantly, the narrator composes the chapter as an address to the jury of Alice's soon-to-be trial and concludes it by asking them: "We cannot understand it, can you?" (97). We cannot understand mothers who kill their children, the narrator emphasizes, because they "challenge our preconceived notions" (97) dictated by the scripts of normative motherhood.

One of the preconceived notions these mothers challenge is the assumption and expectation that motherlove is unconditional and that mothering is always experienced as fulfilling and gratifying. Although the narrator does not kill her child, she does understand why some mothers do and identifies with these mothers through her maternal ambivalence. The narrator explains that while much has been said about the exhaustion of motherhood, there is almost no mention of the hours of boredom: "The succession of gray, amorphous days during which breastfeeding, changing diapers, trying to get the crying baby back to sleep ... that take up your life to the point of suffocating it" (53). The narrator shares the words of author Doris Lessing who abandoned two children from her first marriage: "There is nothing more boring for an intelligent woman than to spend endless amounts of time with small children" (54). Yet society, as the narrator reflects, "tells you that there's nothing more desirable, nothing more revolutionary, than devoting yourself to the other" (53). But "if it were really so beautiful, so desirable, and revolutionary, then by now men would have taken it upon themselves to stay home and send women off to work" (54). However, the narrator then writes: "Sometimes, it can be something beautiful, desirable, revolutionary," like when "the baby returns your smile as you nurse him and then you know that nothing can compete with this moment: the sensation in your nipples, your limitless skin, the trickle of hot milk, the smile, the most honest of gazes" (55). The narrator's words recall those of Adrienne Rich when she describes her maternal ambivalence as "the alternation between the bitter resentment and raw-edged nerves, and blissful gratification and tenderness" (1). In her maternal ambivalence, the narrator identifies with Alice and other mothers who kill their children, and in writing Alice's story, the narrator realizes that "as she was building Alice, [she] was rebuilding [herself]" (57). I suggest that the narrator, through her empathy with mothers who commit infanticide and in rebuilding herself through this alliance, may be read as a feral mother who unsettles preconceived notions of normative motherhood by showing that motherlove is not unconditional, nor is it always experienced as fulfilling and gratifying.

As the narrator is positioned as a feral mother so too is her close friend, Lea. With Alice's trial about to start, the narrator arranges a holiday with her family to meet with Lea, a close friend who also knew Alice from their university days. We learn that Lea, when three months pregnant with her first child, began a "whirlwind affair" with Fabrice, a married father eight years her senior at the school where she was a student teacher (68). Her husband and Fabrice's wife learned of the affair after Lea had ended it shortly before the birth. However, Lea remained "desperate to be with him," and when her third child was born, she called him. She explains to the narrator: "I didn't care anymore. I know there'd be no third chance if [my husband] found out but I didn't care" (77). Lea met Fabrice at a hotel with her six-week-old infant planning to have sex with him but did not only because he was not interested. She explains to the narrator that while she "had been obsessed with having kids, fixated on the idea since [she] was sixteen," when she became a mother she "was hit with all these doubts and needed a release valve to feel alive and Fabrice was there" (76). She explains further that "if it hadn't been for [him] [she] probably would have gone back to puking after meals. Or worse" (76). For Lea, motherhood caused such unhappiness that she had an affair to stop herself from self-harm. However, as Lea explains to the narrator: "Taking a lover while pregnant with another man's baby—

I broke a big taboo, didn't I? Maybe the biggest one of all" (68). The narrator insists that there is "a world of difference between [her] and Alice's situation" (77), but Lea emphasizes that she is more like Alice than not:

> Before I become a mother, back when my idea of motherhood was absurdly idealized, I would hear about women who abandoned their kids ... and I would find the story completely unbelievable... [But I now realize] that it's not like mothers possess some magical essence, an inherent ability to resist absolutely everything.... I'm not saying it isn't horrible ... but I do find them pretty believable now, those mothers who—under certain circumstances—abandon their children. Even those who end it all. (78)

Hearing these words, the narrator recognizes that Lea is right and that "[her] own feelings had shifted in the same direction over the past year" (78). Moreover, as both mothers question "Who could kill a child? No one," they realize that, in Lea's words, "*Since no one can, when a child is murdered, we are all potentially suspect*" (my emphasis; 75). Writing on the case of Joanna Michulski, a mother of eight who murdered her two youngest children, Adrienne Rich shares how the mothers in her poetry group "[felt] a direct connection with her desperation" and "identified with her murderous anger" (5). Lea and the narrator, like the mothers in Rich's poetry group, have known, in Rich's words, "overwhelming, unacceptable anger at [their] children" (xviii) and have dreamed "of going over the edge, of simply letting go ... so that [they could] be taken care of for once" (291). Indeed, as Rich emphasizes: "The expectations laid [on mothers] are insane expectations [but] instead of recognizing the institutional violence of patriarchal motherhood, society labels those women who finally erupt in violence as psychopathological" (272). I suggest that all that separates Lea and the narrator from mothers who kill their children is that each had an "escape valve"—for Lea, it was an affair, and for the narrator, it was writing (76)—that kept them from harming themselves and their children.

On the second to last day of Alice's trial, when a journalist invites the narrator for lunch, she confides that her "heart started to dance" (131), "was trembling" (137), and that she "hadn't felt that way in a long time, maybe not since [she] was fifteen" (137). The narrator further reflects: "From the moment I got pregnant, it was like I'd been stuck in a cold, damp cave where the rays of sunlight couldn't reach. And two years later, I saw myself emerging from the cave, stretching my limbs, warming up my muscles and skin, ready for a whole new range of erotic pleasures" (132). Her description of motherhood as cold darkness and her desire to escape it through romance as her friend Lea had done signify the narrator's ferality and her need to defy the normative script of the selfless and asexual woman of patriarchal motherhood. The following day, wearing lipstick and trembling with anticipation, and having arranged for her own father to pick her son up from daycare, the narrator joins the journalist for lunch, looking forward to "harmless flirtation, a few coquettish smiles [something for] for future fantasies" (144).

However, as they drive to the restaurant, the narrator turns on her phone to discover seven missed calls from the daycare and her husband saying their son was in the hospital. When her mother calls, the narrator realizes there is not much she can tell her: "I was far away, at a trial, no, it was even worse, I was with a man, about to eat with an interesting stranger" (150). When the doctor at the hospital asks the narrator how long her son seemed unwell, the narrator knows but cannot say that her son may have been ill that morning. However, she left him at daycare, put her phone on silent, attended a courthouse trial, and eagerly anticipated a pleasant lunch date. While there had not been a verdict that day for Alice, the narrator understands that "one was going to transpire right here, just for [her]" (151). She will learn the "master class lesson" (151) that while she was "nosing around courthouses and eating Japanese food with an exotic stranger" (151), her "destiny [as a mother] was to suffer" (151). Later, medical tests confirm that her son has viral meningitis but is soon well enough to be discharged from the hospital. As the narrator is on her way home with her husband and son, she receives a call from Jake, the journalist, sharing the verdict: Alice was found guilty but was excluded from criminal liability and would not serve prison time. Significantly, when the narrator sees her husband's curious face as she speaks to Jake, she shrugs to make light of the call: "But not because [she] wanted to hide Jake's existence, but because [she] was ready to assume [her] role as a mother of a convalescent child, everything else was too much" (155). Although the narrator's reflection here may suggest redomestication, an undoing of her resistant ferality, this chapter concludes with the narrator's promise that she will complete her novel on Alice and the infanticide of her twins.

In the final chapter of the book, the narrator confirms that she "has accepted the responsibility and weight" (160) to write Alice's story because she has come "to understand what [her] hands did" (160). The narrator wonders if she would be happier and her life easier if she was not a writer, compelled to complete this narrative, but understands that she must "be a monster, bolt the door, get [her] hands dirty, and sully more innocent souls" (161). The chapter, significantly titled "Alchemy," concludes with the narrator's realization that Alice's story has changed her and hopes that her narrative will do the same for her readers—that they too will be "covered in the muck as [she] is" (161). This muck signifies that although normative motherhood may deny maternal ambivalence and rage and demonize infanticide, these feelings are understandable and even relatable. In confirming and claiming maternal deviance and defectiveness, the novel enacts ferality to resist normative motherhood. The novel *An Unusual Grief* likewise shows how maternal deviance and defectiveness enact ferality to undo normative motherhood in its description of maternal reluctance, ambivalence, discontent, and estrangement and in positioning a child's suicide as generative, releasing the mother's sexuality, which renews and empowers her as a woman.

"She Had to Lose Her Daughter in Order to Find Herself": Maternal Loss as an Enactment of Ferality in *An Unusual Grief*

The novel opens with a woman, Mojisola, having just arrived at an unidentified location from an airport, speaking to Zelda, a landlady, and asking to stay at an apartment and collect unidentified items. No other context is given, but as the novel's opening pages unfold, we learn that Mojisola has arrived at the "home of her dead child, a place she has never been in, was never invited to" (10). The child is her twenty-four-year-old daughter Yinka, from whom Mojisola has been estranged for six months. As Mojisola enters the apartment, she finds a note "in a language she does not speak…. The task ahead is daunting but clear: she must learn the language in which the note is written, and ultimately read the message" (10). The language Mojisola must learn and the message she must read is an explanation as to why her daughter committed suicide. While her husband Titus seeks to comfort Mojisola, saying that "they'll never know why" (231), Mojisola knows why her daughter killed herself. It is because "she failed [as a mother]" (231) and understands that although "[people] may not say the words out loud, they are wondering: 'How did you let this happen?'" (18). "Locked up in her thoughts, tracking through in her life," Mojisola seeks "to find the actual moment of her crime as a mother; the actual second it was that she let her daughter fall ... where her motherness was finally defeated" (230, 231). Mojisola knows that "the failure is plain and unavoidable, because, just two weeks ago, her baby had died, 24 years old and alone" (15). As Mojisola tracks her life to identify and itemize her failures as a mother, the narrative moves between the present, the recent past of Mojisola's marriage and motherhood, and the more distant past of her childhood. These memories reveal that Mojisola was a reluctant, ambivalent, and discontented mother as well as estranged from her daughter. In this maternal defectiveness, Mojisola believes she has failed her daughter and is responsible for her death. Omotoso emphasizes that in her writing she is "obsessed with mothers and death" (qtd. in Dike) and interested in exploring "the equation where life equals death" (qtd in Hill). Although the novel centres on a daughter's death, it is ultimately about a mother's life and how Mojisola, in losing her daughter, ultimately finds herself. As Mallika Ramachandran notes, the novel "is a story of grief but it is also the story of a woman's journey to understand herself, and her relationships—one might even say her life so far." In this novel, maternal loss releases Mojisola's sexuality, which renews and empowers her as a woman and highlights how, in turn, this loss becomes "a catalyst for all kinds of growth" (Jackson). This renewal enables Mojisola to understand that although she may not be the perfect mother, as prescribed by normative motherhood, she is ultimately not responsible for her daughter's suicide. This realization, as it empowers Mojisola as a woman, also allows her to forgive herself as a mother.

From Mojisola's recollections, we learn she became pregnant when she was relatively older, in her mid-thirties. Although the pregnancy "made sense to her husband, and to science, it did not to [her]" (44). Mojisola believed that "her aversion to children should have been contraception enough, and [that] after five years of marriage and nothing, she felt justified and *relieved* to conclude that she was unable to conceive" (my emphasis; 45). When she is in labour with her daughter, Mojisola realizes that she is resisting her body's demand. She hopes the child will go "unborn" and wishes she can "reverse the irreversible and return to a simple existence that had gradually, over the many weeks, disappeared" (48). Similar to the narrator of *Mothers Don't,* who describes the early months of motherhood as "physically and psychologically sucking [her] dry" (17), Mojisola is "flummoxed" and "undone" by motherhood (52). Her husband Titus remembers Mojisola as "a sad wife and mother" (206) who cried every night and could only be comforted by her aunt staying with them. The narrative explains that had Mojisola sought medical advice, she would have been diagnosed with "anxiety, post-partum, schizophrenia, and mental illness" (53). Later, when Mojisola tries but fails to return to her work as an illustrator after her daughter's second birthday, she realizes that she has "lost the mental composure her job required" and will never feel like herself again (53). When her husband tells Mojisola he wants a second child, she tells him "no": "I need another two lives to recover from the first" (50). Undeniably, Mojisola is a reluctant, ambivalent, and discontented mother. Through this defectiveness and deviance, the text positions her as a feral mother who defies and subverts the normative script that she should be happy and fulfilled in motherhood.

When Yinka is born, Mojisola describes her daughter as "a strange, strange child" (49). As Yinka grows, the relationship between mother and daughter becomes more estranged. Yinka became obsessed with drawing at six. She often fell into a daze, once even falling off a chair and cutting her head open. Although a doctor assured Mojisola that Yinka's fascination with drawing was harmless, she nonetheless banned her daughter from drawing despite Yinka's begging and whimpering: "Yinka cried in protest but slowly over the years she both acquiesced to Mojisola's will and resented it. A small hole grew in the space between mother and daughter—it would never close" (58). Indeed, as Yinka grows, the text tells us that "the unconscious part of [her] still remembered, and unable to win the fight that really mattered" (59) she fought with her mother about everything else. Although Yinka eventually does draw again, Mojisola realizes that her daughter has become "strange to her" (72). At fifteen, she shared with her mother that she felt "sad all the time"; Mojisola did not know what to say and could only instruct her daughter to "cover it" (71). But then, as the text tells us "a heavy knowledge came into Mojisola's chest; she knew she had failed, that she ought to have said something and she'd failed to do so" (71). Later, Mojisola explains that in the years that followed "she tried, she really did [to speak to her daughter about her sadness] but Yinka never took it up again" (114).

The mother and daughter are permanently estranged when Yinka discovers that her father is having an affair and that her mother, while knowing about it, chooses to do nothing. After calling her mother a coward, Yinka leaves their home in Cape Town and moves to Johannesburg. The next time Mojisola sees her daughter, she will be dead. Mojisola reflects: "Of all the things her daughter had accused her of (ageist, antifeminist, homophobic, to name a few) coward was the worst. [Mojisola] recalls the disappointment in Yinka's eyes. The sense that somehow, even though he was the cheat, it was her, Mojisola, who had failed" (114). From her memories, it is evident that Mojisola and Yinka's relationship was discordant and distant and that Mojisola did not understand or support her daughter as a mother should. As with her maternal ambivalence, her mothering is presented as defective, positioning Mojisola as a feral mother. This ferality becomes further enacted in the novel's acknowledgement of Mojisola's maternal loss as generative, as it releases her sexuality, which renews and empowers her as a woman and allows her to forgive herself as a mother.

When the narrative moves from past to present, Mojisola is determined to know in death the daughter she did not know in life. Mojisola tries one password after another in an attempt to gain access to her daughter's computer, but she feels she is not "qualified to read her daughter's documents" (69). Eventually, she guesses the correct password, and her daughter's desktop appears, revealing "a much-desired intimacy, however mechanical" (69). What Mojisola finds on her daughter's desktop is an "unexpected" dating profile with Firebabe as Yinka's moniker and Mojisola is "surprised" at how popular her daughter was with both men and women (70, 72). Mojisola "tracks through [Yinka's] various profiles and chatter" (73), unsure how to feel about "[her daughter's] beauty, her wit, and sexuality" (73). Mojisola then decides to chat with a man named D-Man because photos between Yinka and him have not yet been exchanged, allowing Mojisola to pretend that she is Yinka. Mojisola suggests that they meet, and as she anticipates their date, she, like the narrator from *Mother's Don't*, can "almost smell the mounting desire" (103). She then books a "mani-pedi" at her daughter's beauty salon and signs her name as Yinka, reflecting that "She'll never be able to explain this to anyone. They'll say, 'She went to live as her daughter' ... They might call it a mental breakdown ... [but] she doesn't feel broken down.... she feels spirited away ... into a different but necessary existence" (104). I suggest that this "different but necessary existence" is her emerging sexuality, which positions Mojisola as a feral woman and will eventually lead to an understanding of her daughter's life and death and forgiveness for herself as Yinka's mother.

As she prepares for her date with D-Man, Mojisola has a bath in the bathtub where Yinka's body was found and holds the knife she used to kill herself. On the date, she wears a red dress from her daughter's closet. When she meets D-Man, he introduces himself as Jide, and she introduces herself as Yinka. Ramachandran argues that in her attempt "to understand Yinka, Mojisola ends up 'becoming' her and living her life [which] frees her from the bounds [of her own life]." When Mojisola returns home from her date with a man she describes as "too young" (108), she admires herself in the mirror, observing that her lips are full and brown like Yinka's and questions if "she is wrong to enjoy this?" (112) and if "her daughter would disapprove of her sudden delight" (112). On their second date, at Jide's apartment, Mojisola, internally confesses "how much every fiber of her body wants the game [Jide] is offering" (117). She feels desire is "scandalous [as she is] a married woman, an older woman, a grieving woman, a mother woman" (117). Although she understands "the inappropriateness of her internal longings" (117) and feels "shame and loathing" (117), she nonetheless dabs perfume on the bulge of her inner thigh as she prepares for the date. Mojisola arrives at Jide's apartment hoping to see Yinka's drawings there, but once inside, Mojisola discovers a camera and whips in Jide's boudoir and learns that both he and Yinka were into kink (121). Later, Mojisola texts Jide to tell him that she is not Yinka but her mother and that her daughter is dead. She returns to his apartment bringing with her the knife her daughter used to kill herself. After a hard slap across Jide's face to satisfy his BSDM desires, Mojisola strips herself naked, and although she does not use the knife on Jide, Mojisola engages in BDSM sex with him "to consume him in her swell, to obscure and obliterate, to devour" (135). In doing this, Mojisola realizes that she "*has repossessed her own Self*" (my emphasis; 134).

Mojisola continues to visit Jide. She initially believes she is doing so to try and know her daughter, her secrets and "the things she hid away" (176). However, Mojisola realizes that she keeps "returning not for her daughter, but for herself" (174). She enjoys BSDM sex because "when she plays with D-Man she is cut loose from [being] a wife and mother, respectable friend. She is suspended in an enticing void of nothing ... cut loose from civility and the constraints of politeness (174). Mojisola also becomes romantically involved with Wicus Kriel, the proprietor of "We Do Boards," the company Yinka had contacted for framing her drawings. When he visits Mojisola, they share a joint. Mojisola feels "free and dangerous" and leans in to kiss him. As she does so, she feels she has become a cliché: "Scorned wife embarks on a love affair with an unlikely Afrikaans carpenter ... [but] surely [one is] allowed at least one cliché per lifetime" (131). After Wicus leaves, Mojisola masturbates with "strokes [that] are slow and even" (131) and realizes that even though "nothing and no one has taught her this ... everything has brought her here" (131). As Mojisola continues to have BDSM sex with Jide, she, through mas-turbation "finds a way to hold herself, all her parts. There are so many bits to her, many without names, without labels, beyond Biology, beyond explanation. And yet here, now, she can hold them all, she has found a way" (131). Later, Mojisola reflects: "She spent her forties and fifties having bi-monthly mechanical sex with a cheating husband. Now as she climbs into old age, she's beset on all sides: puppy-eyed penitent husband, sulking Afrikaans carpenter would-be-lover and (not to be outdone) BDSM maniac boy-toy" (144). In taking on two lovers and enjoying BDSM sex as a sixty-year-old married woman who is grieving the suicide of her daughter, Mojisola is indisputably a deviant mother. Even more "scandalous" (117) is that Mojisola's newfound kink sexuality delivers "a different but necessary existence" (101), in which Mojisola can finally possess herself, understand her daughter's death, and forgive herself as a mother. Indeed, the novel concludes with Mojisola understanding what brought her to her daughter's home: "to collect her daughter out of her hiding place" (216). And in that process, "she has collected herself" (216). She continues: "It is a strange feeling to know Yinka in death so much closer than she knew her in life. Stranger still to know she had to lose her daughter in order to find herself" (216).

With this understanding, Mojisola realizes that her daughter's interest in BDSM sex was "a fetish" and "her death had nothing to do with [it]" (183). BDSM "wasn't the sickness itself but rather, the search for a cure. She wanted it, no one forced her, she did it for relief, for rescue" (225). Mojisola also comes to understand that Yinka ended her life not because of Mojisola's "failures" as a mother but because Yinka, like her father and Mojisola's husband, suffered from depression. Remembering Yinka's words that she was sad all the time, Mojisola asks her husband about his own depression, which he describes as "endless and with no reprieve. Final. Unbearable" (221). Mojisola finally comes to understand her daughter's depression.

Mojisola starts to draw again and takes on a position as an illustrator for a company that her daughter had worked for, which is "something [Mojisola] could never [have] imagined for herself, something she feels her daughter handed to her, something she took from her daughter's hands" (224). At the novel's conclusion, Mojisola is reconciled with her husband; they have forgiven each other for "being useless at the truth" (220). As the novel ends many years into the future, Mojisola has "learned the fault lies in her thinking" (222) to finally appreciate "what she had been seeing all along but not knowing what she had been looking at" (232) was "not perfection, not people who never faltered, but rather the opposite" (232). And in this, she sees "her shame and her courage, her capacity for failure but also for magic" (232). In other words, while Mojisola once saw herself and her mothering as deviant and defective, she now realizes that the "ugliness and wonder" (232) of her maternal life and self are the inherent and inevitable "resplendent chaos" (233) of motherhood that the normative institution denies and demonizes. Thus, *An Unusual Grief*, as with *Mother's Don't*, claims and honours maternal deviance and defectiveness to enact ferality and undo normative motherhood.

Conclusion: What Is Deviant and Defective Are Not the Mothers Themselves but What Is Expected and Required of Them in the Institution of Motherhood

In the introduction to *Monstrous Mothers: Troubling Tropes*, Abigail L. Palko writes: "An examination of monstrous mothers—those who deliberately or not, fail to live up to the idealization [of normative motherhood]—helps us to understand the pressures under which all mothers mother" (12). In the Coda to this collection, I argue that the trope of the monstrous mother "exceeds the good and bad mother binary by providing context to the mother's life to humanize her character" (269). Texts that enact the rhetorical strategy of contextualization narrate with nuance the intricacies of mothers' lives to elicit understanding and, arguably, empathy. These texts humanize the monstrous mother "to render a complexity that cannot be confined or contained to idealized or disparaged maternal stereotypes" (274). While Palko and I use the term "monstrous" in these discussions, I suggest our observations apply to feral mothers and my reading of *Mothers Don't* and *An Unusual Grief.* The feral mothers of these two novels enable us to understand the pressures under which all mothers mother by showing how commonplace maternal ambivalence, discontent, rage, estrangement, and even infanticide are and how the so-called maternal deviance and defectiveness of these feral mothers are created by and born from the institution of normative motherhood, which then demonizes this behaviour. Indeed, the novels disclose that what is deviant and defective are not mothers themselves but what is expected and required of them in the institution of normative motherhood. The two novels also enact the strategy of contextualization by elucidating how the mothers' lives are not of their own making, but are constructed and constrained by the patriarchal culture in which they live to elicit understanding and compassion. In humanizing feral mothers and demonstrating how commonplace maternal ferality is, the novels reveal and emphasize that what needs to be challenged and changed are not mothers but normative motherhood to unsettle and undo this oppressive patriarchal institution.

Works Cited

Agirre, Katixa. *Mothers Don't,* translated by Katie Whittemore. Open Letter, 2022.

Beyer, Charlotte, and Josephine Savarese. *Mothers Who Kill.* Demeter Press, 2021.

Fraser, Izzy. "Review: A Conversation with Katixa Agirre and Emily Koch on 'Mother's Don't.'" *Epigram,* 19 Oct. 2023, https://epigram.org.uk/review-in-conversation-with/. Accessed 16 Jan. 2025.

Dike, Onyinye. "'I Tend to Write Wildly and Freedly': Yewande Omotoso's First Draft." *The Republic,* 16 June. 2023, https://republic.com.ng/june-july-2023/first-draft-yewande-omotoso/. Accessed 16 Jan. 2025.

Graham, Fiona. "#RivetingReviews: Fiona Graham reviews MOTHERS DON'T by Katixa Agirre." *European Literature Network,* 5 Aug. 2023, https://www.eurolitnetwork.com/rivetingreviews-fiona-graham-reviews-mothers-dont-by-katixa-agirre/. Accessed 16 Jan. 2025.

Hill, Linda. "Staying in with Yewande Omotoso." *Linda's Book Bag*, 22 Aug. 2022, https://lindasbookbag.com/2022/03/22/staying-in-with-yewande-omotoso/. Accessed 16 Jan. 2025.

Jackson, Jeanne-Marie. "Review of *An Unusual Grief*, by Yewande Omotoso." *The Hopkins Review*, https://hopkinsreview.com/features/review-of-an-unusual-grief-by-yewande-omotoso. Accessed 16 Jan. 2025.

Hughes, Michelle Miller, et al. *Bad Mothers: Regulations, Representations, and Resistance*. Demeter Press, 2017.

Palko, Abigail L "Introduction." *Monstrous Mothers: Troubling Tropes*. Edited by Abigail L Palko and Andrea O'Reilly. Demeter Press, 2021, pp. 9–19.

Omotoso, Yewande. *An Unusual Grief*. Cassava Republic Press, 2022.

O'Reilly, Andrea. "Coda." *Monstrous Mothers: Troubling Tropes*. Edited by Abigail L Palko and Andrea O'Reilly, Demeter Press, 2021, pp. 269–78.

Ramachandran, Mallika. "Book Review: *An Unusual Grief* by Yewande Omotoso." *Literary Potpourri*, 22 Nov. 2021, https://potpourri2015.wordpress.com/2021/11/22/book-review-an-unusual-grief-by-yewande-omotoso/. Accessed 16 Jan. 2025.

Rich, Adrienne. *Of Woman Born: Motherhood as Experience and Institution*. 3rd Edition. W.W. Norton and Company, 2021.

Struthers Montford, Kelly, and Chloë Taylor. "Feral Theory: Editors' Introduction." *Feral Feminisms: Feral Theory*, no. 6, 2016, https://feralfeminisms.com/wp-content/uploads/2017/04/ff_intro_issue6.pdf. Accessed 27 Jan. 2025.

Notes on Contributors

Editors

Dr. Andrea O'Reilly is internationally recognized as the founder of Motherhood Studies (2006) and its subfield Maternal Theory (2007), and creator of Matricentric Feminism, a feminism for and about mothers (2016) and Matricritics, a literary theory and practice for a reading of mother-focused texts (2021). She is full professor in the School of Gender, Sexuality and Women's Studies at York University, founder/editor-in-chief of the Journal of the Motherhood Initiative and publisher of Demeter Press. She is co-editor/editor of thirty plus books on many motherhood topics including: Maternal Theory, Feminist Mothering, Young Mothers, Monstrous Mothers, Maternal Regret, Normative Motherhood, Mothers and Sons, Mothers and Daughters, Maternal Texts. Most recently in 2024 she published the co-edited collections *Care(ful) Relationships between Mothers and the Caregivers They Hire*, *The Mother Wave: Theorizing, Enacting, and Representing Matricentric Feminism* and *The Missing Mother*. She is author of four monographs including *(M)otherwords; Writings on Mothering and Motherhood, 2009-2024* (2024) and *Matricentric Feminism: Theory Activism, Practice, the 2nd Edition* (2021). She has published 15 chapters with several more planned on mother-centred novels/memoirs that will be published in the monograph *Matricritics as Literary Theory and Criticism: Reading the Maternal in Post-2010 Women's Narratives*. She is twice the recipient of York University's "Professor of the Year Award" for teaching excellence and is the 2019 recipient of the Status of Women and Equity Award of Distinction from OCUFA (Ontario Confederation of University Faculty Associations). She has received more than 1.5 million dollars in funding for her research projects including her current one on Millennial Mothers.

Casey O'Reilly-Conlin Casey O'Reilly-Conlin has a Bachelor's Degree in Women's Studies and a Master's degree in Environmental Studies, both from York University. Much of the research for her chapter in this collection was developed during writing her major research paper for her Master's degree, entitled *The Feline, Feminine, and Familiar: Co-Histories of Domestic Micro-Rebellions,* which interrogates the conjoined histories of women and cats in Western culture. She has a passion for all disobedient beings, especially of the feline variety. She embraces "the mystical divinity of unashamed felinity," a quote from T.S. Elliot's *Old Possum's Book of Practical Cats,* later developed by Andrew Lloyd Webber into the Broadway musical *Cats.* She resides in Toronto, Ontario with her partner and cat.

Contributors

Dr Laura Bissell is an Athenaeum Research Fellow and Lecturer in Contemporary Performance at the Royal Conservatoire of Scotland. Laura is author/editor of *Performance in a Pandemic, Making Routes,* and *Bubbles: Reflections on Becoming Mother* as well as a poetry collection, *A-Z of Sites of Love and Loss.* Her research interests include: technology, ecology, interdisciplinarity, matrescence, feminism; and performance and journeys. She is currently writing a monograph on matrescence and performance (Intellect) and co-editing the *International Journal of Performance Art and Digital Media*'s special edition: Matrescence and Media.

Caroline Carey is an English writer living in the UK. She waves life stories into illuminating narratives, fostering honesty and appreciation for the complexities of human experience. A writer since childhood, she has published seven books of memoir, poetry, and prose. Through her work, Caroline seeks to inspire, heal, and cultivate spiritual growth. She is the founder of Middle Earth Medicine Ways (www.middle earthmedicine.com).

Alexandra Carter (b. 1985 in Boston) lives and works in San Diego, California. She received an MFA from Goldsmiths University of London in 2015 and a BA from Rhodes College in Memphis in 2009. Recent solo exhibitions include "Monstrous Mothers" at the Middle Room Los Angeles, "Bumps & Grinds" at Rogers Gallery in Las Vegas, "A Sense of Heat in Her Brain" at Luna Anaïs Gallery in Los Angeles, "Berries for

Baubo" at Radiant Space in Los Angeles, and "Tether" (duo show) at Oolong Gallery in Solana Beach, CA. Other solo exhibitions include Fusion Gallery (Turin, Italy), Southfork (Memphis), Projecto'ace Foundation (Buenos Aires), and the Memphis Brooks Museum of Art. She has been selected for residency projects nationally and internationally, including the Kone Foundaton's Saari Residence (Finland), Rogers Art Loft (Las Vegas), KulturKontakt Austria (Vienna), Qwatz (Rome), Graniti Murales (Sicily), Vice~Versa Foundation (Goa, India), RECSIM (Jashipur, India), Galerija-Muzej Lendava (Slovenia), and the Kentucky Foundation for Women (Prospect, KY).

Dr. Martina Cleary is an artist, writer and researcher based in the West of Ireland. She holds a PhD from the European Centre for Photographic Research e(CPR), an MEd from Aalto University of Art, Design & Architecture, and an MA from the Finnish Academy of Fine Arts Helsinki. She currently lectures at The Technological University of the Shannon (TUS). Her research areas include; Photography & Memory, Psychology, Feminist Critical Theory, Immersive Media and Socially Engaged Practices. Over the past two decades her work has been presented in over eleven countries, supported by the Arts Councils of Ireland and Finland.

Hillary Di Menna is a Toronto mother, writer, and creek witch. Hillary takes up space and paints it pink with her daughter, a trinity of black cats, and a little black dog. Hillary writes love letters to the moon, dots 'i's with hearts, and makes cat scratches in her notebooks. Hillary has messy hair and can be bossy sometimes (and she prides herself on both).

Joy Domingo spent most of her adulthood struggling to be a "tame" wife and mother despite her natural disposition and Bipolar Disorder. The marriage was uncomfortable for both spouses. Playing this role became more and more difficult and uncomfortable as the years went by. Staying in the marriage "for the sake of the kids" didn't turn out well. Finally, Joy left the marital home and has been living on her own ever since— discovering, rediscovering, and waking up. Joy has a Bachelor's in History, a Master's in English, and an MSW from Jane Addams School of Social Work, all from the University of Illinois, Chicago. After 10 years of waiting tables, and the next 10 years teaching English at Roosevelt University, she has settled into a private practice as a licensed clinical therapist for the last 20 years. Besides her two adult children, Joy has a

19 y/o turtle and a dog named Max, a therapy dog. Parenthetically, if you are diagnosed with Bipolar Disorder, it's important to take all medicine as prescribed, whether one is tame or feral. Being medication compliant gives you more agency, more choices.

Catherine Moeller is an artist and community mobilizer, who leads seniors into adventure and connection through her arts program in Toronto's Weston area. With the core value of inclusion, Catherine's work is infused with her passion for removing social barriers and interweaving diverse people's voices and stories. Catherine supports the radically inclusive community arts programs at Jumblies Theatre and adores building giant puppets for theatre, parades and festivals. She is presently exploring the world of puppetry as a performer.

Victoria Smits (she, her) is an interdisciplinary artist living in Eugene, Oregon. She studied English, art, and secondary education at Calvin College, holds an MA in English Education with a concentration in creative writing from University of Buffalo, and an MFA through the School of Art Institute of Chicago. Smits has exhibited nationally and internationally, most recently at the Manchester Craft and Design Centre, Manchester, UK, the Old Stone House in Brooklyn, NY, the School of Art Institute of Chicago Gallery, Arc Gallery in Chicago, and Louise Hopkins Underwood Center for the Arts in Lubbock, TX.

Dr. Teela Tomassetti is a Registered Provisional Psychologist and researcher, specializing in birth trauma. After suffering her own through midwifery violence and an excessive haemorrhage almost taking her life in 2021, Teela decided to start the Instagram account @theteaonbirthtrauma, where she breaks the norm and supports thousands of survivors in finding their voices. Her doctoral research was on the activation of the fawn trauma response during birth trauma and its connection to provider mistreatment. Dr. Teela recently opened the Reproductive and Perinatal Trauma Centre, an innovative practice amplifying silenced experiences.

Dr. Jessica Spring Weappa, Ph.D, founder of Mothering Futures®, is a scholar-practitioner specializing in Regenerative Maternal Ethics©. Her transdisciplinary research explores maternal-infant dynamics through a biopsychosocial-spiritual framework, focusing on their societal impact. A narrative therapist with a depth-oriented somatic approach, Dr. Weappa holds a master's degree in human development from St. Mary's University of Minnesota and a doctorate in transformative studies from the California

Institute of Integral Studies (CIIS), where she also co-taught doctoral courses in creative inquiry, narrative inquiry, and arts-based research. Her background in arts education, along with her farming heritage, informs her unique perspective on ethics and future-making.

Dr. Batya Weinbaum received her doctorate in English at University of Massachusetts at Amherst for her thesis, Islands of Women and Amazons: Representations and Realities. She teaches online at the American Public University System, University of Maryland Global Campus, Shadybrook and Lilydale, and sells art and her books at festivals and fairs when working as a psychic reader. She founded and edits the journal *Femspec* available at femspec.org. She was an artist in residence at the Art Annex of the Museum of Motherhood in St. Petes FL where she installed a mural of a fertility goddess, and she volunteers for the Museum in the winter. She is the mother of one young woman, 31 years old at the time of this writing.

Else Werring is a Ph.D fellow in English Language Literature at the University of Oslo, and a mother of two. She is currently working on her monograph *Weaving, Eathing, Birthing: Rhythmic Meditations on (M)otherhood in Jeanette Winterson and Rachel Cusk*.

Dr. Emily Wolfinger Dr Emily Wolfinger is an Associate Lecturer in the School of Social Sciences at Western Sydney University, Australia, and the sole mother of three children. She completed a government-funded PhD in Sociology under COVID-19 lockdowns in 2020. Emily's research examines institutional and public discourses on sole mothers and critiques the undervaluation of caregiving in late-stage capitalist societies. Current projects include an international collection on policies and practices that enable the work of caregiving.

Li Yang (born 1994, China, she/her) is currently a PhD candidate at Leuphana University Lüneburg (Germany), working on the M/Other Project: Creativity, Procreation, and Contemporary Art initiated by Professor Jordan Troeller. She obtained an MA in Curatorship from the University of Melbourne. She was a visiting curator and researcher at Alpha Nova & Galerie Futura (Berlin), funded by the German Chancellor Fellowship (Alexander von Humboldt Foundation). In 2021, she served as a remote intern and guest curator at the Museum of Motherhood (U.S.). Her research and curatorial interests include feminist curating, feminist mothering, motherhood in art, and Chinese feminist art.

About the Cover Art

Materna Sinistra
by Alexandra Carter, 2021

Ink, image transfer, and gold leaf on drafting film,
60 x 48 in (152 x 122 cm)

Materna Sinistra explores the monstrous feminine through themes
like the vagina dentata, combining figures of possession and rapture
with cranberry symbolism to reflect the transformative power of
motherhood in a composition reminiscent of a family crest.